Yetta Blaze de Bury

French Literature of Today

A Study of the Principal Romancers and Essayists

Yetta Blaze de Bury

French Literature of Today
A Study of the Principal Romancers and Essayists

ISBN/EAN: 9783744694735

Printed in Europe, USA, Canada, Australia, Japan

Cover: Foto ©Thomas Meinert / pixelio.de

More available books at **www.hansebooks.com**

FRENCH LITERATURE
OF TO-DAY

A STUDY OF THE PRINCIPAL ROMANCERS
AND ESSAYISTS

BY

YETTA BLAZE DE BURY

𝔚𝔢𝔰𝔱𝔪𝔦𝔫𝔰𝔱𝔢𝔯
ARCHIBALD CONSTABLE & CO.
2 WHITEHALL GARDENS

PREFACE

To run a connecting thread through the sketches contained in this little book were a futile task. The thread would be broken at once; for could Zola be tied to Brunetière, or Anatole France to Vogüé? Reëdited papers, gathered into one volume, are very much like a miscellaneous company of steamboat passengers, each of whom has gone on board independently of the rest. When circumstances thus bring together the censured and the censor, silence among the passengers answers for peace.

In a book like this the reader comes upon the literary portraits that are presented to him, only one by one, as the captain of the boat visits cabin after cabin. Diverse in their tastes, in their tendencies, in their surroundings, the French authors here brought before the American reader will receive, it is hoped, at least a little of the favor which we give in France to the masters of American literature. The aim of the writer of these sketches has been above all to win for her compatriots, from the reading public in the United States, some slight return of the esteem we cherish for Emerson, Hawthorne, Poe, Longfellow. She has sought to make the essence of the French literary genius felt by the readers of a foreign country which she admires sincerely, and which, throughout all its history, has ever been sympathetic toward us politically and industrially.

If the American people shall grant to these portraits a little of the cordiality of reception which they have given so generously to some of the originals, the author's efforts will be fully recompensed.

PARIS, 2 March, 1898.

CONTENTS

	PAGE
PIERRE LOTI	1
GUY DE MAUPASSANT	23
ZOLA AS AN EVOLUTIONIST	37
EDMOND DE GONCOURT	53
JEAN MARTIN CHARCOT	86
PAUL BOURGET	107
EUGÈNE MELCHIOR DE VOGÜÉ	133
FERDINAND BRUNETIÈRE	156
JULES LEMAÎTRE	183
ANATOLE FRANCE	211
MADAME BLANC BENTZON AS A ROMANCE WRITER	239
PAUL VERLAINE	263

FRENCH LITERATURE OF TO-DAY

PIERRE LOTI

" Is this man Loti? Why, the thing is impossible! Such a plain, insignificant-looking person father to Rarahu, to Gaud, to Aziyadé?" and all Paris passes in frustrated disappointment at not seeing the light of genius, the dreams of the poet, and the speculations of the psychologist at once in Commandant Viaud's excellent portrait at the Palais de l'Industrie.

"But, madame, a portrait gives only one aspect of a physiognomy. How can you expect it to give you at once the source whence Rarahu's *morbidezza*, Gaud's virtue, Aziyadé's passion, come? It is only as centuries go by that an Erasmus's picture acquires all the wit contained in 'L'Eloge de la Folie.' Death alone and the imagination of the public make man one with his work. But *à quoi bon? Il y a des banalités immortelles.* Besides, Loti is a poet and a word-painter himself; as great a colorist, pen in hand, as Decamps or Corot; that is to say, feeling equally the cloudy, misty aspects of nature, as those of light. Brittany and the equator, Paimpol and Papeete, Chateaubriand and Théophile Gautier, — *that* is Loti. Not the Chateaubriand of the 'Prose Epics,' but the

Chateaubriand-voyageur, the Chateaubriand of
'Atala' and of the Père Aubry, of whom Loti
reminds one, in interrupting, as he does, Rarahu's
very embraces by reflections of the following kind:
'L'éternelle et sublime prière du Christ, Notre
Père qui êtes aux cieux, sonnait d'une manière
étrangement mystérieuse et mystique au-delà du
vieux monde, aux Antipodes, dite par la voix de
ce vieillard fantôme.' Chateaubriand and Loti are
alike in some aspects of their minds. The analogy
between Gautier and Loti, however, lies in the
æsthetical temperament of both: in their common
worship of the sun. The one, Gautier, a pagan,
bursts into full bloom at the first touch of the
East. The other, Loti, offers his divinity a more
mystical internal cult. Gautier dwells in Olym-
pus amidst gold and glitter, side by side with the
impassible Juno; Loti, on the contrary, of a more
unquiet nature, demands of himself, Whence
comes in the creature man his thirst for belief?"

"Quelles sont ces essences inconnues qui planent
dans les endroits où l'on a prié longtemps? Quelle
est cette oppression du surnaturel?" Both Loti
and Gautier turn to the sun in their own way;
but their ways differ as they themselves differ,
Gautier being above all an Athenian, Loti a
Celt. Gautier finds pleasure in love; Loti, like
Chateaubriand and like all the modern school, sees
in the "fact love" only a creative force, whence
work is conceived in torture and in woe. Loti is
not only in his work the man of his time, but is
so quite as much in his very being. Logical, im-
placable, passionate, and taciturn, will is to him

the supreme law : he counts with sentiment as
with an evil. Without a certain amount of emotion really experienced, he knows the brain cannot
produce the Gauds, the Rarahus, etc. ; such creations being conducive to fame, the emotions have
to be borne. To such men love is only a means.

Self-consciousness has a considerable part also
in Loti's writings ; his reminiscences carry him
back to scenes where the puerilities of child-life
are entirely lost in the poetry of the pictures.
" The days lengthened, the flowers grew, the heat
and light became intense: something unexpected
to me, I felt, was going to take place. It was
summer ; I was then three years old ; all my day
had been employed in mud-pie making. I had
turned these pies into an alley planted with rows
of cut flowers. Notwithstanding my wish to walk
in this garden, I perceived it was too small even
for myself. To admire my doings from above, I
rose on my wheelbarrow, overturned it, and fell.
My nurse took me up, sang to me, coaxed me.
Since, I have understood that had I been coaxed
and sung to on all occasions in life when I failed
for having undertaken the impossible, I should
have suffered far less. During those lovely summer days, in order to express my exultation, I composed hymns to nature, which I sang to myself."
To his home, also, Loti has remained faithful,
through travels and years. In " Fleurs d'Ennui,"
one of his last books, he writes: " This bench on
which I am now is my true home ; here comes
my mother across the courtyard. Oh, the love of
a mother, the only disinterested one, the only love

which breeds no deception, the only love which teaches one to believe in the soul and in life eternal! What madness prompts me to rush constantly from this home to far-away lands!"

Sadness, that latent sadness of things, mentioned by Virgil, expressed by Othello's cry of despair, "O Iago, the pity of it!" that philosophical sorrow born in the thinker from the decay and brevity of all that is human, — such a sadness, enhanced in his sailor-mind by seeing man all over the world subjected to the same misery, is the dominant note of our prose poet. A veil of melancholy drapes all Loti's works: it overshadows Rarahu's hut; filters in Aziyadé's boudoir; dwells at Ploubazlanec by old Mother Moan; and clings to "Un Vieux." As the space fails us here in face of Loti's entire work, we will restrict ourselves to those books which present the most opposed characters, illustrating thus what we said above of Loti's equal understanding of all aspects of nature, whether Asiatic or polar. Born in 1850 at La Rochelle, Pierre Viaud or Loti had just reached the grade of lieutenant de vaisseau when the "Mariage de Loti" appeared, and had already navigated around the world for upwards of twelve years. "Propos d'Exil," which came out in 1885, is the condensation of his Asiatic impressions, a more desolate book than others, as it is written from Tonking, where Loti says, "La France est si loin dans ce pays jaune, qu'on n'espère plus la revoir;" it contains the pathetic narrative of Admiral Courbet's death.

The "Mariage de Loti" was Commandant

Viaud's first book, and was at once noticed. If
Rarahu, the heroine of this romance, differs in herself and in her surroundings greatly from her
elder sisters Atala and Ourika,[1] it is principally
that Loti, her creator, is a physiologist as well as a
dreamer. The days of neo-Sauvagerie, like the
days of neo-Greek dress, are as far from us as
Madame Récamier's turban and Ourika's Christian submission. Though of a less medical turn of
mind than Zola and Maupassant, Loti submits to
the influence of his time; he creates bodies as well
as souls, — bodies endowed, as in real life, with
stronger influence on the moral being than the
moral being ever had on the mere body; hypnotism, in proving that the first condition required in
the subject, for the producing of any phenomena,
is to be hyper-nervously organized, has shown the
supremacy of the body, humanly speaking. However null may be the will in the subject, if the
physical organism does not sufficiently vibrate to
receive the discharge of animal magnetism as its
propulsor, no phenomena are produced.

To the modern school of science the soul is but
an outcome of cerebral forces. Hence springs one
of the chief results of literature — the passionate
study of physiology. When Shakespeare men-

[1] *Ourika*, a novel written by the Duchesse de Duras,
created a great sensation in the days of Napoleon I. It
is the story of a negro girl who, brought in contact with
the highest Paris world, loves with the violence of her race,
and submits to the sacrifice of her love with the passivity
of a Catholic nun. No book can betray a greater ignorance
of physiology than *Ourika;* but in those days physiology
was unknown, at least unapplied to romance-writing.

tioned Hamlet's fatness and short breath, he did
no less in favor of physiology than the modern
French masters. Villemain said, "Pour compren-
dre tout plus clairement il faut d'abord com-
prendre l'homme. Tout écrivain et tout penseur
devrait faire son doctorat en médecine." Maupassant, Zola, Loti himself, though much modified
by the poet which is in him, are more or less phy-
sicians. Their subject is a living one, that is the
difference! Instead of pressing with the finger on
dead arteries in their demonstration of circulation,
these thinkers watch the play of forces in the living subject, man. As they see impulse or instinct
overthrow reason, they look on. Their process of
study is not mischievous, it is merciful, — as merciful as the diagnosis of the scientific man, who
foresees in the abscess of to-day the cancer of ten
years hence ; though he cannot cure it, by careful
advice he prolongs life. Should a novelist, therefore, write only truth, but real human truth, he
would in so far be doing a good deed. No man
would ever have trusted and followed an Æschylus
or a Shakespeare if, before rising to sublimity, he
had not felt that his guide knew him as a man, —
knew him thoroughly and understood him. If genius did not caress humanity first by talking to it
the language of its weaknesses, humanity would
never listen to the teachings of genius. Truth,
whether noble or ignoble, whether realistic or
idealistic, is good when spoken, for truth alone
breeds useful thought in the minds of those whose
thoughts are entitled to command attention.

An imitation savage like Ourika puzzles the

reader; a true little wild being like Rarahu
attaches. She has lovable instincts as well as
savage ones; she is a genuinely interesting object
of study for the critic, because she is herself a
genuine piece of humanity.

Rarahu, the principal actress of the " Mariage
de Loti," dwells in the rivulet of Tataoué, — the
Burlington Arcade of Papeete. She is to be seen
there like a bronze Correggio nymph, either
clothed by the limpid waters, or lounging on the
deep green grass on the shore. Harry Grant, an
English marine officer, whose name has been
turned to " Loti " for the sake of Tahitian pro-
nunciation, meets Rarahu, loves, and marries her,
not by that everlasting bond known to so-called
civilized countries, but according to Papeete customs, which, in fact, differ so little from any others
that marriage lasts just as long — or is as short —
as the *man* wishes!

One evening at a court ball Rarahu has been
dazzled and maddened by the dresses of Tahiti
Europeanized ladies; the next day she appears to
Loti arrayed in a splendid pareo, but a pareo
bespeaking its Chinese origin. Now anything
Chinese means shame, and Loti, having got really
to care for Rarahu, feels sad.

He has gone too far, however, in his conclusions,
and the way in which Rarahu greets a Celestial,
obese, and yellow old gentleman, who desecrates
her rivulet by bathing in it, convinces Loti of his
mistake. Rarahu is confused, she is not culpable.
" She sat on my knees and wept her eyes out, for
in that little wild heart of hers good and bad were

strangely mixed, though her innate sharpness led
her to understand the gap between us, created
by the different views we took of all things in
general."

Rarahu has been adopted by two old people,[1]
but after their death she goes to live altogether
with Loti. The first knell of separation tolls for
the lovers when Loti's frigate is ordered away to
the Sandwich Islands; the distance is short, but
nevertheless it involves a first parting.

Rarahu, inspired by love, applies her knowledge
of writing: " My sorrow is higher than the Paraï.
O my lover, thou hast gone, and thy eyes may now
be lifted to me; mine can no more meet their
gaze, but, alas! every day I feel more that women
like myself are but toys to men of your race."

At his return Loti finds Rarahu has learned
English. " Her voice seemed sweeter than ever
in this language, although she could not pronounce its hard syllables." Loti's knowledge of
Rarahu's weak nature makes him fear that no
sooner shall he be gone than she will become light
and dissipated. " To all my entreaties that she
would keep faithful to the higher mode of life I
had initiated her into, she only sneered, or opposed the most determined silence."

Faithful to Loti she was, though, but in that
measure which was Polynesian fidelity. She had
no European lovers, that was all! and that was a

---

[1] Tahitian parents place their children in the hands of willing persons, who take charge of them as though they were
their own, — rather a terrible argument against the laws
of nature !

great deal, as natives were not counted! To her lover's prayer " that she should go on believing in God as before," she answered, " I believe in nothing more, not even in ghosts, for there is nothing after death, and ghosts themselves only last as long as the body endures." This harshness gives way before grief, however. On the day of the final parting she says, " I am thine, Loti, thy little wife forever. Fear nothing ; to-morrow I leave Papeete and take refuge with Tiahouï" (a dutiful married Tahitian).

The frigate goes back to Europe. Years elapse, and one day Loti lands in Papeete again; he hastens to inquire after Rarahu — she is dead. For one whole year after he left she was a model. But days rubbed away the sorrow, and augmented the wish for pleasure. She gave way: the result was early death.

Instinct had been at the bottom of Rarahu's better qualities. Instinct as well was her ruin! It is the tale of Rarahu which Loti tells us. He is far too much of a disciple of Mérimée to profit by the occasion for moralizing on the "misdeeds of the civilized man"! Loti's moral lessons, luckily for his reader, run through the lives of his heroes. He is too much also a man of the world, pen in hand, to see in Rarahu anything but a lovely bibelot. " Cela plait — on s'en lasse — et c'est fini." A bibelot's life begins and ends with the caprice of the purchaser.

A most direct counterpart to the " Mariage de Loti " is " Les Pêcheurs d'Islande," — a book as eloquent on the poetry of duty as the other was

eloquent on the divers sensuousnesses of tropical
natures.

Not only is " Les Pêcheurs d'Islande " opposed
to the " Mariage de Loti " by the countries where
the action of the story takes place, Brittany and
Iceland, but also because the nobility of the passions within the heroes' hearts offers a more favor-
able ground to the author's psychical temperament;
vouchsafes him more scope for those curiosities
which momentarily raise the novelist to the rank
of a Montaigne or a Bacon. Where are the germs
of thought ? Does man know all he thinks ? Can
thoughts lie unknown to the thinker in the thinker's own mind for a long time ? Is the true man
the one who speaks in the state of unconsciousness,
madness, or dotage ? or is the true man the one
who, knowing his own shortcomings, conceals
them, and acts nobly whilst he feels basely ?
These are the queries which Loti is brought to ask
himself, when old Mother Moan, a model of virtue
for seventy-three years, all at once begins in old
age to shout out foul images. Are these the outcomes of folly? Were they part of Mother Moan's
true self ? Did she know of these feelings and conceal them as long as reason was mistress in her ?
or did she harbor all these thoughts in herself
unconsciously, so that madness alone would reveal
their existence ?

" Avoir été toujours bonne, pure, puis étaler
pour finir une science de mots grossiers qu'on avait
cachée, — mystère moqueur ! " A mystery sketched
out, however, three hundred years ago by Shakespeare when he brought out of Ophelia's mouth,

and out of King Lear's, under pretense of madness, the strange songs of Hamlet's mistress, and the scathing speeches of Lear to women.

Gaud, the heroine of "Les Pêcheurs d'Islande," is all moral effort; her love is all abnegation. Whilst Rarahu's untutored soul tends to the absorption of all else by self, Gaud, on the reverse, throws her own individuality entirely into her love.

" Yann sera pour elle, quoiqu'il arrive toute sa vie, un fiancé qu'elle n'aura pas, un fiancé fuyant. Elle le préférait en Islande car les cloîtres de la mer le lui gardaient. Aucune femme ainsi ne lui prenait! "

At a fair in Brittany, Gaud, a kind of "demoiselle " (her father possesses landed properties), walks leisurely up and down. Seeing a handsome gigantic sailor, she exclaims, " Here is a giant! " The man turns round, takes in her entire person at one survey, and thinks, " Who is this woman so pretty, with the Paimpol coiffe, yet unknown to me? " Thus do the two heroes of " Les Pêcheurs d'Islande " meet for the first time.

Their next encounter happens at a wedding, where Yann point-blank informs Gaud, without any more words, that she, and she alone, in Paimpol — and in the world — is capable of deterring him from good fishing! This is all he says, but it is said with such a look that though Gaud is the richest and the prettiest girl in the place, her heart shall hence be approached by none. When he sets out for Iceland, " le beau Yann " starts without having even so much as called again upon Gaud! At his return there is the same indifference on his

part. Not only does he never come near her, but
he courts many others. Gaud's heart is sinking;
she takes the initiative, and seizing hold of a kind
of business between her father and Yann's father,
she walks off to their house, hoping to meet Yann,
but he is out " tackle-buying," so it is all useless !
Before the next departure for Iceland she knows
he will call at her house, always touching that
same business. This time, happen what may, she
will speak to him. The day comes. After such
an inward battle as to feel herself half dead, she
springs from her room down the stairs as Yann
is going from her father towards the entrance door,
and faces him.

" Monsieur Yann, I want a word with you."

" With me, mademoiselle ? " and as if from fear
of contact with her, Yann effaces himself against
the wall ! Her heart sinks; she could not expect
such disdain on his part. In a voice so husky and
unnatural that she does not know it as her own,
" Monsieur Yann," she asks, " is our house now so
repulsive to you ? The night of that ball when we
first met, you spoke the words 'au revoir' to me
in such a manner that I had reason to believe I
was not quite indifferent in your eyes ? "

" No, Mademoiselle Gaud, we have been already
talked about enough in this country. You are
rich ; we do not belong to the same class. I am
not a man to be continually coming to your house.
Good-by ! " — and he goes.

Oh, had he but listened one moment ! She would
have pleaded, " Forget my money, — let yourself
be loved." She would have said, " I am pretty, I

am honest, Yann. I love you — take me to your
heart!" But none of these words should now ever
be uttered : to attempt another explanation after
this one, how could she ?

The departure for Iceland took Yann again
away. During this journey of his, events happened. An old woman, Mother Moan, a kind of
relation of Gaud, lost her grandson, and through
this almost lost her mind. Gaud's father died,
and unexpectedly left her penniless.

She sold all she had, and took up her abode with
Mother Moan, earning a living for both of them
by her needle. When night came, harassed by
the toil of the day, but firm and courageous, Gaud
lay down in her little bed, still hoping for Yann's
return. She thought, " He cannot escape from
calling on Mother Moan, as Sylvester [the grand-
son] was a sailor in the same crew as Yann.
When he calls, I shall be there, and this time I
will govern circumstances, and try again."

One day she heard that La Marie (Yann's boat)
had returned. Growing feverish before the end
of her daily task, she hurried off her work and
started to walk home. She had not proceeded a
quarter of a mile before she recognized him on
the road coming towards her. She felt her feet
give way. What would become of her? The
same fear and mad heart-beating as at her father's house came over her ; the sudden thought
also struck her that her hair looked unbecoming.
Oh, that she could only disappear in one of the
bushes ! Yann, on his side, was quite as discom-
fited ; but it was not to be helped, and they passed

each other. She gave him one look of entreaty;
he took off his cap, and said, "Bonjour, Mademoiselle Gaud." She answered, "Bonjour, Monsieur Yann." He hurried away, and she felt
stunned. This old heart-breaking game, so often
played since Beatrice and Benedick, never has
been more feelingly portrayed than in these few
touches of Loti. Two utterances, "Bonjour, Mademoiselle Gaud," "Bonjour, Monsieur Yann,"
and the bubble blown by hope has burst. A second before, no sacrifice was above Gaud; but what
was the use now? She was not only to him
"Mademoiselle Gaud," but *a* Mademoiselle Gaud,
like any other mademoiselle! This was the real
end of all! "Alors la chaumière lui sembla plus
désolée, la misère plus dure, le monde plus vide —
et elle baissa la tête avec une envie de mourir."

The time for sailing was again at hand. Yann
had just received his pay from his employer when
he caught sight of a mob near Ploubazlanec. An
old woman stood gesticulating with her stick,
screaming and menacing, whilst boys laughed and
mocked her; they had killed her cat! Yann, in-
furiated, dispersed the mob. Gaud, coming back
from Paimpol, hastened to the group, and lifting
her eyes to Yann in one touching look of inquiry,
said, "The mother has been dragged along, I assure
you, Monsieur Yann; her dress was all neat and
clean this morning, when I left her." And whilst
she spoke, Yann kept looking at her as though her
poverty enhanced her charm. Her mourning surrounded her with a halo of dignity. Yann walked
on with both the women.

Poor Gaud's heart was on her lips; she felt as though it would burst. What could be the meaning of such attentions on the part of Yann? They had reached their door — what would happen now? Was he going to leave them? Or was it possible that he would pass their threshold? Some grand decision was about to be taken — each of these three felt it.

Happiness had come to Gaud at last. They married. For six days Gaud was Madame Gaos. Then came again the Iceland departure, and Gaud was left behind.

Summer passed, and in September the boats began to return; October, November, December, — neither Yann nor any of the crew were seen. A year went by; none of them ever reappeared.

One ominous night Yann had celebrated his nuptials with the sea. "An unspeakable mystery had presided over the monstrous wedding; the sky, draped in black, overshadowed the feast. The bride gave tongue in order to smother the victim's shrieks. Thinking of Gaud, his earthly wife, Yann had battled hard, till, vanquished, he had opened his arms and given himself up to the fatal embraces."

After the tales of love, of despair, of passion, Loti, some years ago, gave the readers of the "Revue des Deux Mondes," under the title "Un Vieux," the most pathetic narrative of the sad moment when the state orders its old servants to their rest. An old sailor is sent to repose not only because he really *is* old, but because the state has declared the time has come when he must be so! Kervella, the sailor, has been all over the world; his frame is wiry and looks strong, yet he is internally worn by fifty years' seafaring.

"When the day came for the sailor to part with his life of activity it was a day like any other, and none of the men seemed to notice whether this faithful servant went or stopped," writes Loti. With a pang, at night he put away his uniform, shut up his old tattooed body in a black overcoat, and, all accounts settled, the state having sufficiently paid him for his life, he walked out of the barracks.[1]

Now indeed bliss had come to him! there were no more dangers, no more duty, no more troubles. A good bed, in a comfortable little house bought with his economies, having a view on the port and a lovely little garden to care for, the wish of all his days fulfilled at last, — this was happiness! Yet the tears kept washing his face, and his heart yearned for death!

On mild Brittany summer days, to give himself the illusion of being in the tropics, he put his water in a cooling-bottle, dressed himself in a nankeen suit, brought down his parrot, and fanned himself with a palm-tree leaf. Though he appeared to the passers-by as if in sleep, his brain was in reality living over again all his past. He remembered — he remembered he had once been young, strong, handsome; now his limp arms hung on both sides of his long empty body, overspread by a net of blue veins like a corpse overspread by worms. He remembered he had had

---

[1] In Brest some of the men sleep in barracks, like soldiers.

mistresses; he had been longed for and knelt to.
Women had swooned under the kisses of these
withered, faded lips; this dark face or that blonde
one passed through his mind. Still he regretted
none. Love? The mouths pouting of themselves
toward caresses, the eternal charm drawing creatures toward each other, blending them in passionate embraces — all that was gone! and he cared
not! His food was now his everything — what
he would eat for supper. He remembered having
had a wife. His married life lasted one spring.
All the generosities of his heart, all the energies
of his unemployed fondness, he had showered upon
her. For her he had become timid and reserved
as a child; to woo her he had trained himself to
refined modes of courtship quite out of his habits.
Duty had called him away; when he returned,
his wife was living with a rich old man, spending
all he gave her upon fine clothes. He remembered
having had a daughter, whom death had robbed
him of, a certain May evening. The remembrance
of this child brought tears to his eyes. A hideous
little faded photograph of her as a "première com-
municante," taper in hand, brought pangs to his
heart. Thirty months had he counted and recounted in that last expedition to China, till he saw
her again. Scarcely had he reached the shore,
before he ran to the woman who kept her. De-
positing the bag full of presents for his child, he
flew up to her room. She was dying. He for-
gave, and paid high prices for a nurse, who poi-
soned her with a drunkard's care. There still
remained the holy grave; so from Hong-Kong he

sent the woman in Brest a big sum of money to
get a marble slab and an inscription to be laid
on the grave. But the woman, having become
imbecile, spent the money for drink, and when
Kervella came back, his daughter's sacred little
bones were being jostled with others in the "fosse
commune." Years and years had passed; wounds
and feats of courage had carried him to the notice of an admiral. Ambition helping, he became
master, the highest grade a "man" can ever attain to in France.

Thus he remembered; and now that he had
come to his rest, sleep had gone. His nights were
filled with horror; his body was broken and de-
formed; the sea had left him to remain a solitary
old man whose tears fell unnoticed by all. Why
had he not died young? An animal keeps his
shape to the last; man alone is condemned to wea-
risome old age — derision of life!

One night in March, Death, who was hurrying
on to Brest, tarried to twist Kervella on his bed,
turn his eyes inside out, and his mouth all awry.
Coming in the morning the Mère le Gall, his char-
woman, said, "Tiens, mon vieux est crevé!"
Whether in Papeete, or whether in Morocco,
Loti's philosophical sadness leads him to the same
queries as Monsieur de Vogüé before the Sphinx,
as Chateaubriand before Jerusalem.

To really thinking minds the Sphinx is everywhere, most of all in the mysterious sufferings
of innocence! Why shame to this pure one, why
honor to this lower soul? Why slavery to a poor
negro girl, born with every instinct of modesty

and dignity? That is the question Loti asks himself at Fez in the depths of Africa.

"'The slave-market is low?' I asked the dealer.

"'There still remains to be sold that negro woman there in the corner,' answered he.

"A form closely hidden under a gray veil, crouched on the earth, rose at my bidding. It was that of a girl between sixteen and eighteen; her eyes, brimming over with tears, bespoke infinite despair; her mistress stood by her side, as miserable as herself. Though much attached to the girl, she had to dismiss her for want of money to keep her: it looked like the sale of a child by a mother!"

Fatou-gaye, the "négrillonne" of the "Roman d'un Spahi," is another excellent type of the negro, in her wildness, and also in her capacity of feeling "black melancholy." Fatou-gaye is a kind of Rarahu, rather comical at first. "Her head," writes Loti, "was entirely shaved, save five rats' tails sticking out, and gummed with little bits of coral hanging by their ends — and one sequin which served as a kind of tonsure." Setting apart this grotesque coiffure, Fatou-gaye's face was that of an exquisitely fine little Greek statue, with a skin of polished onyx, wonderfully white teeth, and eyes of an excessive mobility.

Fatou-gaye was a child slave of the Spahi's first mistress; her dress consisted only of one row of gris-gris. One night Jean (the Spahi) had seen the proof of his mistress's infidelity. Stunned with grief, he had fallen at her door, and risen again to rush madly toward the sea. The thought of his body becoming the prey of crabs had prevented his

drowning himself. Vanquished, however, by feverish drowsiness, he had fallen asleep on the burning
sands, to find himself, when he woke, protected by
a sort of tent. Fatou-gaye had followed him, and
this tent was made of her best " pagne." For many
hours she had watched him in a trance, covering
his brow with kisses as he lay quite motionless.
She would not have minded much if he had died,
for " I would hold him so fast in my arms,"
thought she, " that none could separate us." But
the palms of Fatou-gaye's hands were roseate, and
Jean looked upon her as on a kind of ape. To
Loti, Fatou-gaye's hands are of no consequence;
her heart is the main object, and his treatment
of it is masterly.

Loti's career has far too close a relation to the
particular nature of his talent, and his adoration
of his commanders is too illustrative of his professional qualities, for us to omit quoting some passages in his narrative of Admiral Courbet's death:

" The admiral was to me the incarnation of the
sublime old words, ' honor,' ' patriotism,' ' heroism,'
' abnegation.' He had evidently the secret of making himself loved, but he was at the same time
rigid, inflexible to himself as to others. His orders
were imperative and dry. ' You have understood
me, my friend. Go.' A pressure of the hand, a
kind frank look, and with that one went — one
went anywhere; so long as one obeyed him, one
felt on the right road. Here he lay now, vanquished by the two maladies of this yellow country, dysentery and hepatitis, and at the same time
heart-sick at the small echo his great victories had

had in France. Death in these extreme regions
allowing of no lying in state, the body of the
admiral had been embalmed, and, wrapped in his
shroud, lay on the red carpet of his state cabin.
After the 'défile' came the religious ceremony,
during which time a small bird obstinately sang,
perched in the folds of the flag. Never yet had I
seen sailors weep whilst on duty. Here, however,
all those of the piquet d'honneur gave way."

We pointed out in the beginning of this study
of Loti how much resemblance was to be found
between certain characteristics of his style and
that of Théophile Gautier. This would in no
way tend to lessen our author's individuality. Although decidedly more poetical, Loti's talent is not
as robust as Théophile Gautier's, not as robust
either as Maupassant's, or as powerful as Zola's.
It is of a more psychical turn, and some of its
dreamy features may be attributed to his sea-life,
while its irony at times seems almost an echo from
the Boulevard. Loti is an outcome of the Boulevard, such as it was, in the past; when the peri-
patecians Gautier, Méry, Gozlan, and others issued
their literary decrees while walking up and down
from the Librairie Nouvelle to the Rue de Riche-
lieu. There are no more Gautiers, no more Mérys,
no more Gozlans; but there remains a Loti, an
aristocratic-minded Loti, who talks little, and never
converses but with his equals, sufficiently full of
hatred for the "philister" to express his disdain
as did Heine.

"Vous devez me trouver bien sot aujourd'hui,
mon cher," said Heine to one of the collaborateurs

of the " Revue des Deux Mondes ; " "c'est que je viens 'd'échanger' mes idées avec X."

Loti's vein of irony is often that of Heine ; it is dry, cruel almost, as is shown by Kervella's adventures. Heine, however, had known of fights of all kinds, pecuniary and others. Loti is now rich (through his marriage), and from the outset of his career he has never known anything less than comfort, which sufficiently shows that temper depends, not upon circumstances, but upon temperament and personal disposition. Melancholy by nature, and by his almost Breton origin, the morbid spirit of his work is the outcome of his own feelings.

Loti's despair and sombreness are more those of satiety than those of undervalued literary efforts, as was the case with Verlaine. Elected to the Académie Française while yet in the full power of youth, Loti reached almost at once equal fame and popularity. His pessimistic disposition is therefore, above all, the natural outcome of the Schopenhauerist atmosphere which is breathed by our modern writers all over the world, and much more in France than anywhere else.

GUY DE MAUPASSANT

MAUPASSANT was born August 5, 1850. More of what is commonplace and ephemeral about him — his successes and his adventures — is known than of his intimate family life, so honorable and so full of filial devotion. One of his former chiefs (at an early age Maupassant was a private secretary in one of the Ministères) said of him : " He has never been guided in his social relations but by tact, affability, and generosity." Maupassant's beginnings were modest, his official salary in 1872 not rising above 1,800 francs a year, but the compensation for this was a certain amount of leisure, enabling him, after office hours, to pursue his literary labors. The difficulties of helping to maintain a home were great, notwithstanding which his respect for his pen never swerved, and he waited to make his début till his master Flaubert was satisfied with his productions. Flaubert lived near Rouen, Maupassant's family in the neighborhood of Croisset. From childhood the great man had watched over the boy's mind, setting him certain themes to exert himself upon. " You will go to such a street, where you will see a concierge and his parrot ; you will then write down what you saw and read it me ; " and till Flaubert pronounced, " Now I *see* the picture," Maupassant had to work and destroy. " Boule de Suif," which appeared in

1878, was the first outburst of a success which
never waned. Then our author began that life of
personal experience which he paid for so cruelly.
It should be remembered, however, that whilst
common men go uselessly through the same "feu
de la vie," it is the privilege of talent only to turn
these games into fertile literary productions. Few
men, be it said to Maupassant's honor, retain after
the lessons of pleasure the strong and lofty filial
sense of duty out of which was carved "Pierre et
Jean." We shall return to "Pierre et Jean"
later, when we have first skimmed through some
of Maupassant's short stories, where he becomes
unconsciously a rival of Mérimée and of Balzac.
In the volume entitled "Clair de Lune," La Reine
Hortense exhibits the highest knowledge on the
author's part of that firmness of will and dignified endurance which are so characteristic of the
Frenchwoman. At Rueil lives a tall, gaunt, severe
old maid. Her martial demeanor toward a herd of
divers animals over which she reigns has brought
upon her the name of Reine Hortense. She falls
ill, and only through delirium does the leading
sorrow of her life express itself; for through unconsciousness she calls to a husband and to a host
of children. Husband and children are both the
mere outcomes of a deep-rooted anguish and sorrow. Her life has been one long effort at disguis-
ing what her secret wishes were, and now that she
controls herself no longer this wish expresses itself,
and the horror of her solitary life is made evident
by this outburst of nature. Solitude at heart has
been to the miserable Hortense the unbearable

burthen, and as she is about to die will and effort
have been overcome by fever. Nature has the
last word above conventionality.

In another of Maupassant's tales we find L'Infirme just as ironical in its conclusions as Reine
Hortense, though far less heart-rending, for this
time the sacrifice is voluntary and the broken-
hearted man rises by self-denial. We see a victory, not a defeat. L'Infirme is a very perfect
miniature of the noblest type of the Frenchman,
of that type where strength is accompanied by outward gentleness, and where virtue is clothed in
grace of manner and personal charm. Two men
going to St. Germain get into a railway carriage.
One is a magistrate, the other a retired army officer. They had formerly been acquainted, but had
lost sight of each other. After being wounded,
the officer left the service. He is plethoric, like
one who lacks proper exercise. His face, though
bloated, still retains beauty through the nobility
of features and expression.

As L'Infirme gets into the carriage his valet
helps him to place a number of parcels. "There
are five parcels," says the servant, "the bon-bons,
the doll, the drum, the *pâté*, the gun." Furnished
with these materials, the magistrate builds up a
story. "When I used to know him," thinks he,
"he was a fine man, a brilliant officer, engaged
to Mademoiselle de Mandal. She has evidently
married him, spite of his wooden legs." On the
strength of this story, the magistrate asks the officer whether he is a father, and gets his whole fictitious building blown up at once. Mademoiselle de

Mandal has become Madame de Fleurel, and is not in any way to be coupled with L'Infirme. It is a wife's duty to live every hour of her life by her mate, and L'Infirme declares that his own irritation against himself when he hears the clap of his sticks on the floor is far too great for him to think of getting a woman whom he loved to share life with him. "Any form of sacrifice," says L'Infirme, "is acceptable for a time, however long; but it should be for a time only, not for life." As the men arrive at St. Germain the door is thrown open, and, besieged by Monsieur and Madame de Fleurel, and by the Fleurel children, who encircle L'Infirme, it is evident that the lover of yore has now become the friend. The halo of accomplished self-sacrifice is around L'Infirme, making this tale one of the most noble and pathetic.

Turning to quite a different note, we will sketch out "Le Retour" and "L'Abandonné," two of Maupassant's deepest short stories. "Le Retour" is drawn from low life among silent and undemonstrative peasants. "L'Abandonné," on the contrary, is taken from society, where words and actions are only the means of concealing thoughts.

Madame de C. has a "friend," who some forty years ago became the father of her son. Tied legally by marriage, Madame de C. cannot recognize her illegitimate son. She wishes, however, to see this son before she dies. He was torn away from her on the day of his birth. One very hot afternoon Madame de C. goes with the friend to the farmhouse where this son of hers lives. The farmer's wife, *une femme à la figure de bois,*

receives her grumbling. Whilst she is arguing,
urging Madame de C. to take her departure, the
farmer passes by, his head buried in his shoulders,
dragging a cow behind him and emphasizing the
animal's obstinacy by a tremendous oath. Madame
de C., who from sheer exhaustion has fallen upon
a seat, grasps the friend's arm.

"It is *he*," says she, "it is our son! Is that
what you have made of him? Let us go! Come
away; I cannot bear this." "I settled a farm
and 80,000 francs on him," answers the friend.
"Many a legally born son of a *bourgeois* would
wish for the same." And father and mother both
rejoin the husband, who seeing them coming, calls
out: "Well, my dear, . . . I hope you have had
a sunstroke!" "No, indeed, a delightful walk,"
says the friend.

In "Le Retour" the scene is among peasants,
whose impassibility is real, not feigned; for the
peasant not only feels less acutely than educated
mortals, but he ignores the means of transmitting
his emotions even when he experiences them. He
is like a substance without a shadow. If he feels
a shock there is no outward rebound; if he suffers
he knows not how to depict his pain. His joys or
his grief ignore the play which in the educated
being is often the unconscious echo of stage re-
membrances. Trained from her earliest infancy
by sheer imitation of her elders to put her facial
expression in harmony with the sentiments she
wishes to convey, the woman of the world is an
actress whose movements complete her thoughts.

In "Le Retour" a man named Martin is lost at

sea. His widow, the mother of two children, marries another sailor, by name Lévesque. Twenty
years elapse, and one day the wife is troubled by
the persistence of a beggar at her door. In the
evening Lévesque returns from his day's work, and
speaks to the beggar, who turns out to be no other
than Martin, the former husband. Both husbands
agree to go to the curé ; no small indication this,
on Maupassant's part, of the great prestige still
held among peasants by the priest. No less a
trait of peasant physiology is the attitude of the
woman, who in point of fact falls into the arms of
Martin, calling him "Mon cher homme!" whilst
at the same time she remains devoted to Lévesque.
The curé lives at the other end of the village. On
their way the men enter the tavern. There both
husbands tarry sufficiently long to agree that law-
suits are costly, and that the curé's decision might
lead to a suit. A pleasant state of friendship
between the two husbands is therefore determined
upon by both men, and the story closes with the
true and characteristic ejaculation of a peasant
recognizing Martin after twenty years : "Tiens,
c'est tè!" (*tè* being the country slang for *toi*).
That is all, but coming from a French peasant it is
enough, as it implies all in the way of queries and
wonderment which it withholds.

Maupassant's picturesque narratives of Africa
and Arab women are no less interesting than his
French stories, but as space limits us to his psychical studies above all, we will end our consideration
of his short tales with a few words about one of
his last, "L'Inutile Beauté." The Comte de Mas-

caret has married a penniless and lovely girl. His
love for her is of a realistic sort. From jealousy
principally, and to keep her at home, he has made
of his wife a slave to maternity. In the space of
eleven years she has had seven children; but she
takes her revenge. "Your conduct has made me
hate you," says she to her husband, "and I have
had my revenge against you. I swear solemnly
by the heads of my children that one of them
is not yours — you shall never know which!"
Mascaret begins to suffer torture; he neglects
his wife; his club friends remark that he looks
like one eaten up by a secret sorrow. After six
years' martyrdom, during which he never goes
near his children without the horrible thought
that one of them is not his own, he entreats his
wife to take pity on him. "For mercy's sake, tell
me which is not mine? I will swear to love him
as the others." "I told you a lie," replies his
wife; "I never had a lover. I have always been
faithful to you." This only aggravates matters,
as now the husband is at a loss to know which
statement he can rely upon. The suffering he
undergoes is so evident that the wife is touched,
moved to pity, and says: "I see that you have
suffered enough. I assure you I am now speaking
the truth. All these children are yours. But
had I not acted in this way, I should by this time
be the mother of four more! Women are members of a civilized world, and we decline to be
treated as mere females to repeople society!"

As she spoke he felt instinctively that the woman who thus addressed him was not made solely

for the sake of perpetuating the race, but that she was as well a strange, unfathomable outcome of all the complicated desires amassed through centuries; that she had diverged from the primitive and divine intention of her existence, and was developing a mystic and indescribable beauty, such as we dream of, surrounded by all the poetry and ideal luxury with which civilization endows her, a statue of flesh, appealing to the senses and yet ministering to the mind. Emotions filled the husband's breast far more stirring than the old simple form of love.

"Pierre et Jean" and "Fort comme la Mort" are the author's masterpieces. Let us consider them briefly.

Madame Roland has two sons: Pierre, the elder, a doctor; Jean, the younger, a lawyer. As to Roland, he is a mild grotesque, given up exclusively to the seafaring mania, and keeping a boat, with one boatman as his "crew." One fine day, unexpectedly, Jean is advised that an income of 20,000 francs a year has been left to him. Rejoicings on this account are high in the Roland family, till an old druggist strikes a knell in Pierre's heart. This inheritance, according to the druggist's views, is so detrimental to Madame Roland's past that Pierre, who worships his mother, is brought to actual despair. Pierre now remembers Monsieur Maréchal, the testator, and gradually becomes his mother's spy. One day when Madame Roland is gazing at Maréchal's miniature she sees herself watched by Pierre; hence she knows him to be possessed of her secret. Pro-

gressively the relations between Pierre and his
mother · become so strained that the unfortunate
woman clings violently to her younger son. The
very day when Jean takes up his abode in new
rooms, where he is to carry on his legal practice,
Pierre, unable to control his sorrow any longer,
tells Jean plainly that he is living on the proceeds
of his mother's shame. Madame Roland, con-
cealed in the adjoining room, hears everything;
she throws herself on her younger son's bed and
swoons. The ensuing scene between Madame Roland and Jean is of the deepest pathos. "If you
cannot look upon your poor father as my true, my
only love, leave me!" Pierre's reprobation haunts
her; she cannot bear it.

Pierre is made to undergo nothing but trouble,
whilst Maupassant bestows on Jean, the inferior
mortal, every happiness that fortune, love, and
maternal affection can bring. Pierre goes off as a
doctor on an American steamer. His mother is
relieved at his departure, and none regret him —
not even the Polish chemist, Markrosko, who, having counted upon him to help his trade, only rages
against his departure. Pierre's further attempt
to raise some regret in a girl he had once loved
merely brings him her felicitations for going to
America, — "A beautiful country, as I hear."

Next to "Pierre et Jean," "Fort comme la
Mort" is certainly Maupassant's *chef d'œuvre*. The
painter Bertin has become famous after painting
the portrait of Madame de Guilleroy, one of the
leaders of Parisian elegance. He falls in love
with her, and struggles bravely with his passion,

whilst she on her side never comes to the sittings but accompanied by her little girl. She tries to frighten away love by making fun of it; asks Bertin how his passion fares; in fact, has recourse to light gayety, till one day passion is strongest, and . . . when she leaves the studio (having that day been unable to bring the child) she feels her life is given forever to Bertin. If she ceases the sittings her husband will wonder, so she bravely goes back the next day and asks Bertin to forget. . . . She promises she will try to do so herself. The painter submits . . . and long remains in the bonds of distant friendship; but *she* feels what he is undergoing, and enters with him into a *liaison* which never swerves one instant on both sides for above twelve years. Guilleroy swears by Bertin, and Bertin never during these years looks at any other woman but the comtesse. Nanette, the little girl of fourteen years ago, is now a woman. She is presented and betrothed, and her likeness to her mother is still enhanced by her being in mourning, as Madame de Guilleroy had been when she first met Bertin. When Nanette stands under her mother's portrait it is obvious to all that she is its model. Without analyzing his emotions, Bertin strangely feels himself becoming younger. At one time he used to suffer cruelly from his solitude at home. . . . But time has diminished that feeling. Now all at once he begins to feel the same again. He wishes she was ever with him, and that he could always hear her crystalline voice. (Nanette's voice and her mother's, like their faces, are easily mistaken for one another.) Bertin, seated in the comtesse's boudoir, watches her and Nanette close to each other under the lamp-shade, and the thought of his solitude becomes more and more oppressive. As he gazes at Madame de Guilleroy his heart is filled with the words of former days, which he would like to utter now. He wishes she would send the girl to bed, for his heart has suddenly leapt back fourteen years, and he wants to give her fresh happiness.

The comtesse is summoned unexpectedly to the country to her mother's death-bed. Tears and sorrow make her believe that she has lost her beauty, and she reaches such a pitch of anxiety on that subject that, madly frightened at the arrival of Bertin, she takes refuge in her house instead of meeting him at the train, for fear of the indiscretions of broad daylight. Once back in Paris, this anxiety becomes a fixed idea. She gazes and gazes at herself in the mirror, breaking her own heart over the sad inspection of her wrinkles. At night she lies awake; rises, to begin again the perusal of this sad, lovely, careworn face, dreading that insomnia may only add to the havoc. She prays, kneeling before a crucifix (a gift of Bertin's), that respite shall be granted. Many and many women have been allowed to remain long beautiful. Why not she as well? With a woman's tact she has discovered the nature of Bertin's sentiments towards her daughter, but she forgives. She even pities Bertin. One day, overwhelmed by feeling that he has grown old, and desperate because he cannot get the better of his love for Nanette, wounded to

the quick, moreover, by a critique in the "Figaro,"
Bertin puts an end to his life, and the comtesse,
summoned in time, receives his last words.

This story of a love equally long and profound
on both sides is dignified and interesting. Though
Maupassant's heroes generally submit too easily to
the call of their nervous system, "Fort comme la
Mort" gives no instance of this habitual weakness.

Our author's last book, "Notre Cœur," is the
story of the moral rise and fall of a lover whom a
coquette raises for a time above mere pleasure,
and who, deceived by his mistress, falls back to
Anacreontic devices. Why all of a sudden society
should have been so severe upon the lover in "Notre
Cœur" is a matter of great wonderment. There is
a little book called "Le Lys dans la Vallée," a marvelous little book, in which Balzac took up the
sketch of a certain Beaumarchais and made a portrait out of the mere outline of the comtesse (Mariage de Figaro). In that wonderful little book
one sees a highly respected man of the world re-
sort for ambition's sake to the same source as the
hero of "Notre Cœur." Félix de Vandenesse,
Balzac's hero, is and remains, notwithstanding his
failings, favorably regarded by the reader; why,
then, this great severity toward the similar character in "Notre Cœur"?

Who knows, after all? French morals are perhaps more in the ascendant than is generally believed; but Maupassant's art is our purpose, and
his art, more than that of any of his contemporaries, is the outcome of his own nature, of a nature
expressing the temperament of his time. Loti is

tho poet of romancers, Zola is the Darwinist, Maupassant the physiologist, the man of the amphitheatre, the surgeon who, after cutting through the outer envelope, carefully handles one nerve after another, measuring, studying, weighing, appreciating the influence of each upon the group, the reaction of the local phenomena upon the whole system. Like Bourget, Maupassant is the "romancier-médecin," the man of prompt diagnosis, the real exponent of his time, which is with us the age of science.

Maupassant, in a word, is the artist as well as the scientist, and his success came to him, according to Madame de Lafayette's saying, still more from "what he is than from what he does." His gifts are as abundant as his requirements, for " he knows as much as he guesses."

Yet the different appreciation which is given by our public to analogous facts, the disapproval to-day of ways of life which were acceptable in 1835, rather enhances the documental worth of Maupassant's tales. These become somewhat akin to an average pulse of the moral status. Few writers, also, have struck so many different chords as Maupassant, passing from the most talented picture of the lowest moral surroundings, as in "La Maison Tellier," "Une Vie" (prohibited in the railway library), "Bel-Ami," "Les Sœurs Rondoli" (between 1880 and 1886), to such books as "Pierre et Jean" and "Fort comme la Mort," — real epics from the point of view of depth of feeling.

Flaubert was not the sole inspirer and master of

Maupassant. Mérimée's short tales, it is very evident, also guided him. Though perhaps less imaginative than Mérimée, and more turned to psychology, Maupassant has a style which at times reminds one of Mérimée's. The majority of the heroes, too, are the same pessimistic, ironical personalities as in Mérimée, though Maupassant's irony is perhaps more tempered with generous pity than is the case with the author of "Carmen." We should not forget either that Maupassant, who died in 1893, was taken in the prime of his years ; so that his pessimism was a fruit of his own mood, a result of the atmosphere which he breathed, rather than, as with Mérimée, the outcome of disillusion and of the tedious monotony of things and of life generally.

ZOLA AS AN EVOLUTIONIST

To attempt in the space of a short article a general sketch of the work of any writer of romance is always somewhat of an impertinence; yet more so when the object of the sketch is Zola, the man of his time who has evolved in his books the greatest number of original ideas, the man who has combined in the highest degree the elements of saturation and radiation.

No personages are to a greater degree than Zola's creations the outcome of the organic forces, climate, temperature, and soil; that is, the outcome of surroundings and heredity. No personages, either, surpass those of Zola in offering to organic forces their own personal intellectual and emotional energies; man receiving and man giving; human vibration, which answers in direct proportion to the calls made upon it.

Such is the particular side of Zola's work which, to our mind, leads this work straight to evolution, Darwinism, Spencerism. This is the feature of Zola's literary temperament, leading him to the scientific conclusions which are the basis of these pages.

" The Paradoux till then had only been visited by the sun; the love of Serge and Albine first infused life into the Paradoux ! " he says in " La Faute de l'Abbé Mouret." Further on : " The birds, the trees, the very frogs paid homage to the lovers. This was their kingdom — the Eden where they reigned supreme ! "

Here are the processes of organic fecundation merging into life. Flowers, atmosphere, the natural calling of all forces to each other here culminated in the love of the two children of Eden united in the Paradoux. The desert has in return received from them by radiation the gift of life. Thus is the parable complete ; no less complete than the blending together of all the essences, psychical as well as physiological ; in fact, biology applied instead of theoretic. If, in the effort of finding out, as Descartes says, "where a thought is lodged in its author," I ask myself, What is in reality Zola's own intellectual climate and temperature ? I am at once struck by the very complexity of the scientific atmosphere in which our author lives, — an ambient complexity of atmosphere so very oppressive that we cannot help feeling the results of it in his books.

Though Zola's books differ in the quality of the human weaknesses he satirizes, they are alike in their physiological essence. All of them tend more or less to the outburst, in each member of the one Rougon Macquart family, of some particular manifestation of wantonness, avarice, or mad vanity. Psychical or physiological shall be the manifestation, but it shall take place. From 1870 to 1880, from the " Rougon Macquart," on through the " Conquête de Plassans," the " Curée," and " L'Abbé Mouret," to the " Bonheur des Dames," —where at last noble Denise is born, a Rose among all these Thistles, — nothing buds upon these human plants but sin and brutality. In 1893 "Docteur Pascal" expresses the bodily weaknesses of the whole race. He is neither unscrupulous like the Rougons of the "Curée," nor ungovernably ambitious or licentious. His bodily health, not his soul, is compromised, and disease under the form of tuberculosis does away with all his fighting powers.

Son of an Italian engineer, the builder of "Pont Zola" at Aix, Emile Zola, who was born in Paris in 1840, when Louis Philippe was on the throne, began his literary life in journalism. He was the press intermediary between Hachette and all the Paris papers : hence his work on the "Globe," the "Temps," the "Petit Journal." The influence of this early work has prompted him constantly during the last five or six years to mix himself up with politics and public matters, accusing or absolving in a way which, to say the least, is rather indiscreet.

His rate of work has been about six hundred pages a year for the last quarter of a century. This implies little enough leisure for judging men and things in a general way. In 1893 "La Debâcle" showed us what the same virtueless people were capable and incapable of in front of the foe. His last books, "Rome" and "Paris," have not added to his literary status. As a quarter of a century rarely sees the same public turned to the same literary appetites, it may be added that the readers of to-day incline more toward delicate satirists of the quality of Lemaître, or of France, than toward descriptive and even sometimes prolix *naturalism*. It may be said also that Zola's effervescent zeal to get into the Academy — trying uselessly for the seats of John Lemoyne, Marmier, and Renan — has considerably hurt those who loved to see in him one of those literary artists too proud ever to be vain.

Mentioning Zola in his "Contemporains," Jules Lemaître has certainly struck with his ordinary skill one of the truest notes of his talent, in saying, "Zola is no critic; no more is he, as he insists upon being, a naturalistic romancer. He is a pessimistic poet; a poet because with a view to his description, whatever it be, he transforms realities and modifies them for the benefit of the amplifications of his story. Compare him with the author of ' Nabab: ' the naturalist is Daudet far rather than the author of ' L'Assommoir,' which implies that Zola's paintings are, perhaps, all the stronger, because they are bigger than the human size."

Though a man may differ in his own private thoughts from the general psychical atmosphere of his time, his genius or talent will seldom fail to be coherent with the period in which it has developed. No one could imagine Dr. Johnson at the court of Charles II., or Voltaire in the same salons as the Bishop of Meaux. Returning to the apparently sweeping proposition above expressed, that our present period in France is, scientifically speaking, one of great complexity, we may illustrate this by the fact that one of the leading men of the day in French physiology, Dr. Charles Richet,[1] is at the

---

[1] Dr. Charles Richet is Professor of Physiology at the Ecole de Médecine. He has organized in France the first serious scientific researches and inquiries on the subject of psychology.

same time the leader of all psychical researches in the same country. What such a double power of brain says for the man who possesses it, we are not called upon to consider here. Dr. Charles Richet, though the youngest of illustrious French scientists, is as well known to the English public and as highly thought of in England as in France. The object of our remark here is simply that a time when the same mind can on the one hand lead other minds to the precise conclusions of the " Anatomical Table," and on the other hand simultaneously lead these minds, and others with them, into the realm of psychical speculations; that a time when powers so diverse can lead to successful efforts toward knowledge, is necessarily to be termed a complex period. Thus can we say that, if 1789 was the epoch for lawyers, 1889 was the period for doctors, scientists, and biologists. Hence the medical psychology of Bourget, the scientific physiology of Maupassant, the psychical physiology of Zola.

This first point conceded, namely, that Zola is a physiologist above all because he submits without rebellion to the pressure of his time and surroundings, we will proceed to add the following : From physiology to chemistry, that is, from the study of man's organs to the study of his fluids, and of the way in which these organic fluids combine with the atmospheric fluids; from the theory of the dissipation of energy in man to sheer naturalism, and from sheer naturalism to mythology, there is but the distance measured by Zola's power of imagination.

Mythologist, have we said? Yes, mythologist through the pressure of physiology and biology, and evolutionist through the latent unconscious Spencerism which fills the atmosphere of these days; mythologist by the enforcement on his personages of those penalties, after the defeat of will and the triumph of the lower self, which pagan antiquity reserved for its victims.

Earth with Zola — the earth earthy — is so far the foe of all that is elevated, the cause of all failure, that not only in " La Terre," but in numbers of other instances, we see the soil and its fluids play the part of the vanquisher, and wreck the higher promptings of the soul.

"Zepphrin hésitait encore, mais de chaudes bouffées de terre d'automne fraîchement remuée le grisèrent, il s'enhardit," he says in "Une Page d'Amour." And in another passage : " Elle avait son visage dur de femme jalouse, car la mort venait, la terre montait à elle pour la reprendre."

This idea of sending back to the lower elements the man in whom the divine element is blurred ; this idea, curiously enough, in its outer mythological " allure " has merged into the "pulvere reverteris" of Catholic orthodoxy, — an orthodoxy to which earth, the soil, is death, corruption, the very reverse of Cybele, the fecund deity of the Greeks. Above ideas stand habits, customs, for customs order the doings of man, whilst ideas only inspire them. Physiology has now entered the French mode of thought. She keeps as close company with all the writers of our day as did philosophy with those of the eighteenth century. High pres-

sure and overwork have forced physiology down
from her former exalted position, in which she was
to be approached only by the initiated; and though
I will not venture to affirm that all writers of fiction in France read Huxley, I can safely say that
they all discuss him, and are well acquainted with
the substance of his teachings. The close contact
brought about in our time between writers and
doctors, owing to nervous exhaustion and hard
work, has been the origin of all the contagion of
physiology among laymen — among novel-writers
above all. If we once concede the force of the evidence of the dominance of physiology in modern
literature, we concede also the preëminence of the
laws of atavism in the same field, the very basis
of Zola's work. Balzac, in fiction, had invoked
atavism long before Zola, — no need to discuss
that, — but Balzac had introduced atavism as a
means conducive to the interest of his stories.
He never used atavism like the scientific biologist,
as a demonstration of truths which till the present
day have belonged only to science. Balzac was
a novelist, — the greatest creative genius of his
day, — but not a scientist.

Balzac would create a Madame Marneffe, and
provided she stood the test of the events which
she had to go through, provided she was sufficiently supple and grasping, Balzac and his reader
were satisfied. Who in those days would care to
ascertain the temperature of Madame Marneffe's
blood, or whether she was nervous, or "nervo-
sanguine," etc.? But now we are the servants of
science — of physiology above all. Atavism is in

itself no novelty; the Greek drama lived on it, and Shakespeare as well. The only novelty lies in the way in which atavism is handled by our author; in the application to creations of the imagination of the facts of experimental physiology; in fact, in the tracing out, with the help of physiology, of the origin of creatures of fiction in the same way as Michelet would apply the science to the study of a great figure in history. To accuse Zola of being immoral because the effort of will in such creatures as Nana or Lantier is inferior to the power of the appetites, is as unjust, relatively, as it would be to accuse Michelet of partiality when he shows the assassination of Henri IV. as a result of Marie de Medici's lymphatic sensualism. Whether fiction or history, truth is truth, and if the development of atavism is the basis of the study of a human character, this delineation of character must be faithful to the promptings shown by physiology as the determining motives of the character under consideration.

Still, to be a physiologist or a biologist, as Zola shows himself in many of his writings, in no way implies that he is also a materialist (a word now rather meaningless, as positivism is the keynote of modern scientific philosophy). In France, the materialist, if there be any, should evidently be as indifferent to the evolutions of man's soul (whatsoever they were) as to natural phenomena of any kind. Moral hurricanes, or cyclones, should not have the power of stirring the true materialist to anger; the very fact of his being a sincere materialist would as its first result make him satisfied

with all nature's solutions, and render him averse
to any possible amelioration. Now, Zola's han-
dling of his characters is so far from betraying
indifference that his anger at their frailty and
weakness amounts to hatred, and he never treats
of their misdemeanors otherwise than in scorn and
in wrath.

Real, thorough Materialism is, therefore, as rare
at the present time in France as genuine Atheism.
The true materialists were the men of forty years
ago, — Broca, Trousseau, Davesne, all of them
more or less pupils of Cabanis and Condillac, who
were in turn, philosophically speaking, grandsons
of Locke. And even these were sensualists, not
materialists proper; they adhered to the doctrines
of sensation in Locke and Condillac, dead and
exploded systems since Darwin's appearance : for
Darwinism teaches evolution, that is, immortal
movement and life persistent, whilst, on the other
hand, the theory of mere sensation leads to death,
to death coincident with the extinction of the
body.

All modern science in France indorses Littré's
proposition : " Life properly so-called escapes all
man's efforts at classification or researches ; it cannot be reduced to any chemical or physical laws."
Littré is a positivist, and the day is gone when
Descartes could affirm that the soul lay hidden
under " the ninth lobe of the brain," as the day is
also gone when it could be asserted that life is
matter, and matter alone !

Forces, the combinations of forces intellectual,
moral, psychical, and physiological, these are the

pillars on which now rests the theoretic philosophy
of French scientists. Above all, in questions
which pass from physics into metaphysics the present generation is eclectic and decidedly opposed
to dogmatism. Scientifically speaking, we have
tried to show that Zola is no materialist; it remains for us to try to sketch his methods in the
field of morals. If in relation to science Zola
keeps pace with the age and with his surroundings by his treatment of the duality in man, we
may well say that in regard to morals Zola goes
back to very simple divisions and to very old
devices, — so old in reality as not to differ much
from those of the twelfth century. The Dragon
and St. Michael at war together within the same
being, this was the mediæval conception of man;
it is also at times that of Zola. St. Michael kills
the Dragon when the personage is Angélique or
Albine; the Dragon devours the soul when the
personage is Lantier, Nana, or others of the same
weakened nature.

Symbolism and allegory underlie many of Zola's
works; especially is this the case in " La Faute de
l'Abbé Mouret," where the symbol of paradise is
not the only basis of the theme, but where a secondary personage, a side figure, Désirée Mouret,
is a most eloquent symbol of moral nullity. Désirée is the living demonstration that brain-life,
even to our realistic master, is really life *par excellence.* Beautiful, healthy, with every physical
gift in exquisite proportion, Désirée Mouret, the
Abbé's sister, is a psychical nullity. No thought
stirs her soul; her mind is torpid. She is a very

statue of Condillac.[1] Zola has not described Désirée as in active opposition to intellect, but as
simply, naturally null in her mind and will, and
therefore through that very nullity assimilated to
the inferior creatures who court her, and associate
with her, feeling her to be very nearly akin to
themselves. The mere fact of her nullity makes
Désirée no more than a statue to all irrational
beings. Birds perch upon her, animals brush up
against her ; she is the type of form, and of form
only.

The philosophical scheme of Zola in his general
work (admitting that he is conscious of having
such a scheme) is worked out by his personages
rather than theorized on by himself. The objec-
tion to this has been its unreality. Our vices, it
has been objected, are not the sole guides of our
conduct, and to depict human nature from its evil
aspects only, is not to represent it fairly. The
answer is that Zola depicts what appeals to his
particular genius, and that this genius is neither
that of Berquin nor that of Florian. Genius applies itself to its particular calling ; no one finds
fault with Rosa Bonheur for choosing animals
rather than historical subjects. Why, then, blame
Zola for the view he takes of humanity ? He
paints what he sees, and provided the picture be
living and talented we should say with Voltaire,
"There are no bad books ; there are only books

---

[1] Condillac's " théorie de la sensation " is demonstrated by
his illustration of the statue, where, taking an automatic
figure, he shows how moral life and thought penetrate it
progressively by means of the senses.

badly conceived and badly expressed, and also bad readers." Novels and romances are not copies of real life, but rather translations — interpretations of life. To interpret a life for the public benefit is to draw from it its proper meaning. To write a novel or a play is to set forth the meaning of a character in one or at most two of its phases, phases which in the novel must necessarily be successive, for the sake of the reader's comprehension, whilst in life they would be simultaneous. The novel can depict the human heart only as the painter depicts the human form, in one of its phases at a time. The painter decides upon a three quarters view or a profile, and, once fixed upon, this will go down to posterity as a portrait, whilst instead of being properly a portrait of the whole person, it is but a likeness of one side of his appearance. Novels are the same; they can convey only fragmentary aspects of the human soul; therefore the novelist must choose, and though his talent may lead him to mingle corruption and innocence as exquisitely as l'Abbé Prévolt in "Manon Lescault," his art will ever force him, like Balzac, to portray a certain type of woman under the name of Madame Marneffe, and another type under the name of Eugénie Grandet. The least educated and cultivated beings are the least complex. In the scale of humanity a peasant is necessarily less complex than a city workman, and a city workman less complex than a thinker. Hence Zola's taste for taking his types so frequently from the people, as they are simpler and less disguised than their superiors. As to the question of strict morality in literary fiction, it is difficult for this not to become a question of relativeness; otherwise what would become of all the classics? Paganism is not an answer, for paganism had its stoics and its mystics, — Marcus Aurelius, Plato, and others, — as Christianity has its sensualists, its epicures.

The first care of a book-writer is, therefore, the literary and philosophical excellence of his book. The writer is the baker: his business is the quality of the bread, not the results of digestion. Provided the bread be nutritious and the book suggestive and true, — in fact, of a kind to arouse and promote thought in the reader, — the mission of the writer is accomplished. Heroic tales may generate heroic deeds, but the processes of the mind are diverse and incalculable; it is almost impossible to declare from the nature of the seed what will result as flower or fruit.

A thought is a shell; it may burst before reaching its aim. Hence good deeds may spring from indifferent soils; the chemical combinations in the realm of psychology, from which spring actions good or bad, are far too intricate and too personal to the beings themselves ever to be laid to the responsibility of any author. Thoughts may turn to good whose first origins were just the reverse, and *vice versâ*. It is therefore moral and worthy to sow good seed; but it is unjust to charge one or two writers of genius with the laxity of morals which exists in their time. Besides, of perversity there is no trace to be found in Zola's work, though the same work is undeniably interspersed with very grossly naturalistic details.

To return to the tendencies of Zola to symbolism, which are so very evident in some of his books, and which lead him to deep poetical feeling, no passage is more eloquent in this respect than chapter xiii. in " La Faute de l'Abbé Mouret." A more perfect combination of modern color and archaism than the landscape of the Edenic garden of Paradoux has never been produced. Something in the landscape is very much like the work of Turner's brush, modified by a touch of Gustave Moreau, and peopled with figures drawn by Burne Jones. Nowhere, perhaps, in all Zola's work does Love, the god, play such a divine part as in the Paradoux, spreading his rays of life on dead nature all around him, whilst nature in turn bends in humble obeisance before him ! Love, it will be said, is not the only subject for the novelist. Certainly not ; and Zola, above all others, takes that view, since ambition, cupidity, revenge, are portrayed in his different works.

No, love is not the only passion, certainly, with which the novelist has to deal, but it is the passion of all others which finds most favor amongst readers, for it is the one passion above all that has power of life and death.

To write truly upon this subject it is of first importance to analyze love, relegating to the animal side of nature what belongs to it, but never forgetting that love, like death and like life, escapes all man's curiosity, and that its origin and its end are alike hid from his inquisitive eye. Its birth is divine, its death enveloped in mystery. According to these laws it is well for Zola to paint such beings as Albine and Angélique, but they present humanity under only one aspect, and he deals with all aspects. Besides, Zola's supreme merit is to show the evolution of passions, to impersonate rather than to discuss them.

Although our author has not the highly-strung perception of the pathos of love which Loti possesses, he has a greater diversity of gifts than any of his contemporaries. Poetry, science, the knowledge of all characteristics, and thoroughness in whatever he touches are his, and so much his own that to find one equally gifted we could cite Tolstoï alone.

To return, in closing these remarks, to their original subject, evolution, we would say that Tolstoï, Ibsen, and Zola have been the missionaries of the doctrines of Darwin and Spencer, applying the theory of evolution throughout their books under the form of atavism or heredity. Zola does not hint, like Tolstoï, at the question of psychical evolution. Zola keeps to the physiological side of heredity. He watches the working of the germ in the being, its growth, expansion, decay, and re-birth; in fact, Zola keeps fast to the law of life and its eternal transmutability, a doctrine entirely modern and in every way antagonistic and opposed to the teachings of the eighteenth century.

One of the best examples of the re-birth of force springing from decay is given by Angélique in "Le Rêve." The mother is as perverted in her mind as she is corrupt in her person, perversion and corruption neutralizing each other. A lily rises from the mire, and Angélique is the fresh plant of a thoroughly exhausted stem. She is life springing out of death, sunshine arising in darkness.

Ibsen's conclusions are the more desperate; Tolstoï's conclusions the more cruel; Zola's conclusions the more brutal. Immoral, philosophically speaking, they are not. For the "Kreuzer Sonata," "Nana," "L'Assommoir," or "Ghosts" are none of them the apology, but the dire and bitter condemnation, of vice. The philosophical side of a book, however, belongs but to the few; the majority do not rise above the story. When the story is horror-striking or revolting, the reader turns away, going no farther. But what then? Is the naturalism of the writer too forcible, or is the reader not strong enough to bear the truth?

"L'homme est un composé de matière et d'esprit. Il ignore la matière, il ignore l'esprit, il ignore le bien qui réunit la matière avec l'esprit; et c'est là tout l'homme!" says Pascal.

Why not, then, with Voltaire lay the fault at the door of the "bad reader"? The reader, however, departs scatheless; the writer remains to bear the burden. Writers of Zola's power survive the shock; this is their revenge.

EDMOND DE GONCOURT

I

THE last letter addressed by Edmond de Goncourt to Madame Alphonse Daudet, in which he asked her to receive him on a private visit, without any friends, — this last letter, after twenty years' friendship, is not much more familiar than the one written in 1881, in which the same Goncourt announced to the young household (" le petit ménage "), as he called the Daudets, that soon " Renée Mauperin " would be copied, and that friend Céard would ask them to fix an evening for him to read it to them. Then followed these words, addressed especially to Madame Daudet : " You condemn me, who have often spoken ill of the female sex, to write a novel in honor of the good woman, the intelligent woman, the gracious woman ; disguised at a distance beneath a velvet mask, this woman will be the portrait of the wife of my best literary friend, your husband." The Goncourts — this plural will remain necessary, since death itself did not sever one brother's talent from the other — were, first and above all, historians ; this quality remained paramount even when they wrote novels. They were inspired by the curiosity of documents, we might call it restitutive curiosity, whether manifested in their historical or their psychological studies. Where Balzac created, the Goncourts reconstituted. Germinie Lacerteux, Renée Mauperin, are human reconstitutions, much more than creations ; the pretty attracted them, and conformably to the suggestion of their nervous temperament, they reproduced the surroundings of Madame du Barry and Madame de Pompadour by means of picturesque flashes, as they reconstructed poor Germinie Lacerteux by means of traits and chiaroscuro. Their style, in spite of Monsieur Faguet's [1] opinion to the contrary, is preëminently a gift of the painter, though it certainly betrays a nervous character. " Sister Philomena, slight and aërial, moves gently around the beds of the dying; her soul is felt in every breath she breathes." Again, consider this sentence with reference to Marie Antoinette : " She had the rhythmic step that heralds the approach of the goddesses in the ancient poems." The brothers were " colorists in their style because they were nervous," and similarly they may be called historians, because they possessed, both in history and in the novel, curiosity of the restitutive order. We should be judging by appearances only if we were to consider such realistic books as " Germinie Lacerteux " and " Renée Mauperin " as contradictory to their historical work. Physiology, the anatomical side of human phenomena, was always a subject of preoccupation to them. Let us not, however, confound what is contemporary with what is life ; though Germinie Lacerteux and Renée Mauperin are more properly contemporary,

[1] In the *Revue Bleue:* " The Goncourts."

they are to no greater extent life-studies than
Madame du Barry and Madame Pompadour. In
the former, as in the latter, the consideration of
the physiological contingents which affect the
psychological ones was paramount in the minds
of the writers. In order to pass judgment on
the Queens of the Left and Right, the two brothers made use of no other means, inductive or
deductive, than those employed in studying and
classing the hearts of the heroines in their novels.
The Goncourts differed but little from each other
except in externals; Jules being so delicate, so
pink and white in complexion, that when he was
on walking excursions with his brother, the latter
was always taken for some gay Wilhelm Meister
traveling with a disguised lady. Edmond was of
military bearing, looked like an officer, elegant and
precise. Notwithstanding this dissimilarity in their
outward person, their minds were the complements
of each other; their artistic apprehensions tended
towards the same choice. They agreed in this:
"That the history of a period is written by means
of its outward fashions and manners; that supper
menus and adornments manifest the inward state
of mind of a period." Thus it was that the brothers succeeded in dealing with the mind of the
eighteenth century with the same dexterous, artistic touch as that with which they fondly handled a
figurine of Coesvox or Cousto.[1]

With regard to this dexterity of manipulation
of the eighteenth century there are few more inter-

---

[1] Two sculptors of the eighteenth century, whose statues
are among the masterpieces of French art.

esting studies than that of Honoré Fragonard; it
is also one of the most convincing testimonies to
the artistic and color-loving nature of the Goncourts. We may remark, by the way, that some
of Taine's qualities are found in their work, partly
in the management and selection in their dealings
with art or with personalities. It is Taine, however, without his philosophy; for they lack general ideas, and linger more willingly over the
dissection of an individual or a branch of art,
than over the task of noticing, in a period, all that
its contingent of ideas has furnished to certain
attitudes of thought in the aggregate, during the
years it includes.

Jules de Goncourt died in 1870. " He was
slain by style," his brother writes, seeking to make
the French language express all it can and even
more. Literary form devoured him. " I remember," writes Edmond, "after hours of ceaseless
night labor passed in revising, and in efforts after
perfection, which wore away his brain, — I remember the anger of impotence, and, in fine, the
strange, intense protestation with which he let
himself fall on the divan, and how silent and over-
whelming was the smoking that followed." Here
was the same agony as that suffered by Flaubert,
but differently confronted; and while the giant
of Croisset roused and trained himself for the
struggle by scanning sentences in Chateaubriand's
" Atala," Jules de Goncourt ransacked his mind,
torturing its hyper-sensitive organism; and, vanquished, died at last in the full tide of youth, at
thirty-nine years of age, from congestion of the

brain, caused still more by the uncompromising severity of the "artist" than by over-work. It was the artist in him which made him pitiless of himself, and which never ceased spurring him on toward a greater perfection.

Together with their friends they formed a fine group of intellects. At the Sunday receptions held in their home at Auteuil, in the "Garret," as the house was called, the giants, the polar bears of genius, Flaubert and Tourgueniev, shaking their manes, stalked up and down the room filled with works of art, while, lounging on divans, Daudet, Maupassant, and the two brothers replied to their arguments. Each discussed, in his own mood, "Madame Bovary" and "Germinie Lacerteux," "La Faustin" and "La Maison Tellier," "Le Roi Lear de la Steppe" and "Fromont jeune," opposing one another, coming to close quarters in the persons of the authors, and finally appreciating one another with all the wise gradations that made each put himself in his true place, without braggadocio as also without false modesty. In 1852 Jules started a paper, to which for a year Gavarni supplied a daily illustration. This paper, with which Edmond naturally had quite as much to do as his brother, was yet more especially Jules's work. Among those who wrote for it were Méry, Gozlan, Alphonse Karr, Montépin, and Théodore de Banville. In 1853 an imperial ukase stopped the publication, which was called "Paris"; and the Goncourts, being somewhat anxious about their first novel, "En 18—" (which had been published on the 2d of December and whose leaves had been

scattered by the cannon of the "Coup d'Etat"),
as also about their play "Zemganio," bade adieu
to journalism. In the last number of their newspaper, they announced their intention of devoting
themselves to a book of historical biography,
"The Mistresses of Louis XV." Such was the
beginning of the reconstitution of the eighteenth
century, in which the brothers went from Queen
Marie Antoinette to the portrait-painters of the
day, and from them to the courtesans. These last
particularly were placed before the modern reader's
eyes with all their detailed characteristics. The
Goncourts had already at that period fixed their
attention on one side of their subject, and were
seeking for the spirit of the age they described,
above all, in its manners and customs. In an excellent article written on the morrow of Edmond's
death, Henri Fouquier asserts that Edmond was
especially the novelist. Now, as the novels, no
less than the works of history and the plays, were
joint productions, what can be the ground for such
an assertion? "La Faustin," one of Edmond's last
books, had but little success, and would scarcely
serve to prove what Fouquier says. If Edmond
were more decidedly the novelist of the two, why
did he not show it by writing some work quite distinct from that which was common to both? and
how is it possible to draw the line between the respective contributions of the two brothers to their
common labor, when we can no longer question
the authors themselves? In "Sœur Philomène,"
as in "Nos Hommes de Lettres" and "Madame
Gervaisais," there are studies made simultaneously

in the same environment, either medical (" Charles_
Demailly," for instance), or mystical, or licentious.
But whatever be the environment, the two brothers
fix their spy-glasses on the same phenomena.
After a number of years it is really impossible for
the reader to determine what belongs to one or the
other in the building up of the characters, or in
the development of the story. Before coming to
their work, which I shall divide into two parts,
I beg to be allowed a sketch of their family and
surroundings; after which, I shall point out, in
the historical works and the novels, the portions
best calculated to indicate the merits of their style
and art. One of their most characteristic traits
is a sense of deep pity underlying their irony, —
a sense of pity which extends beyond the mere
persons of those who are being painted. An
instance of this is seen when Sœur Philomène
returns thanks to God in her evening prayers, "O
Lord, what have I done for so many blessings,"
whilst Romaine is blaspheming the sufferings of
which she is dying.

II

In the year 1830 Monsieur and Madame de
Goncourt were temporarily settled in the Rue
des Carmes, a faubourg of Nancy. Their family
name, which was Huot, belonged to the old parliamentary *bourgeoisie*. The De Goncourt title had
been conferred on the family by letters patent from
Louis XVI. Documentary proof of these letters
was produced by the Goncourts at a time when a
newspaper controversy had led Louis Ulbach to

write, " Edmond and Jules de Goncourt call themselves by the name of their village, but they have
made sufficient protest against those that accuse
them of using a false name, for this name to be
attributed to them." These letters patent, consti-
tuting them " Seigneurs de Goncourt," date from
1787, are marked with the seal of the town of Bar,
and are signed by the king.[1]

Edmond was born in Paris in 1822; Jules
eight years later, in 1830. At the boarding-school
of Goubaux, Edmond studied with Dumas *fils*,
without, however, injuring his health by any undue
application. He tells us in the " Journal" how
he first acquired a taste for collecting : —

" My uncle," he writes, " had in 1836 some property at Menilmontant ; it was the ' Petite Maison
pleasure house,' formerly inhabited by Mademoiselle Marquise, a celebrated courtesan of the eighteenth century. Every Sunday we used to go out,
and this is how we spent the day. Toward two
in the afternoon, after lunching on raspberries, my
mother, my aunt, and another sister-in-law, clad in
pretty dresses of light muslin, and wearing plum-
colored shoes with satin cross-bows, such as Gavarni
paints, would set out for Paris. They formed
a pretty trio : my aunt, a dark beauty of the intellectual and witty type ; her sister-in-law, a blond-
complexioned creole, with blue eyes, light hair, pink
and white skin, and of languid manners. They
reached the Boulevard Beaumarchais. My aunt

---

[1] The most accurate documents on the brothers have been
collected in a valuable volume (*Les Goncourts*) by their eminent friend and executor, Alidor Delzant.

was one of the four or five persons in Paris, at this
period, who had a passion for old things, Venetian
glasses, objects in ivory, Genoa velvet, Alençon
point-lace. We arrived at the shop of a brica-
brac dealer, where, as it was Sunday, everything
was closed, the light entering only through the
half-open door. In the demi-obscurity of this
vague and dusty chaos there was a hurried and un-
canny sort of rummaging, and, as it were, the noise
of pattering mice, amid all this rubbish, while
hands were stretched timidly out, lest the clean
gloves should be soiled. Little toes poked out this
or that object; then there were sudden bursts of
joy at some fortunate discovery. Those Sundays
certainly made of me the collector of knickknacks
I have been all my life."

In 1849, to refresh themselves after the agita-
tions of the Revolution, the two brothers under-
took a walking-trip in France; it was on this
occasion that the blond and rosy-cheeked Jules,
by the side of Edmond, looked to those who saw
him like a woman in disguise. In 1852 they made
another journey together, this time to Italy, where,
at Milan, and again at Venice, they found themselves in the midst of Mazzini's revolution. On
their return they avenged the failure of their first
novel, "En 18—," caused by the political crisis,
by the bringing out of a second edition, which
Jules Janin welcomed with the warmest praise, —
praise we believe well justified, as will appear from
a few lines we quote, describing a scene on the
Seine near Meudon: "The river gurgles; the
humming of insects, the chirping of the crickets,

the whirring of wings in the tall poplars, the
smothered notes of far-off songs, the rustling of
germs shooting into life, joyous crackling, all filled
the silence with the murmuring hosanna chanted
by a beautiful summer day." Grumbling classicists
might ask how a " hosanna," which is an outburst,
can at the same time be a murmur ; however such a
license may astonish us, the passage is none the less
picturesque. It is a romantic effusion adapted to
a precise and rigorously exact picture. A cousin
of the Goncourts, Pierre Charles de Villedeuil, a
"musketeer of the empty sack," went into part-
nership with the two brothers in order to establish the " Eclair " newspaper. But at the end of
a year, during which the " Eclair " had struck
down too many government officials, this newspaper was obliged to disappear, and was replaced
by the "Lorette," which, by a singular irony of
circumstances, was published by Curmer, the religious publisher of the day. After the disappearance of the " Eclair " and of the " Lorette,"
the Goncourts published in book form, in 1856,
under the title " Quelques Créatures de ce Temps,"
a collection of articles that had already appeared
in these two newspapers ; and this was one of their
last steps before "introducing into history," as
Jules Janin wrote when speaking of the woman
of the eighteenth century, " what is not history."
Such is the work of the Goncourts, when they
sketch the portrait of the old woman of the eighteenth century, when they place the old lady's tub-
chair as the social pillar of society at this epoch,
when they show to what extent the influence of

those who *were* bears on those who *are*, and how
useful to the young of both sexes were these old
ladies, "living memories," who knew how to in-
struct and love those that were to come after them.

" In her poor, broken-down body was the low
rippling laughter of the mind's mirth ; over her lips
flits the past and flourishes once more in its reminiscences, whilst a lively, boyish speech decks with
a lost charm this old woman of the past. Around
the silk tub-chair [*tonneau*], where she ensconced
herself during the winter, see how many young
dark and blond heads throng; the old woman
pairs these young folks, comforts their worries, consoles their griefs by bantering them, breathes into
the rosy ears bent toward her a thousand lessons
of life, a thousand counsels of social morality and
of amorous directions, a thousand teachings at once
airy and profound. She is a beneficent fairy con-
cealed beneath a mask of wrinkles, and her young
smile, her amiable reason belie her white eyebrows.
She is the father confessor overflowing with abso-
lutions, she is the mother of loves, she is a bridge
between the two sexes, or, more justly, an old man
with the bewitching characteristics of a woman."

In the way the brothers Goncourt have treated
history, there is more than one point in common
with Taine, yet with this difference, shall I say
again ? — that Taine does not content himself with
arranging the human mosaic, what the English
call the "cumulative " evidence. Taine concludes ;
he unites pieces of evidence into a whole which he
comments on, and from which he draws conclusions. Taine is a philosopher, a deducer, a receiver

of ideas, whereas the Goncourts are only observers, delicate pryers into the secret movements of a century.

They were lucky finders; engravings, libraries, newspapers brought them treasures. Now it is the " Mémoires de Sophie Arnoud," [1] now the " Mémoires du Marquis de Calvière," in which latter the marquis, like Hérouard for Louis XIII., notes down, hour by hour, all the sallies and childish prodigies of Louis XV.; another time it is a Watteau, one of the least written-about painters of his time, for the simple reason that, being very poor and dying very young in the hospital, he had no time to frequent society and to obtain patrons. " Thus," writes Michelet, " their lucky discoveries have permitted them to deliver to the public still-quivering passion, wet traces of tears, imprints of tender hands," all, in fine, that forms the fragments of history, the blocks from which is formed the statue. With certain Marie Antoinette documents they have constructed an admirable and living figure. Leaving aside the queen's abandonment by the various foreign courts, a fact painfully brought out by Mallet du Pan's saying, " The foreign courts have paid so little attention to this catastrophe that the public has quickly ceased to be impressed by it;" leaving aside policy, they have revealed beneath the brilliant exterior of the Princess of Versailles the mien of grandeur and nobility which the woman opposed to the blind fury of

---

[1] Sophie Arnoud was one of the wittiest actresses of the end of the eighteenth century. Her preferred lover, the Duke de Lauraguais, was quite as witty as she was.

a maddened populace. They tell us that " the queen possessed all the characteristic marks which men's imagination requires from majesty in woman : a serene benevolence; a figure made to fill a throne ; hair forming a diadem of pale gold ; the most beautiful and brilliant complexion possible ; a perfect neck, perfect shoulders, and perfect hands; the rhythmic step that heralds the approach of the goddesses in the ancient poems ; a royal poise of the head ; a superb air of welcome and protection, the dazzling remembrance of which strangers carried away with them. Her mind manifested in private society a facility for complying with others, the habit of belonging to them, the art of encouraging them, the science of rendering them pleased with themselves. If any one took liberties with what she said, or put a malicious interpretation on it, the queen grew angry in her kindly way, or showed a childish alarm at the innocent sallies that escaped her, poutings that were forgotten in a moment in presence of a sad face, fits of laughter that swept away all disgrace, and, mingling together, queenly indulgence and womanly pardon." Neither Michelet nor Carlyle, nor yet Tacitus, had introduced impassibility into history; and when the model is at once the most attractive and the most unhappy of queens, and this model is painted by colorists as ardent as our authors, one need not be astonished at the enthusiasm of the tone.

The eighteenth century, which, underneath its furbelows, powder, and patches, its frivolous artificial fripperies, its outrageous crinolines and head-

dresses, was about to give birth to the picturesque
naturalism of Rousseau, and which colored the im-
pulsiveness of Diderot, — the eighteenth century,
more than any other period, was that of which the
Goncourts could say, " A period must be known
by its dinner-menus, a courtly period must be
sought out amid its fêtes and its attire." Moreover, the two brothers, who handled the engraver's
burin as they handled the pen, were peculiarly
fitted to sketch, out of the descriptions they gave
of the eighteenth century, the coming period, as it
were the outcome of its predecessor.

They were among the first to introduce the *living
document*, and thus, in drawing up the indictment
of a century, they call in the aid of all possible
witnesses ; none are unworthy or puerile in their
eyes. In the France of the eighteenth century the
Goncourts see forthcoming the present equality-
loving and democratic France in its slow elabora-
tion as expressed by the claims of the Beaumarchais " Figaro," the hybrid production of an epoch
in which Voltaire is the last classical death-rattle,
as Rousseau is the first breath of romanticism.
One of the original ideas of the Goncourts was to
revive the vivid and sprightly art of Moreau, Fragonard, and Watteau, at a time when the French
school of painting was living on the academicism of
David and Ingres. It was by the " melancholy "
of its gayety that the Goncourts understood to
what extent the eighteenth century was the an-
cestor of our own. The smile of Watteau's figures, the veiled gayety of grace of " Qui sait? "
revealed to them all the various kinds of boldness

in the sculpture and engraving of the century, the troubles, the preoccupations of that period from which were to issue all the movement of modern ideas and all the complexities of our time.

Side by side with the beautiful portrait of Marie Antoinette, I will place one of Louis XV., which is no less telling.

" The young king appears in one of the inner rooms at Versailles, a tall, peevish-looking, and melancholy lad, with signs of an unaffable and malicious nature. Though in the flower of his youth, he is wrapped in the shadows and suspicions of the Escurial, harrowed by the fear of hell, which betrays itself in his trembling speech. A feeling of emptiness devours him, together with a great hesitancy of will; he experiences imperious physical needs, the violence of which reminds one of the ancient Bourbons. He awaits with anxiety the rule of a woman who shall be either passionate, intelligent, or amusing. He consumes himself with ennui and idleness, while appealing to the outbreaks of passion or the riot of pleasure. Deliverance from himself is what the queen fails to give him, and what he has sought all his life in adultery."

The three sisters Nesles make their appearance to charm away his listlessness, and the Goncourts draw portraits of them, of Madame de Mailly and Madame de la Tournelle, which, without mentioning other qualities, are too brilliant not to be quoted.

" Madame de Mailly, with her bushy eyebrows and eyes so black that they had a somewhat hard

expression, was one of those beauties of the provoking kind. With rouged face, gauze-covered
shoulders, star-adorned forehead, flushed cheeks,
tumultuously coursing blood, large brilliant eyes
like those of Juno, bold bearing, and flowing
dress, she comes forth from the past with superb,
unblushing graces, like goddesses at the feast of
Bacchus."

Being anxious to keep the royal favor in her
family, Madame de Nesles had brought her sister
Félicité from a convent-school, and married her to
the Count de Vintimille. Félicité was plain and
badly shaped, but her wit had completely detached
the king from her sister, when a miliary fever
carried her off in a few days. The family, however, had not lost all its chances. Madame de la
Tournelle remained. She was quite different from
her two sisters, being unaffable and malicious, but
beautiful.

"She had a dazzling complexion, an insolent
gait, witty gestures, an enchanting look in her
large blue eyes, the saucy, impassioned, sentimental smile of a child; her breast panted and
throbbed, unceasingly animated by the ebb and
flow of life; she possessed an incomparable art of
bewitching people, a mind that seemed to come
forth from her heart whenever any one spoke of
tender and affecting things."

One of the best of the Goncourt portraits is
that of Madame du Barry.

"Her hair was of the most beautiful pale tint
imaginable, and curled like the hair of a child;
it was such hair as stamps on a woman's forehead

an adorable continuation, as it were, of girlhood. Her blue eyes, which were hardly ever seen open, were shaded with dark curling lashes and stole the most voluptuous glances ; her skin was like a rose-leaf, her neck like that of an antique statue."

There is the same charm in the sketch of Madame de Pompadour :

" Marvelous aptitudes, a learned education such as few could receive, had made this young woman a virtuoso of seduction. Her complexion was of dazzling whiteness, her pale lips disclosed wonderful teeth, her eyes were of an indefinable color, her figure shapely and of moderate height, her gestures sparing, and all her body full of life and passion, a changing and mobile physiognomy into which her woman's soul passed continually, in turn tender, full of feeling, imperious, noble, or roguish."

The conscientiousness with which Edmond ransacked the archives will appear still more clearly in the letter addressed by him to the eminent collector Burty, when he was working at the series of the eighteenth century.

" MY DEAR FRIEND, — I no longer go to see anything or anybody ; . . . it is the fourth day I have worked from morning till night without going down even into the garden. I am beginning to find that history, conscientiously written, is too exacting a mistress, . . . and to want to go to the Exhibition; and yet when I get out, what a fate, to be compelled to pass all the day at the Archives ! "

The history of the eighteenth century, more

than the history of any other, was discovered by
the Goncourts in outward events, and even in the
least living facts of the nation. In pamphlets,
portraits, toilets, almanacs, drawings, education,
they made a regular hunt for all elements from
which they might bring to life again "the woman
of this age." In France, where, more than anywhere else, woman has held an important rank,
to write the history of the mother, the wife, and
the mistress during a given period is very lucidly
to explain and sketch the man of the same time,
and his particular idiosyncrasies. At an epoch
when the Abbé Prévost created the most touching
heroine of the day out of a *marchande d'amour*,
it cannot be without interest to seek, in the origins
of some of the royal mistresses, for peculiarities
analogous to those of Manon Lescaut or of the
women of Laclos,[1] and that is why, before speaking of the Goncourts as novelists, it was necessary
to give the above quotations.

III

At the outset of their career the brothers inhabited the much mentioned apartment of the Rue
de St. Georges, where, buried beneath heaps of.
papers, books, and pamphlets, they might be seen
consulting for their historical work. While engaged in this task, or in water-color sketching
along the banks of the Seine, they found time to

---

[1] Laclos, the author of *Liaisons dangereuses*, drawing upon
documentary evidence, has described in this book the cold-
blooded libertinism of his time as graphically as the Abbé
Prévost its sentimentalism.

try their hand at the drama. The Vaudeville represented "Nos Hommes de Lettres," which was
withdrawn almost immediately. Contrary to the
usual custom, which is to make a play out of a
novel, the Goncourts had made a novel out of
their vaudeville. Their diary for 1860 relates
how they wrote their second work of imagination,
"Sœur Philomène."

"Sunday, 5th February, 1860, lunched at Flaubert's. Bouilhet related to us this story about a
sister of the hospital at Rouen, where he was
house-surgeon. A friend of his was house-surgeon
like himself, and this sister was in love with him,
in a Platonic way, he believed. His friend hung
himself. The sisters of the hospital were cloistered,
and went down into the courtyard of the hospital
only on days when sacrament was celebrated.
Bouilhet was watching beside his dead friend when
he saw the sister enter, kneel down, and say a
prayer which lasted a full quarter of an hour,
without paying any more attention to him than if
he were not there. When the sister rose from her
knees, Bouilhet put into her hand a lock of hair
that he had cut off for the dead man's mother,
and she took it without thanking him or saying
even a word. After that time, whenever they met,
she maintained the same silence as to what had
taken place between them, but on every opportunity showed herself most serviceable and devoted
to him."

This story took almost absolute possession of
the minds of the Goncourts. For a whole season
they walked the Charité Hospital and watched

the operations and the consequent nursing of the
patients. Their delicately organized natures in no
wise accustomed themselves to the miserable horror
of the flesh-torturings they witnessed, and it was
while they still retained their shuddering impressions that they wrote "Sœur Philomène." The
adorable, ethereal creature familiar to all readers
of the book, — her slender form, crowned with the
high cap of the sisterhood, moves gently about the
beds of the dying. One sees her gestures, one
feels her breath, one surprises her soul in its discreet action. Love burns in her as the lamp of
a sanctuary. " This love," writes Paul de St.
Victor in the " Débats," "appears as melancholy
as a fire in a desert." Writing to Flaubert the
Goncourts said, " We have placed the birth and
childhood of our sister in an environment of the
people, with manners and minds of somewhat vulgar stamp, in order the better to clip her angel's
wings. Tell us then," they continued, " if the
figure we have created seems to you to stand upright." Flaubert replies in a letter dated July,
1861 : —

" Received your volume this morning at eleven,
and had devoured it before five this afternoon.
Notwithstanding some little repetition of words
that I should quibble with you about, the book
thrilled me. I read it through at one sitting.
Philomène's childhood, and her life in the convent,
dazzled me. It is true, it is delicate, it is profound ;
many a woman will recognize herself in the portrait. One feels the body beneath the mysticism.
. . . Your patient's conversations, your physiog-

nomies of students and house-surgeons, that of the
head-surgeon Malivoire, are exceedingly well done.
Tell me how your book is received, how attacked;
let me hear from you. Accept my affectionate
greetings, and rest assured of the love I bear you.
                    " GUSTAVE FLAUBERT."

Some years later their relative success having
brought their books more into notice, they record
that, whereas " Nos Hommes de Lettres " had cost
them a thousand francs, " Sœur Philomène " has
been sold. " We are making progress," wrote
Edmond. They once more felt the pulse of the
public with " Renée Mauperin," the modern girl
of the Second Empire. The heroine is, at the
same time, pure and free in manners, tomboy and
virtuous ; she is preserved from love by her surplus of brain, and restored to her sex only by the
death of her brother, Henri Mauperin, whom she
loves sincerely, accusing herself of having killed
him by an untimely piece of news. The death of
this brother restores her to her woman's nature.
" The soul of Renée is transfigured amid the ruins
of her body ; the bold, scoffing child becomes a
bashful virgin. Like a wounded Amazon asking
once more for her woman's clothing, Renée reas-
sumes before dying the weakness and gentleness
of her sex ; her elfish wit still hovers on her lips,
but tender now and melancholy ; the filial sentiment which has filled her life inspires her last
moments ; she feigns to be calm, acts as if she
were convalescent, exhausts herself in false smiles
and vain projects ; her words, however, become
rarer, there are long intervals of silence in her

bedroom, one hears no longer aught but the sighs
of her who is suffering and the sobs of him who is
watching."

The portrait of Renée at the outset enables us
to realize the evolution that had been accomplished;
and her return home shows likewise how she recovers through the agency of sorrow her woman's
nature which she had voluntarily disguised, under
the influence of her father and Denisel. The inspiration of the portrait came from a lady friend
of the Goncourts, who has elsewhere been described
in the "Journal."

"Mademoiselle . . . possesses the cordiality
and loyalty of a man, allied to the graces of a girl;
a ripe reason; an ingenuous heart; a taste for the
most refined shades of intellect and art; a contempt for all that is the ordinary topic of woman's
thought and conversation; lively antipathies and
sympathies at first sight; smiles of bewitching
complicity for those who understand her; a clear
understanding of the studio-mind; a passion for
riding or driving; and withal a childish dread of
Fridays and the number thirteen; in fine, an amiable woman's foibles mingled with original co-
quetry."

One of the characters of the book is the Abbé
Blancpoix, who desires to deliver the *Bon Dieu* of
the rich from all the ugly severities of the *Bon
Dieu* of the poor. The authors were accused of
having copied him from the Abbé Carron, whom
Veuillot reproached with "driving a two-horse
carriage when cabs were to be had." However
this may be, the Abbé Blancpoix furnished Ed-

mond with an opportunity to write a letter sparkling with wit, in which his arguments tending to
whitewash the good Abbé are of the most ironical
vein. He says: —

" We had no intention of painting a portrait,
we have no taste for personalities, and not being
in the habit of attacking the dead, we did not for
a moment think of the Abbé Carron. Our design
was to depict not an individual, but a type; not a
priest, but the priest who directs high-born con-
sciences and *places Paradise within the reach of
the rich,* — the priest who out of the ugly, harsh,
rigorous religion of the poor evolves, as it were,
an amiable religion of the rich, at once airy,
charming, and elastic; the priest who out of the
idea of God forms something that is comfortable
and elegant."

We may be grateful to the Abbé Carron's heirs
for having extorted from Goncourt so elegant a
sally of wit and such acute irony.

In 1865 the two brothers — Edmond, as always,
supplying the solid, documentary portion — offered
to the public " Germinie Lacerteux." This is a
new period of the novel. Hitherto medical science had dealt with the physiology of the body's
ills, and philosophy had contented itself with the
therapeutics of the mind's troubles. Thirty years
before Robert Louis Stevenson the story of Germinie Lacerteux furnishes us with a case of moral
and physical reduplication no less precise and ver-
ifiable than that of " Dr. Jekyll and Mr. Hyde; "
moreover, the study of the double life in Germinie
is based on fact. For fifteen years the Goncourts

had in their service a servant without reproach.
She was a woman whose honesty and devotion had
never swerved. At her death their surprise was
great to discover, that beneath the upright and
blameless conduct of the servant, there had been
another existence of debauch and daily licentious-
ness. Such a study of a double life, in which the
merit of the servant was grounded on no moral
principles, and failings and virtues seemed equally
the result of the unconscious promptings of fatal-
ity, was bound to arouse the conservative press
reader. The most moderate of this section characterized " Germinie Lacerteux " as being " putrid
literature." Others accused the authors of wan-
tonly provoking a scandal, and of wishing to bring
about a demoralization of the people. The friends
of the Goncourts, Monselet and others, spoke of
the book as being "sculptured slime." In truth,
all this wrath was quite unnecessary over the appearance of an innovation, which after all was only
a somewhat different and less common way of writing that human history which the novel claims to
be. There is a taking into account of the whole
being on the dissecting-table, a noting of *all* the
contingents, physiological and appetitive, generous
and self-sacrificing, and an absolute separation of
the movements, so that the two beings which
exist in Germinie live separately. Each runs a
different career. It is precisely the diversity in
these two careers of Germinie, and the non-con-
fusion in her of the contradictory elements of her
nature, which constitutes the curiosity and truth
of the study. It is the coëxistence in this soul

of morally morbid elements with others that are
sound, the absence of contagion between the good
and the bad, the inward flourishing together of
poisonous plants and other perennial ones; it is
the juxtaposition in the same ground of decompo-
sition and vigor, of purulence and purity, which
makes this study so singular, and yet, we dare to
say, so true to life. Cases such as that of Germinie, or, indeed, that of Dr. Jekyll, are not frequent. Of the two, Dr. Jekyll is the more culpable, since he is more conscious, carried away
as he is by voluntary combinations of his brain,
whereas Germinie obeys only natural appetites.
Germinie is a fallen character, Jekyll a powerful
one; and though the double life of these two beings is directed toward absolutely different aims,
the one acting entirely from instinct, the other
from perverted reasoning, I make a point of comparing them on two grounds: first, in order to
claim for the Goncourts the initiative of a new
kind of study; next, to show up the inanity of
those virtuous cries of shocked feeling, from people who confess without shame to an interest in
Stevenson's sketch, while they boast of their shame
in reading the Goncourts' study. Since Jekyll is
an assassin and a thief whose *état d'âme* none will
deny having contemplated, why shudder at the
mention of Germinie? Jekyll is a man who in the
so-called unconsciousness of hypnotism steals and
kills; the other is a wretched woman who, in the
rush of a physical life of which she has not the
guidance (and that is also a sort of hypnotism),
sinks into degradation, while yet preserving in her-

self a capacity to perform a certain distinct class of
duties. They are both in turn guilty and honest
people, two of life's vanquished ones and two workers. Whence comes it that Germinie, whose de-
bauches and downfalls have their cause in innate
appetites, appears unworthy to be discussed by
those who take pleasure in subtle criticisms over
Jekyll? Are we an adolescent civilization, to recoil like children from the profound study of the
soul's ills? Are there cancers so foul that the philosopher should turn away from them? Why in
psychological studies the loud pharisaical rebuke
before the spectacle of the open sores of lechery,
when similar sores produced by reason and money-
interest find us all attention? "Germinie Lacerteux" is not a bad book, since it is a humane book,
in which the heart is torn with pity in presence of
so much inward misery. "We are in a hurry to
finish with the proofs of our 'Germinie Lacerteux,'" writes Edmond de Goncourt on the 12th of
November. "Living through this novel again puts
us into a state of nervousness and sadness. It is
as if we were again burying our dead servant. Oh!
it is a most painful book, and has come forth from
our inmost being. It is even materially impossible for us to go on correcting it. We no longer
see what we have written. The facts of our book
in their horror and misery conceal from us even
the mistakes and printer's errors." And the proof
that the nervous state they speak of causes them
real suffering appears from another mention of it
made by Edmond on the publication of the book.
"Our 'Germinie Lacerteux' appeared yester-

day," he writes; "we are ashamed to have to confess to a nervous emotion. To feel in one's self the
moral strain that we now experience, and to be
betrayed by one's nerves, by a cowardly sinking at
the pit of the stomach, by a sort of 'rumpling'
feeling, is the misery belonging to our natures,
which are so firm in their boldness and their efforts
towards the true, but are nevertheless betrayed by
that ill-working bit of machinery called the body."
They were not far wrong in fearing the coming
conflict with the public. It was, in fact, a great
struggle they were facing, quite as great as that
of the romantic school against the classicists.

"Germinie Lacerteux" sold like wildfire. In
order to make this success serve for their dramatic
work, the two brothers started on "Henriette
Maréchal," one of those stories that society people
prefer to experience in their own persons, rather
than to hear or to read. Henriette Maréchal, who
might figure in the "Golden Legend," since she
is a martyr, was not so successful as Germinie.
Though Henriette, to save her mother, springs upon
the stage declaring her mother's lover to be her
own paramour, — though she is thus heroic, Henriette was condemned by the public, as she pre-
viously had been by the censor. In the "Journal"
the Goncourts have given an account of the reading of "Henriette Maréchal" to the members of
the Comédie Française. "Here we are, seated before a green baize table with a desk and something
to drink. There sit ten of the members, impassive and mute. In the first act, the scene of the
opera ball finishes amid laughter and sympathetic

murmurs. But shortly after, seriousness is once more the order of the day. Thierry [1] takes us into his private room; we hear Got's voice. We wax anxious. My eyes are fixed on the clock, which tells us it is five-and-twenty minutes to four. I am so absorbed that I do not see Thierry re-enter; a caressing voice says to me, ' Your play is accepted and cordially approved.' We ask his leave to run away in order to get a breath of fresh air, without our hats, so intensely are we absorbed!" Thierry, who dared not ask for anything to be cut out, trembled for such expressions as "paillasse en deuil," "tourneur de mâts de cocagne en chambre," "abonné de la Revue des Deux Mondes." (The last of these expressions is equivalent to the famous "Vieillard stupide" of Hernani.) It would need only an excited audience to produce an outburst and a storm of hissing. Monsieur Rouher, one of the ministers, proposed that Henriette Maréchal should only be wounded, and afterwards marry *l'amant de la famille*. But Marshal Vaillant, the Minister of Fine Arts, decided with military thoroughness that the final pistol-shot should remain in the play.

"Madame Plessy alone of the actors," writes Edmond, speaking of those who interpreted the various rôles, " possesses the real literary instinct. She understands from the very first, and renders the spirit of the part. She feels at once all she observes. With her the comprehension is immediate, always intelligent, sometimes sublime. Her only failing is her instantaneousness of intuition,

---

[1] The manager of the Français.

which does not fix itself. She understands so
quickly that every day she understands something
fresh. Each time she acted our play in a superior
manner; but each time she was superior in a part
she had neglected the day before, and which she
abandoned on the morrow. As to the other actors,
they repeat at first like children, they grope after
the intonation, they fail in the gesture. They need
to be prompted and urged on. At every moment
they make mistakes in what has been written, and
are an unconscionable time before getting into the
'skin of the personage.'"

The "Journal" of the Goncourts, which is one
of the most contemporary and sprightly fragments
of their work, has raised, and will always raise,
discussion. Has any one the right to cast abroad,
for generations to come, conversation freely indulged in, among private friends? It is the Goncourts themselves who have given a reply to this
question by establishing their accounts of the
eighteenth century on notes, fragments, diaries,
gossip, and indiscretions of all kinds, in which the
century was so rich. Their historical work is built
up out of the men and women whose portraits they
have painted; and these portraits are the outcome
of divers journals of the eighteenth century. That
is their answer.

IV

As long as their books are read there will be
the joint work of the Goncourts to take into account; and it would be a barren task to separate,
in what is left us of them, the two minds whose

every intellectual movement was executed in married unity and harmony. The foundation of the "Academy of the Goncourts," which dates back some fifteen years, owes the initiative of its final expression to Edmond. The elect of this academy, in which talent was to be the only title of admission, were ten in number. Among them figured Alphonse Daudet, Léon Hennique, Huysmans, the two brothers Rosny, Octave Mirbeau, Paul Marguerite, and Gustave Geoffroy. Some of these are completely unknown to English letters, though none the less men of real worth, whose willful eccentricity (not to say exaggerated verve) has kept them out of the circle of European notoriety.

He whom Gaston Deschamps called "the nervous, morose old man" had no other rôle in this academy, however, than that of allotting and distributing the capital. Every member was to receive six thousand francs a year, on condition, if he were already a member of the classical Academy, of quitting it before entering the other.

What do the Goncourts represent from the literary point of view? They represent "work," an incessant amount of work, labor without respite, the work which Zola extolled in his appeal to young men : —

"The ideal is work. In all my struggles and fits of despair, I have had but one remedy, work. How often have I sat down to my table in the morning not knowing what to do, full of bitterness, and tortured by some great physical or moral pain ; and yet each time, in spite of the revolt of my suffering, my task has been a comfort and relief

to me; I have always been strengthened by my
daily task."

The Goncourts were workers. Edmond worked
longer; it is difficult to determine if he worked
better, since practically all that he did after his
brother's death was the accumulation of documents. I select at random out of the "Journal"
a note of the 9th November, during the siege of
Paris. He is speaking of Victor Hugo, of his absence of taste, of his being in some things a slave
to the body, for instance, of his indiscriminating
appetite.

"I remember one day when Neffbyer Vacquerie,
Proudhon, my brother, and I had given up expecting him to dinner and had dined without him, our
leavings had been thrown into a corner, an unclean
medley of stewed veal, ray-fish, etc. Hugo arrived,
and literally devoured it, while we looked on in
stupefaction. . . . He eats like Polyphemus!"

I cannot finish this sketch without quoting the
fine portrait — drawn by Sainte-Beuve, and one of
the best pieces of writing this critic has left us —
of the illustrious friend and patroness of Edmond,
who telegraphed to Daudet on hearing the fatal
news, "I cannot believe it; I am prostrated." I
mean the Princess Matilda. Already in 1862,
when the two brothers were still struggling, the
princess, struck by the novelty of their talent, drew
them into her circle, employed her credit on their
behalf, and remained their friend.

"The princess has a high, noble forehead, and
her light golden hair, leaving uncovered on each
side broad, pure temples, is bound in wavy masses

on the full, finely shaped neck. Her eyes, which
are well set, are expressive rather than large, gleam
with the affection or the thought of the moment,
and are not of those which can either feign or conceal. The whole face indicates nobleness and dignity, and, as soon as it lights up, grace united to
power, frankness, and goodness; sometimes also it
expresses fire and ardor. The head so finely poised,
and carried with such dignity, rises from a dazzling
and magnificent bust, and is joined to shoulders
of statuesque smoothness and perfection."

The friends the Goncourts had, and merited to
have, form perhaps not the least part of their glory,
when it is remembered that among them were such
men as Théophile Gautier, Flaubert, Delacroix, and
Daudet. The friendship of Monsieur and Madame Alphonse Daudet, of the true woman who is
also a woman of talent, the friendship which con-
soled and sustained Edmond after the death of
Jules, and in which the Daudets maintained, notwithstanding their admiration, a right to advise, —
honors Edmond's memory no less than the last
lines of Zola's funeral oration.[1] When in the case
of a man who preëminently possessed a cerebral
temperament one sees the existence of such a gift
of friendship, it reveals the tenacious vigor of the
sentiments, the coexistence in him of an emotional
activity as intense (a rare thing in men of cerebral
temperament) as that of his brain.

"All Edmond's consolation was in his work,"
said Zola, "To-day he is at rest; and we cry to
him, like Daudet, sobbing and distracted with

[1] Edmond de Goncourt died July 16, 1896.

grief: ' Go, dear grand workman, go ! Thy task is achieved ; go to rejoin thy brother in the tomb and in glory.' "

As for " glory," the centuries to come shall decide. The two brothers instigated, influenced, and guided the movement of a whole school of young writers, and that is saying a great deal without anything else. Glory is shy. It is her prerogative to give or withhold the kiss her lovers pray for. Her fancies are unanticipated and sometimes surprising to herself. Will Edmond de Goncourt be one of those temporary favorites ? If so, in spite of the Goncourts' voluminous work it would be an exceptional piece of good fortune, more than an expected one.

JEAN MARTIN CHARCOT was born in 1825. His father was a carriage-builder of small means, yet an artist rather than an artisan, for the workman's profits in business only served to defray the cost of the artist's dreams. He designed wonderful chariots, and executed them so well that even to-day the great men of his craft study his work. From him the eminent physician inherited his taste for artistic surroundings, as well as his love of the beautiful in all things. His house in Paris was full of works of art, and all who knew him remember well the splendid mantelpiece at Neuilly, copied by himself from the original, of the fifteenth century, discovered near Limoges.

Charcot obtained his appointment as Interne des Hôpitaux in 1848, simultaneously with his best friend, the surgeon Vulpian. Through the earlier part of his career his master, Reyer, knowing that he was poor, helped him by placing him in a rich family, with whom he travelled through Italy as attendant physician. It is curious to note that he failed in his first examination for "lack of eloquence"! At the second trial, however, he brought to bear all the resources of his newly acquired modern languages so effectively that he astounded his examiners by the wealth of his quotations. In 1856 his articles on the "Disorders of

the Liver," which appeared in the "Bulletin de la
Société de Biologie," marked him as a coming man.
He felt the impulse, and rose with giant strides.

Gout and rheumatism were his next subjects.
Cornil and Charcot were among the first to ob-
serve and study the influence of these diseases
upon the kidneys, and these studies lasted until
1862, when Charcot took definite charge of that
microcosm, the Salpétrière. Henceforward he
could not complain of lack of variety or quantity
of subjects. It was at that time a huge disorgan-
ized institution, known to the literary world at
large through the medium of Prévost's "Manon
Lescaut." From the end of the sixteenth to the
end of the eighteenth century, it harbored all the
incurables of mind or body, in addition to the
modern Magdalens in France. Up to the time of
the Revolution it was Bedlam; nor was there any
very noticeable improvement until Charcot took
charge in 1862. He left it an organized, rational
institution.

It may be asserted as an axiom that all great
men of science have worked backward. From
the study of the parasite they have been led to the
study of the afflicted root or essence. Gout and
rheumatism led Charcot back to the study of their
concomitant nervous disorders and to the research
for the possible causes. In 1872 he began a
course of lectures on hysteria, so thoroughly supported by proof, so patiently elaborated point after
point, with such a plethora of observations and
notes, that his disciples were both amazed and
carried away with enthusiasm, — not the enthusi-

asm born of oratory, but that of conviction. The
laboratory and its indisputable results furnished
the only arguments. Every experiment told, and
every experiment was proved by repetition; its
results were strengthened by a series of developments, each one helping to clinch the final result.
This was Charcot's method; he could never feel
satisfied to teach or make public his personal
theories until their value was thoroughly demonstrated beyond the possibility of doubt even to
himself. Indeed, this very conscientiousness, this
very thoroughness of research, are alone accounta-
ble for the charges of cruelty so often brought
against him; and it must be admitted that, for
the sake of truth, he often considered the case as
more important than the subject, the disease more
interesting than the individual. The admirers of
Vesale are loud in their praise of his studying
"man by means of man himself." Charcot studied
"woman by means of woman," and shall this be
called a crime? In the former case the man, to
be sure, was dead; but Charcot's patient was
asleep. When, as often happened, the charge of
lack of pity towards his patient was made, or
when, again, he was accused of putting his hysterical subjects to unnecessarily severe and frequent
tests, he invariably answered: "It is by facts, and
by the study of facts alone, that I can reach the
truth and obtain valuable results."

It was not till 1882 that Charcot was appointed
professor of nervous diseases. For twenty years
he had been at work in the hospital systematizing,
organizing, classifying, coördinating the various

departments and the documents of his cases. The
catalogue was an important one and complete. He
had subdivided his patients into distinct categories,
headed " senile," " chronic," " beginners," etc. ; and
(as is now done in large modern libraries) each
patient had her card on which the case was analyzed and finally indexed. Newly arrived patients,
suffering from some apparently novel form of disease, were at once examined and classified; after
a few leading questions, Charcot knew exactly
what had been their hospital history and their
pathological evolution. His capacity for work was
extraordinary ; he superintended everything himself, and every autopsy was carried out according
to his directions, after he had made a personal
examination of the body.

Every morning at nine he left his hotel in the
Boulevard St. Germain, and in less than twenty
minutes his stout Percherons brought him to the
door of the " City of Misery," into which he had
introduced so many improvements and such a perfect system. His influence was felt directly in
every department, and his advice became law even
as early as 1866, when, the lecture-hall having
proved too small, he annexed the hospital kitchens,
and provided room for an additional daily attend-
ance of five hundred students.

He was unusually clever with his pencil, and his
facility in drawing was of great help to him in
his lectures on hysteria. Without interrupting
the spoken text he would draw figures on the black-
board — say, for instance, two woman's bodies,
the one a face, the other a back view, and without

a pause in his delivery he would mark on the first
the fourteen hysterical points, on the second the
four centres of pain.   With rare method he classified the phenomena probably attributable to inherited taints or deducible from any other cause,
and divided them under two main headings — the
higher and the lesser (or simple) hysteria.   At
all times he was careful to refer epileptic phenomena to a class of their own, distinct from hysterical phenomena.   Under simple hysteria we find,
for instance, the very common case so distressing
to parents.   A young girl of eighteen or twenty,
in apparently good health and endowed with
a strong constitution, suddenly takes it into her
head to refuse food.   At first it appears to be a
mere whim; the patient seems to be neither weakened nor affected in other ways by her fasting; she
continues to dance, go out, and amuse herself as
usual, and her health remains apparently normal.
However, little by little, she becomes languid and
her strength begins to wane.   The initial — passive — lack of appetite has now developed into an
active abhorrence of any form of nourishment,
as violent as the abhorrence of liquids produced
by hydrophobia.   The mere sight or smell of food
causes her to shrink and shiver.   She becomes
morbid, torpid, suffers from shortness of breath
and general lack of strength; her nerves are
unstrung, and the slightest cold develops into
pleurisy; she faints frequently under no apparent
provocation, and the fits last a long time; they are
sometimes followed by convulsions akin to epileptic
fits.   She is on the brink of death, and yet, techni-

cally speaking, there is nothing the matter with her. Now is the time to consult Charcot, and his advice will be as prompt, as valuable as that of a Dupuytren, who without a moment's hesitation called out "Cut that man open — here!"[1] In the case of our young girl any treatment based on the presumption of epilepsy would prove fatal. Charcot brings a new force to bear; the hysterical patient has contracted habits of resistance, which must be broken by still stronger insistence, yet indirectly: by complete change of surroundings; by a rigidly enforced isolation from the home atmosphere in which the disease developed. In other words, a psychical treatment is required, and very generally succeeds.

A physician who is not at the same time a philosopher is not worthy of the name. Pity on the one hand, the apparent cruelty required by the treatment on the other, must both be met, understood and satisfied. Neglect of either consideration involves failure, often death. The slightest excess of sympathy for the individual may prove fatal, but too rigid an enforcement of the treatment may prove so as well. Therefore, to deal with such diseases, the practitioner must at the same time be a thinker, and an observer of humanity of no mean capacity; Charcot possessed both the skill of the one, and the instinct of the other, to a remarkable degree. Indeed, one may say of some of his lectures that they are important con-

[1] This was a celebrated case in which Dupuytren's divination *saw* the existence of an internal abscess which had escaped all the doctors.

tributions to human history rather than mere technical dissertations; for example, his study entitled
" Parallèle entre la Médecine moderne et la Médecine de l'Antiquité."

The meddling jade Fortune — often such a mis-
chief-maker here below — happened in Charcot's
case to shuffle the cards knowingly. As once she
had dropped an apple before Isaac Newton's eyes,
she this time caused the so-called Pavillon Sainte
Laure to drop to pieces. Here the idiots, the
epileptic, and the hysterical patients of the Salpétrière all lived together indiscriminately. When
new quarters became necessary Charcot distributed
them in different groups, and this imperfect, partly
accidental classification was the starting-point of
the great discoveries he made later, to which his
name will forever remain attached, and which
established once and for all the fundamental distinction between hysteria and epilepsy.

The daily lectures at the Salpétrière soon became inadequate, and Charcot accepted the presi-
dency of the Société d'Anatomie, where the reports of his staff were added to the vast amount
of documents at his command. It has been said
of him that one of his chief characteristics was an
undue thirst for notoriety, and that the quality
of his work was impaired thereby. So far is this
from being true that we must, on the contrary, lament the paucity of his publications. His first
lectures on hysteria we owe entirely to the insistence, tact, and devotion of his wife, who took
notes, and edited the lectures. She also organized
his household so that he never knew a care or

worry in his home life, but always found the absolute rest and change without which he could never have made such constant and mighty draughts upon his energy as the Titanic character of his work demanded daily. It was not until 1887 that Charcot was able to carry out a dream of many years' standing, namely, the publication in two profusely illustrated quartos of his work on two departments of human misery, "Les Malades et les Difformes dans l'Art" and "Les Hystériques et les Démoniaques." In the first of these two volumes the pitiful history of the victims of rachitis, of the dwarfs, of the victims of syphilis and all such as cringe and suffer under the tyrant lash of similar curses is unfolded systematically. Sculpture as well as painting gives its testimony and is cross-examined. The grotesque figure of Santa Maria Formosa, which in "The Stones of Venice" Mr. Ruskin attempts to crush under the weight of his displeasure (the gargoyle, by the way, is still in place), is so true to nature that Charcot declares it is accurately copied from life: "I have that man under treatment at this very moment, and his facial convulsions are absolutely the same as these." Compare the two sketches, the one of the mediæval monster, the other of the modern man, and the resemblance is striking.

Constantly bringing to bear the documents of the past on the living documents of to-day, Charcot works out the history of human monstrosity; the story of the dwarfs he traces downward from the Egyptian god Bes to Tom Thumb, through the Bayeux tapestries to the mosaics of Ravenna, classifying, numbering, docketing the dead patients exactly as he treats his living ones. Instancing "The Triumph of Death" (in the cemetery of Pisa), where Taddeo Gaddi has so well depicted various forms of human misery, he analyzes them and gives his diagnosis, pointing out the absolute realism of many figures supposed to be only fantastic; and scientifically he compares the blind man of the Scriptures, so often drawn by Raphael in his Biblical compositions, with the blind patients under his direct observation. The "king's evil" is less abundantly portrayed in art; nevertheless, through his friend Dr. Keller[1] Charcot was able to obtain a copy of the picture signed by a contemporary of Albrecht Dürer and hanging in the museum of Colmar; it represents a case so truthfully that any doctor could prescribe for the painted patient. The heroic friend of the lepers — Miss Marsden — would find food for thought in the page representing St. Elizabeth washing with her princely hands such ghastly wounds as even the disciples of Miss Nightingale might fear to touch; and on another page a student of the plague — the black death — could analyze in detail the sufferings of St. Roch.

This volume, as well as its companion, was written by Charcot with the help of Dr. Paul

---

[1] Keller is the Preissnitz of Paris; besides being unrivalled in his application of hydrotherapeutics, his knowledge of art and of the history of art is deep and varied. In his work he is seconded by his wife, a woman of unusual attainments, whose philosophical essays and criticisms, signed "Jeannine," have attracted admiring appreciation.

Richer (who should not be mistaken for the eminent professor, Charles Richet, whose psychological work is as well known in France as that of Charcot himself), and the work marked an epoch. Before Charcot's day, psychology was barely recognized by a few of the most independent scientific men; it was absolutely excluded from the universities; and among the people it was generally supposed to be connected with sorcery and the black arts. This connection — or I should say apparent connection — with magic and the occult suggests a few words on Charcot's second work on nervous diseases, "Les Démoniaques," a curious book, fascinating not only on account of the wondrous lore contained therein, but equally so because of the Janus-like attitude of the author. As long as Charcot is dealing with the past — with the "obsessed," the "possessed," the seers, the prophets, the hallucinated subjects of history — he speaks with an echo of compassion in his voice, and even perhaps of sympathy; and without these gentler qualities to temper criticism the scientific book falls dead, lacking the human element. The man as well as the *savant* has signed these pages, and the curiosity of the practitioner, the eagerness of the analyst, the selfishness of the discoverer, are softened by a certain recognition of kinship, of regret for the unnecessary suffering endured, the pity of the man who might have helped for the very helplessness of mankind. This is the sentimental note in the book, where the author looks back, platonically, impersonally. It is an artistic retrospect, and we are taught to understand and

appreciate certain affinities of suffering, their persistence, their uninterruptedness throughout the
long history of the human family, as described to
us in the Bible, or painted for us by Raphael.
But suddenly this genial current is interrupted ; we
reach the present, the experimental age, — the Sal-
pêtrière; and the expert, the professor, the impersonal manipulator of subjects and cases, takes the
place of the man.

As long as the author is commenting on a case
through the medium of a picture, or some artistic
historical records, be it as far back as 1230, when
Quinto Pisano painted the saints or the picture
of Francis of Assisi casting out devils; be it
the more realistic picture of St. Zéno canonizing
the daughter of a Roman emperor; or be it the
somewhat coarse St. Vitus's Dance of the Flemish
painter, — the directness, the lucidity of his diagnosis is tempered with pity, a certain unexpressed
but implied commiseration. As soon, however, as
the evil is represented not by a work of art, but
by a work of God, a suffering subject, the last
vestige of fellow-feeling vanishes before the eagerness, the anxiety, the morbid craving for new data,
new discoveries. The plates of Dr. Richer retain
their intensely pathetic interest, but in the text we
cannot find one ray, one degree of human warmth ;
we cannot restrain our own pity, nor on the other
hand rebuke our amazement. Human beings,
beings like ourselves, are shown to us, bent double
in frenzied contortions, heads and heels meeting
after a wild struggle of passionate, writhing resistance to some superior will. Every attitude is ex-

pressive of agony, and yet the subject is treated here as a mere phenomenon; its antics are chronicled, or rather registered, like the reading of the thermometer or the variation of the aneroid. And the pity of it! This impassive attitude of scrutiny offends and wounds our better sense, for some centuries ago there came among the poor, the sick, the maimed, and the halt, One who was a great Healer, and His ways were different from these ways, and we have learned to love His ways and admire them.

Charcot's life was so full that it is not easy to condense or epitomize it in a short article. He was a many-sided man; after the physician and the professor comes necessarily Charcot in his relations to hypnotism, and Charcot the head of the modern neuropathic school, and also Charcot at home and in society.

In speaking of hypnotism we must first recall that in France the line is very rigidly drawn between scientific psychology, pathological psychology, and speculative psychology. Indeed, psychology was not recognized in France as a science until well-known men had established its relations with physiology and proved the bearing of the one upon the other. Charcot was one of the first to repudiate the "marvelous" element in psychology, which the public persisted ignorantly, but doggedly, in mistaking for the science itself. In 1882, when he assumed the specialty for "nervous complaints," he said in his opening speech: "The study of psychical phenomena is absolutely dependent on the knowledge of anatomy and of physiology, for without such knowledge it is out of the question to propound a rational solution of psychical problems. The progress of knowledge, based on facts, is fast reducing the meaning of the word 'marvel' to a lame explanation for the ignorant; soon the word will have become obsolete."

It was only through its connection with physiology, therefore, that psychology obtained a standing at the university, and only on the basis *mens sana in corpore sano*, the two, body and mind, being interdependent. Charcot, apparently a skeptic, but at the same time a profound student of the feminine mind, understood early what a mighty lever faith might become, if ably exploited, above all in relation to women's ailments. In his admirable essay " La Foi qui guérit " (Faith the Healer), he refers not to the faith in things beyond, but to the personal faith of the patient in his doctor, adviser, and ultimate curer. His knowledge of the feminine heart enabled him to found a whole system of healing upon the innate love of woman for her particular functions in life, functions of servitude and self-sacrifice. Her simple faith and love enable her to forget or lay aside the mere animal functions of the mother material, and to realize in spite of them the higher ideal of the mother spiritual.

Charcot's insight into woman's moral organism predestined him to his mission as woman-curer. There were two origins of woman's nervous disorders, he believed, unequally interesting sentimentally speaking, but scientifically of parallel importance, — excess and abstinence. In the second case the disorders are mostly reactions from the moral feelings to the organism. Far from asserting the sole supremacy of physiology, he willingly admitted that the initial cause of the physical unbalancing of woman is more often in the moral nature; hence his mode of treating most of these ailments by a primary appeal to faith in the curer. This mode rarely fails where the disease above all is principally the outcome of sorrow and heartbreak. Charcot's school has taken from its head that grand, humanitarian, philosophically Christian understanding of its duties, and the men who have received Charcot's impetus have remained faithful to the generous feeling of pity and interest toward the patient, which is a trait of the modern scientists.

The great Healer, Christ, asked His patients: "Have ye faith in Me?" Charcot commanded, "*Have* faith in me and I can cure you." For the majority of cases there was no specific remedy; the remedy that cured was the practical one. His patients were mostly hysterical women, who, like a ship at sea without a rudder, were drifting helplessly to leeward. He began by saying: "I know your case thoroughly and I know that I can cure you, but you must have utter confidence in me and in your cure." Often this was all the treatment needed; faith was in itself a relief; faith in the man was a help, and eventually the patient's own imagination, aided by the ordinary hygienic methods, completed the work begun. Speaking in a general way, hysterical patients are of two kinds, the honest and the dishonest; and I use

the term *honest* because it is a flexible word covering certain distinctions I cannot well make here.
Of the *dishonest* class — the most difficult to cure,
because of the unreliability of its patients — we
could cite cases only, not types, and here faith and
self-respect alone can be of the slightest use. It
is with the *honest* class that the influence of men
like Charcot is most needed, most quickly felt,
most beneficial. The healer brings with him "the
faith that heals," and the apparent miracle is
wrought : if the patient listens, obeys, and is convinced, the cure is assured.

The mental trouble has apparently killed the
body ; now the mental trouble must be set aside,
and the mind itself will repair the ravages it has
wrought. However, few men are qualified for
such work. Apart from deep and varied knowledge, they must possess an unusual, singular character made up of apparent contrasts. Iron-handed,
velvet-gloved, they must rigidly carry out their
motto — *Suaviter in modo, fortiter in re.* They
dare not make a single concession, nor yet be
guilty of the slightest violence. The personal interest of the master — for in this case he is a master — must be recognized by the patient, but this
interest must be kept within such exact bounds
that no personal reminiscences are ever revived,
no suggestion of even the remotest personal risk
is evoked ; yet the flattery of being studied by a
master-mind must be used as a tonic. I have seen
many such resurrections, and among them I remember two cases, one where the moral being was
practically dead, and there the physical complica-

tions were such that a single crisis of insomnia
lasted eleven days and nights, during which the
patient was never for one moment free from fever
or delirium.   I am not at liberty to name the
eminent professor who treated her; I can merely
mention that he was of the school I have been
describing.   The treatment lasted three years, and
to-day the patient is able to do intellectual work
of the highest order, and for so many hours a day
that few men could stand the strain.   Compassion
was the initial remedy, faith the first result.   This
patient was a woman of strong character, of a
highly strung temperament, of intelligence and
acquirements, the child of nervous parents.   About
the same time — and I have given these details
for the sake of contrasting the two cases — the
same physician was treating a case of equally
complete prostration; but here the patient sprang
from a different race.   She was a delicate, rather
lymphatic, unexcitable creature, whom sorrow and
the misery of her life had reduced to a mere skele-
ton; her physical weakness was such that she
could leave her bed but for a few hours at a time,
and yet to-day, after a course of treatment that
lasted two years, she teaches and lectures six hours
each day during ten months of the year.   The
master who achieved these resurrections is no ordinary physician.   The man is a more important
factor in these cures than the doctor, and he rarely
fails in his attempts.   He is at the head of one of
the great hospitals of Paris, where his cures among
patients of the lower classes are as astounding and
complete as those I have quoted from among his

clientèle élégante. La foi qui guérit is responsible for the good achieved in these cases, as much as therapeutics and hygiene.

To achieve such results, however, no mean attainments are required. To begin with, the man; next, wide and reliable technical knowledge; a clear insight into human nature; perfect tact and absolute inflexibility of purpose and direction. Of this school of men Charcot was the founder and high priest. There are many—as there yet will be many—who owe their life and their interest in life to Charcot's work, and for whom it will be impossible ever to forget that the university professor, a skeptic by right of surroundings and profession, was the one to preach the faith that was to make them sound. To heal the body through the mind, to make the body again the physician of the mind, was indeed an inspired conception. Not that the treatment is new, for many a case might be quoted from the Scriptures. But this is not quite the same kind of faith cure, nor the same kind of faith. Charcot was the missionary of the new science which in our days has worked marvels in the dark province of hysteria. Before his day it was a forbidden waste, on the threshold of which Dante's desperate lines could have been written; now the liberator has come.

Hypnotism and hypnotic suggestion are no new themes. We have records of such practices in the very oldest annals of human history, but the compassionate element was usually neglected and the effect or cure was rather fortuitous than scientific. Charcot imagined the test of sympathy. None

love suffering, few are not eager to be relieved
therefrom. The suggestion of Charcot is one of
relief, hence acceptable at the outset, to say the
least. Whether suggestion is, however, really beneficial to the patient or the reverse will for some
time to come remain scientifically a disputed question, to be solved only by means of the results
which may be obtained.

Now that we have sketched Charcot as doctor,
professor, and therapeutist, as the propounder of
doctrines new and the destroyer of doctrines obsolete, it seems opportune to say a word of Charcot
the man of the world. Like all men predestined
to rule over others, — and few monarchs have ruled
" with right of life and death " as Charcot did, —
he was born with an innate love for art and refinement. He had read deeply and travelled much;
his grasp of new and varied subjects was as remarkable as the keenness of his observation. His
personal appearance was that of a chief: he carried his head high, and there was something very
proud, even domineering, in the poise of the mas-
sive head and finely chiseled profile. He was at
home on Tuesday evenings, when all the intellectual lights of Paris called; to each he talked his
own language, as an equal. The professor, the inquisitor, vanished before the enthusiast, and it was
then that you learned to know the man. Impassive, keen, even hard in manner before the patient,
whom he dissected mentally as coldly as the surgeon performs an operation, he was singularly open-
hearted and sympathetic at home. He talked well,
with the vivacity of youth and the enthusiasm of

the artist.[1]   There were no small or mean traits in his character, and whatever he did, he did in a large, noble manner, with a fine energy upheld by a powerful, inflexible will.   His gaze was singularly fixed, stern, somewhat hard, but clear and unflinching ; he looked *at* you, not above or beyond you, — indeed, through you.   He loved his home, where he was serenely happy in the love of an admirable woman and of their two children.   On that threshold the professor disappeared ; the man, the kindly philosopher, the animated artist alone remained. His work will endure because it is not founded on mere hypotheses, but is the result of long, keen, and critical observation of life itself.   Nervous diseases, as I have said above, are not a recent discovery, for the Bible and the histories of all ages quote innumerable examples ; but the disease was merely as yet mentioned, not understood.   Charcot classed the ailment, analyzed it, and established its true significance and importance.   His discoveries compelled the creation of a special professorship for the teaching of the phenomena at the university, and there he proclaimed the individuality of epilepsy, insanity, and hysteria, showed their apparent relations, proved their real differences.

Alexandre Dumas *fils* once said to one of the most eminent critics of the "Revue des Deux Mondes : " " After the generation of heroes of my

---

[1] Indeed, he was an artist himself ; from his travels he brought back remarkably fine sketches, and himself drew the designs, suggested by these sketches, for the decoration of his dinner service.

father's day, it was rational to expect a generation
of nervous sufferers." But this generalization is
not sufficiently broad, and the whole romantic
school should be included. We cannot well imagine how Antony, Lelia, Rolla, could have produced
healthy, well-balanced children, endowed with normal constitutions. The generation of fathers who,
as they put it, had "followed the impulses of their
hearts," in reality merely the dictates of their passions, weakened the following generations. The
grandfathers had been men of a different mould,
sanguine, plethoric, suffering from an excess of
vitality, so that blood-letting and debilitants were
as much in vogue then as are iron, the coal-tar
series, and tonics of various descriptions now.

A man's living to-day depends rather on seden-
tary work than on active, out-of-door exertion. It
is the brain rather than the body that must be
trained, and the body pays the expense; the doctor
is a tutor or adviser. And as supply and demand
seems to be the fundamental law of human production, there has arisen a generation of men like
Broca, Claude Bernard, Charcot, who examine the
anatomy of the mind as well as that of the body,
needing philosophical instruments unknown to
Ambroise Paré and Fagon. It would seem that
the philosopher Marcus Aurelius, even though
surrounded by the darkness of his time, had foreseen this evolution when he wrote: "The higher
soul must use the eyes of reason to see through
matter."

Among modern scientists Charcot is perhaps the
one who saw through matter with the clearest

vision. His work is as important to the human
family as the work of Pasteur. Could anything
more be added to his praise? Charcot in reality
has been the revealer of a mode of treatment which
yearly sends back to usefulness and duty human
beings whom former methods would have sterilized
by shutting them out of activity. The great professor has eminently localized into "phases" an
ailment which by its nature, and in woman's case
above all, is mostly ephemeral, and of a transitory
nature. Science has received much from Charcot,
but woman has received more. The mother, the
wife, who, after a short period of care, comes back
to her hearth a happy woman, should bless the
great professor's name; for to him, and to him
alone, she owes her escape from confinement in
some asylum, where in former days so many were
placed and where they remained, forgotten, long
after the ailment had disappeared forever.

PAUL BOURGET

I

SUAVE elegances; little barons and countesses;
white-and-pink tailor-dressed blondes; swells who
sport themselves with equal "sveltness" under a
Palermo sun or in a London fog; dreams of deep
foliage in gorgeous conservatories; soft lamps,
capped by shades of supple silk; yachts, resplen-
dent with golden ornaments, replete with luxuries
of all kinds, and bright with feminine beauty of
various types, — real floating strong-boxes, the
property of wonderful Americans whose hearts are
as rich in beautiful and delicate feelings as are
their bank-accounts in redundant ciphers, — such
are the personages and the surroundings Bourget
loves to introduce and describe in his novels.

An intense care for *souls* seems only to have increased our author's preoccupation about *things*;
and though physiology has not with him, as with
the Goncourts and with Zola, encroached upon
psychology, yet upholstery, dress, fashions, and
"five-o'clocks" occupy a most prominent position
in all his books. Thus it happens that most of
Bourget's personages express their inner being
more by their tastes than by their feelings; these
tastes themselves being so strongly influenced by
the atmosphere of frivolity surrounding them that,
freed from its pressure, their possessors might be-

come quite different persons. We can imagine a
Noëmie Hurtrel (L'Irréparable), for instance, an
Hélène Chazel (Un Crime d'Amour), or an Ely
de Carlsberg (Une Idylle tragique) entirely other
than what they are, if the surplus of money and
leisure which leads to their errors were taken from
them — especially Noëmie Hurtrel, who, betrayed
by a libertine, proves herself victorious over the
commonly resulting deterioration of character;
thus showing what elements of real individuality
resided in her, could she but have freed herself
from the empty frivolity of her surroundings.
Bourget's heroes and heroines follow but too often
the moral bent of their circumstances. This sub-
ordination of the inner personality to the outward
pressure of *entourage* leads at times to strange
conclusions; as in the case of Hélène Chazel, when
she speaks admiringly to de Querne of her past
purity: "Quand je me suis donnée à vous j'étais
si pure. Je n'avais rien, rien sur ma conscience."
If Hélène Chazel, the prototype of hysterical amorous fantasy, and de Querne, the perfection of cold-
heartedness, are true representatives of modern
lovers in the France of the nineteenth century, the
depopulation of that country should be looked upon
as a blessing. The posterity of such a couple could
only be regarded as calamitous. As to Mme. de
Carlsberg, who is introduced as a romantic type
of the woman à *grandes passions*, what shall the
reader infer of these *grandes passions* when, before he has reached the third chapter of the book,
he discovers that she is already entering with
Hautefeuille on her third love experience? Now,

without going back to Mérimée's "Carmen," it
would be a matter of difficulty to find among the
fathers of romance in France one who would trust
in the reader's good will enough to beg for his
interest and sympathy in favor of a lady whose
grandes passions are as multifarious as her ca-
prices, and who really designates as "passions"
what scarcely deserve a name at once so grave and
so implicitly tragic. Incoherence of character is
met with in Bourget's novels not only with regard
to women, but quite as commonly with his men.
De Querne, for example, is sketched as a *roué* and
a Lovelace; but he suddenly becomes a Vincent
de Paul, and this transformation of a Don Juan
into a henpecked lover is no less a matter of wonderment to the reader than the curious quality of
the *grandes passions* of Mme. de Carlsberg.

Regarded in the treble character of poet, critic,
and novelist, Bourget strikes one as being truer to
himself as a critic — in his studies of contemporary
writers, for instance — than he is as a novelist.
His essays on contemporary psychology are truer
to life and less characterized by contradictions than
the psychology of some of his fictitious personages.
The emotional world is not his natural fatherland:
the world of passion comes to him rather through
the imagination than through the feelings. It is
in the brain-world, in the intellect proper, that he
dwells more naturally. "Beauty," he writes, "is
made up of lyrism, of the splendor of what the eye
can see, of the magic of dreams." Dreams, power
of evocation, lyrism, — three decided operations of
the brain rather than of the feelings. The gift of

observation itself, according to him, is but the result of the atavism of confession among Roman Catholics, the outcome of the habit of self-examination, — another brain-sport, which in his eyes has led to the knowledge of others through the study of self.   This last conclusion, as to confession leading to depth of observation, appears dubious, inasmuch as it is uncertain whether the parents of Balzac, of George Sand, or of Dumas were practicers of the rite.   Moreover, what would become of all the English school of romancers — Richardson, Fielding, Sterne, George Eliot — if Protestants, who do not confess, were to be bereft of the literary gifts which, according to Bourget, confession alone can confer?   Whether or not the practice of self-examination, in view of such religious act, is beneficial to the romancer's mission as an observer of humanity, remains unanswered ; but that the power of observation in itself is held by Bourget as the main gift of the novelist, his works sufficiently show.   With Bourget the intellectual effort is held above the impulse of natural inspiration.   A man of great parts, of observation ; a reproducer of what he sees, a sketcher of what he reads, far more than a sensitive philosopher who, subordinating his emotional capacities to the modification of his reason, writes the history of incidents gone through and of passions experienced, — such appears Bourget the novelist.

Men and women the luxury and leisure of whose social position naturally lead to a life of emptiness are those whom Bourget chooses most frequently

to depict. Vainly in all his works should we seek
the study of a rural individuality such as Balzac,
Mme. Sand, George Eliot, have immortalized. Let
us but alter in imagination the worldly circumstances of a Suzanne Moraines (Mensonges), or an
Ely de Carlsberg, and we at once strike at the
very source of their moral life. If we suppose
these ladies deprived of money and overburdened
with home duties, we at once destroy the very
essence of their passion-life ; as this finds its root
only in the outward worldly exchange of parties
and meetings, which cannot exist without an abun-
dance of money and with no work to do. Every
incident in the heart-life of Bourget's heroes and
heroines is subservient to this or that worldly
circumstance, which will bring together or tear
asunder the loving couples whose reunion or separation is generally dependent upon social evolution. On the other hand, what has the world to
say to an Eugénie Grandet's feelings, to an Adam
Bede's emotions, to an Emma Bovary's desires?
These characters are human. They bear the stamp
of no period, the fashions of no epoch. They who
invented them searched for their patterns among
human hearts. Bourget's personages, on the contrary, are essentially factitious ; they move in an
atmosphere redolent of opoponax and musk. Their
emotions emanate from their brains long before
they are felt by their hearts.

The social *milieu* in which Bourget's men develop is, it should be mentioned to a foreign reader,
the least really French that can be imagined.
Long before he wrote his " Cosmopolis " our author

lived in, and inspired himself from, the rich Israelitish colony resident in Paris. Money, beauty,
culture, are to be found in that society, and
precisely in the order in which I mention them:
namely, money, as the autocrat; beauty, as the
means to money; and culture, as the servant of
both — or more truly as the spice, the relish which
comes in opportunely to testify to the omnipotence
of money and to show how well-arranged dinners
and ably-managed receptions bring the pride of
Horaces to compromise in our days, as they did in
the time of Augustus. From this very "goldy"
society, where truffles pave the road to orders for
paintings, and the smiles of love buy at a cheaper
rate the homage of Academicians; from this particularly un-French society, where the only fatherland is wealth, has Bourget taken most of his
types. As Emma Bovary, Germinie Lacerteux, or
Denise ("Au Bonheur des Dames," by Zola) are
unmistakably good or bad, yet nevertheless *true*,
types; just as these personages are French, and
necessarily French, so, on the other hand, Suzanne
Moraines, Hélène Chazel, Noëmie Hurtrel, are
cosmopolitanized Frenchwomen, — women who,
though brought up and living in Paris, have been
thrown so much among un-French elements as to
lose the characteristics of their race.

"La Française est avant tout une femme de
tête." I will not discuss here the question of the
merits or demerits which this assertion involves:
I simply state the fact. In following her reason
the Frenchwoman comes to self-denial as often as
she might do in following nobler feelings; never-

theless the basis of her character is reason. In
the name of reason she marries; in the name of
reason she hoards; in the name of reason she
even lies. Now, reason being eminently opposed
to mere sensual enjoyment, none can be farther
from an Eugénie Grandet or a Mme. Marneffe
than an Hélène Chazel or a Noëmie Hurtrel. Balzac's heroines, whether in the order of passion or
in the order of virtue, always fight, and sometimes
conquer. Bourget's heroines are mostly possessed
of that Semitic indifference and *laisser aller* in the
moral world which is a remnant of Orientalism.

Enjoyment by all bodily means is the natural
tendency of modern Jewish society, newly admitted
to and intoxicated by the privileges of equality
with those who, not a century ago, burned and
hanged them; and from this society Bourget drew
the concepts of most of his feminine types. Of
the austere, mass-going, humbly dressed *grande
dame française*, Bourget's novels are ignorant.
Cosmopolis is his world. His mission has been to
initiate the French reader into cosmopolitan Paris
society. Even when his ladies seem French they
are not so, in their souls or in their habits.
Bourget is a subtle psychologist; but the psychology he practices in most of his types is the
psychology of a rather newly modified French personality. A foreigner, after reading his books,
would fancy he had there approached real French
society, and, being unable to reconcile in any way
the outlines of Balzac's personages with those of
Bourget, — the difference of time and period not
accounting sufficiently for the gulf between them,

— would naturally conclude either that these romancers cannot have painted personages of the
same country, or that one of them is inexact.

Another peculiarity in Bourget, very suggestive
of the modifications undergone by young *viveurs*
of our time, is the way in which his heroes, de
Querne and du Prat, for instance, before ending
in a vague humanitarianism, turn to a no less
Tolstoï-ism, — in fact to that kind of idealistic anxiety which has come to novel-writers in France
through Ibsen and the Northern School.   Flaubert
as well as Balzac, and Maupassant equally with
Flaubert, — both being French to the core, —
have introduced metaphysical suggestions in their
human studies; but more than any other, the
psychologist of modern modified Frenchmen and
Frenchwomen is Paul Bourget.   Let the foreign
reader see in him the very faithful painter of a
fraction of Parisian society essentially modified
by Israelitish and cosmopolitan elements; of a
world which is not what the French call "la
société;" of a world where wealth plays the part
of birth in the Old France, and of brain-power in
the rising democracy.   Remembering that the
pleasure-mad ladies and their empty-headed and
empty-hearted lovers whom Bourget portrays are
illustrations only of a very small minority of what
Paris can boast in the way of un-French French
people, foreigners who read "Mensonges," "Un
Crime d'Amour," "Une Idylle tragique," etc., run
no risk of believing that Suzanne Moraines and
Hélène Chazel are types of the ordinary French
bourgeoise in good society.   That there exist num-

bers of Suzanne Moraines among the best and choicest of social groups is not to be denied; but to assert that venality in gallantry is as common with a certain order of the French world as in other countries would be a great error.

The world which Bourget has mostly painted is, as I have said, very un-French: it is a world of pleasure and of pleasure only. Bourget does not dwell, like Flaubert or Balzac, among all species of humanity, among provincials and Parisians, among poor and wealthy, among nobles and burghers; no, Bourget is the psychologist of *a* society. He very subtly, very delicately, and very powerfully paints the men and women of his country who, by living as much as they can out of the sphere of their own natural surroundings, by rushing to Monte Carlo, to Cowes, to Rome, or anywhere, drawn away by their own ennui and frivolity, become as unlike their native race as can well be imagined.

Psychology proper is Bourget's best field of work; and, therefore, before considering his novels, I shall first examine his studies on his contemporaries. His "Essais de Psychologie contemporaine" are certainly among the best titles to fame of a writer whose critical faculties are far superior to his powers of imagination.

II

Bourget is a living antithesis to Zola. There is not a personage, not a situation in his books, but is radically in opposition to what Zola would

have made of it. Zola deals mostly with the un-
educated classes; Bourget's first care, on the contrary, seems to be that his heroes shall be wealthy
and uncommon. Remarkable has been the success which has greeted Bourget, from the very
commencement of his career; no long fight with
ill fortune, but success from the appearance of
his first verses, "La Vie inquiète," "Les Aveux,"
"Edel," etc. Indeed, all his earlier writings met
with immediate appreciation. Of the "Essais de
Psychologie contemporaine," the studies of Baudelaire, of Taine, of Renan, are the best.

In his "Baudelaire" our author starts with the
destruction of all the received theories about
healthy or unhealthy literature. "There is no
such thing as health, or the contrary, in the world
of the soul," writes Bourget to the unmetaphysical
observer. Our troubles, our faculties, our virtues,
our vices, our sacrifices, our volitions, are mere
changeful and variegated combinations, — normal
because changeful. There exist no healthy or unhealthy loves. Why should the loves of Daphnis
and Chloe be in any way healthier than the loves
described by Baudelaire? An overcrowded and
meanly furnished boudoir is in no wise more or
less healthy than the trees under which Chloe
meets her pastoral mate. In humanity health is
never transferable to the psychological regions.
Baudelaire appears to Bourget as *the* one who has
understood and painted the ennui of his period, —
the yawnings and gapings of the refined monster,
due above all to the complications of modern life,
the over-refinement of our tears, and the sophisti-

cated nature of our gayeties, which have made us
morally euphuists of the inner life. "C'est de la
préciosité morale." Bourget's Baudelaire is a living and very true likeness because quite a literary
one, devoid of any cantish *redites* about Baudelaire the man.

Our author's taste for wealthy society betrays
itself in an aristocratic preference, which makes
Renan dear to him above all others; for Renan is
an enemy to the illiterate. With regard to Renan's exegetic performances, Bourget disclaims
any enthusiasm. Faith to him is and must remain
simple and childlike. Renan's dazzling rhetoric
is too literary; meaning by that, perhaps, rather
unevangelical. But, then, Renan is such a writer!
And style is in itself an aristocracy.

Whatever the gap between Baudelaire and
Renan, it is not greater than the distance between
the classically critical ability of a Bourget and
the powerfully creative gifts of a Flaubert. Still,
Bourget's admiration for the "Norman bear" is
deep and sincere; and if his natural bent necessarily leads him to the cult of cleverness rather than
to that of spontaneous genius, Flaubert nevertheless receives, under Bourget's pen, a treatment in
no way offensive to his worshipers. Flaubert
should have been seen pacing his study, Chateaubriand in hand, quoting aloud whole passages of
"Atala." One of his favorite paragraphs was,
"Among the secular oaks the dazzling moon in-
discreetly reveals to the wild old shores the mysteries of nature." "Images," writes Bourget,
"with Flaubert, always preceded the actual expe-

ricncc." Flaubert painted chiefly from his own
intellectual conceit rather than from remembrance.
Images and sound, *i. e.*, the sonority of a written
phrase, were the inspiring principles of the author
of "Salammbô." "I know," he would say, "the
worth of a phrase only after I have sung it to
myself." This undercurrent of lyrism in Flaubert
himself accounts for the dreams and aspirations
with which he has imbued Emma Bovary's wishes.
In fact, lyrism is a fundamental *leit motif* in
"Madame Bovary" and in "L'Education sentimentale: roman d'un jeune homme." Flaubert's
personages are overthinkers: they die by living
their thoughts. St. Anthony dies of too much
thought and love for his Christ; Emma Bovary
dies of living her divers dreams. And one of the
best scenes portraying this over-activity of mind is
depicted in the passage quoted by Bourget from
"Madame Bovary," where the heads of husband
and wife, though meeting together on the pillow,
wander so far from each other in their imagination. Charles Bovary dreamed he was listening
to the breath of his child. He loved to think of
her, — how she would grow and develop. Emma
imagined she was tearing away at the gallop of
four vigorous horses, hurrying on toward a country
whence they would never return, — her lover and
herself. The quotation is not only humoristic, as
showing the discrepancy between the grandilo-
quent dreams of Emma and the homely realities of
her surroundings, but it evidences the existence in
Flaubert himself of that untiring activity of mind
with which he endows the personages of his inven-

tion. Style was Flaubert's tormentor: and, though
he has not said of himself what Edmond de Goncourt said of Jules, " He died of style," yet style
was his constant preoccupation. He touched and
retouched, arranged, altered, and worked whole
nights hunting after perfection. " The word and
the thought," he often repeated, " are one; the
thought is not outside the word: it is as inseparable from it as the word is inseparable from the
phrase."

If Flaubert's personages think more than they
act, if with them speculation destroys action,
with Bourget the reverse is often the case. Had
Noëmie Hurtrel, for instance, applied more of her
meditative faculties to her own personal case, she
would not have been driven to despair and suicide.
The same with du Prat. Both are victims to absence of thought: they are mastered by events
because they follow them with the impulse of
their natures.

Taine appears to Bourget only as the philosopher. Of Taine the historian, the critic, the ini-
tiator of foreign thought in France, Bourget is
utterly neglectful. The philosophical principles
of Taine and Bourget with regard to literature,
however, are as contradictory as the methods of
Zola and Bourget in novel-writing. Bourget is a
decided separatist, — one who, like Descartes, entirely separates in humanity the promptings of the
person and the suggestions of the soul. In the
same being, according to Bourget, are two distinct
impulses, and not only distinct, but opposed: the
promptings of the spiritual being, and the prompt-

ings of the bodily being; seldom meeting in the same conclusions. Taine's views, on the contrary, go to affirm that man is the result of a climate, of a group, of a pressure of ideas, of an atmosphere moral and real. The characteristic of Bourget's philosophy and psychology is minutiæ, — minutiæ to a defect; minutiæ to which Beyle would have certainly applied his remark, "La minutie en psychologie peut aller trop loin, lorsque, par exemple, elle transforme en hommes de simples manches à sabres! "

A "tonified" Baudelaire, a Renan freed from all anti-religious aggressiveness, a lion-like Flaubert in search of perfection, a softened, tender Beyle,[1] — such are the modifications that Bourget's delicate and subtle psychology has imposed upon the well-known writers whom he has studied. One of the excellences of these essays is their comprehensiveness. In all his models Bourget has shirked nothing. He has taken account of all contingencies; of the heart qualities and gifts as much as of the brain gifts. He writes: —

"There exist souls of election with whom the development of the mind and of the intellect is in no way detrimental to the full swing in them of the life of passion as well. In such natures, cerebral fever and creative powers are but an addition to the fermentations of natural normal life. The capacity of such natures for affection and love is increased instead of being destroyed by reason of their consciousness."

[1] Bourget's sketch of Beyle ("De Stendhal") gives quite a new and lovable aspect of the great critic.

As Bourget's novel, " Le Disciple," is rather a work of pure dissective psychology than a romance of passion, its natural place is here, immediately after the psychological sketches, and before his other novels.

III

The theme of " Le Disciple," — well characterized " the diagnosis of others through the magnified study of self," — such as it is, fastened itself upon Bourget's mind through a most tragic criminal case which happened in Algiers in the year 1889. A young man named Chambige, belonging to the French bureaucratic middle class, killed his mistress ; failing afterward in his attempt to kill himself. During the interval of imprisonment between his arrest and his trial, Chambige addressed most dithyrambic letters to Bourget, charging all the contemporaneous novel-writers with having instigated his crime by the spirit of pessimism prevalent in the modern literature of fiction. The verdict on Chambige was one of " irresponsibility ; " and, shortly after this true and terrible case, appeared " Le Disciple." Robert Greslou, the " disciple," is the acme and essence of the egotist. The vaguest movement of his own lungs is to Greslou a matter of the intensest significance. He has kept a journal of his every palpitation since his childhood. He writes : —

" At the age of twelve my faculties of observation were such that one of my dearest wishes was to be in possession of the opinion my mother had formed of me. I wished to compare what I really was with what was thought of me. I waited for the occasion; and one day I listened to my mother's estimation of myself in a conversation with a friend of hers. The conclusion I drew from that day forward was, that between what I was and what she thought me to be, there existed no more likeness than between my real visage and the reflection of it in a colored looking-glass."

Robert Greslou, an obscure professor, recriminates against the whole world; and, knowing no limits to his aspirations, he considers himself frustrated in all his desires simply because he fails in the satisfaction of his ambition. "La psychologie de Dieu," a book written by one Professor Sixte, who, under Bourget's pen, represents the modern pessimistic doctrinarian, has made Greslou the passionate disciple of Sixte. This book is one of pure speculation, the professor being essentially one of those innocent scientists after the fashion of Jean Paul Richter's Maria Hilf — innocent, but dangerous. He plays with the most intricate cobwebs of moral life, quite unconscious of the perturbations that his conclusions, born of speculation purely, may induce if transported from dreamland into real life. In this book, which theorizes on the passions generally, Greslou discovers elements which he resolves upon applying in his own life, — methods, so to say, indifferent or curious, and, speculatively speaking, in both cases harmless; whereas, ripened and working in an over-excited brain and a discontented mind, they may become nefarious, if from the world of speculation they are transferred to the world of action. Greslou

becomes tutor in the household of the Marquis de
Jussat-Randon, where he promptly decides upon
playing to Charlotte, the daughter of his patron,
the part Saint-Preux played toward Héloïse in the
work of Rousseau. His success is followed by the
death of both, for Charlotte poisons herself and
- Greslou is shot dead by her brother.

"Le Disciple" is not only an implicit satire
upon the danger of philosophers' writing platonically upon passions which they have not experienced; it also shows what havoc pessimistic doctrines of any kind may make among discontented
souls. Love of self, carried to morbidity and
crime, is the essence of "Le Disciple." Preoccupation of self, carried almost to monomania,
forms the basis of Noëmie Hurtrel. With Noëmie,
also, despair takes the place of remorse; but
Noëmie was sufficiently armed by Bourget: she
had brains and moral energy enough to rise by a
strong effort of will above the unique and deleteri-
ous contemplation of ego which absorbs her very
essence. False sensitiveness, taking the form of a
sustained worship of "I," is the "case" of Noëmie
Hurtrel; and such cases are common with our
author; so common, indeed, that almost all his
personages are moral cases: in de Querne there
is such absence of feeling that he cannot love; to
Madame de Carlsberg, fidelity in her affections is
an impossibility; Chazel has such utter trust in
those particularly who betray him that it is akin
to lack of penetration. Noëmie Hurtrel's error
of losing herself in over-meditation upon her own
destiny prevents her from any useful undertaking.

She leads a fruitless life, through the impossibility
of tearing herself from herself.

IV

The brain, I repeat, is with Bourget the main
dwelling of all the concepts of his heroes and
heroines. Consequently the loves of these personages are oftener loves of the imagination than of
the heart. "Un Crime d'Amour," which might
as appropriately be entitled "Lack of Love," is
the story of an artificial brain-love on the part of
the hero, of a headlong caprice on the part of the
heroine. "La Terre promise" tells of a little girl
who will only know real love long after she has
outlived the mild schoolgirl tale she hears at first.
"Une Idylle tragique" is the story of a neurasthenic lady in search of passion through divers
essays of dreamy fancies. The case of Hélène
Chazel in "Un Crime d'Amour," as cases go, is
far from being a new one : it is the hackneyed
narrative of the husband's best friend alienating
the wife. The only novelty in the matter is the
descriptive mania of Bourget, — his dwelling upon
screens, lamp-shades, bookcases, carpets, upholstery
of every known kind, long after the reader is entitled to expect that the portrait of the heroes
should replace the sketch of things belonging to the
surrounding frame. If the errors of moral insight
which abound in "Un Crime d'Amour" happened
only to Hélène and de Querne, love might justify
them ; but Robert Greslou, Madame de Carlsberg,
Hautefeuille, err in the same way with regard to

their own inner status. Is this, then, the error of
the author himself? Or do the falsified views of
the characters of his imagination impose their own
crooked conclusions on the novelist? It is easier
in such matters to estimate results than to perceive
causes. The results of these strange morals are
that women betray the most trusting husbands,
believing themselves angels, and that Lovelaces
turn to Vincents de Paul. Unexpectedly strange
and curiously unsound, to say the least! A beautiful feeling of humanitarian sympathy gleams
through "Un Crime d'Amour" toward the close,
however, making it end more pathetically than it
began. De Querne, speculating on the difficulties
which exist for the philosopher who would rest
assured that the explanation of earthly life is to be
given in Paradise, and on the emptiness of man's
destiny when deprived of future rewards, concludes that the solidarity of misery is in itself a
sufficient cause for man to brace himself to the
short-lived and dolorous effort of living. Noëmie
Hurtrel, in "L'Irréparable," is a variety of de
Querne, in so far that the key of her nature is a
morbid brooding over a tragic event of which she
has been the victim.

An impulsive, unconscious creature is Noëmie,
— unconscious, at least, of any effort to rise above
the events which assail her; and though Bourget
has at first shown her to the reader as a woman of
culture and intellectual aspirations, his opinion
of her species is so willingly, so purposely, a mis-
estimating one that he endows her with no wish to
abstract herself from self-absorption either by study

or by humanitarian deeds of any sort. We are informed by the author that Noëmie Hurtrel is one of those modern dabblers in philosophy who meddle in Schopenhauer and Kant, mix with the subjective and the objective; one of those who read, perhaps, rather than assimilate, and whose only wish, if they do assimilate, is to talk what they have absorbed. Though the woman who should cure a heartsore with an application of Plato would be very unwomanly indeed if she proceeded thus in the acute period of her trouble, yet a woman whose mind is at all developed, as Bourget insists in telling us Noëmie Hurtrel's was, might at least make an effort of some kind. The self-abandonment of Noëmie can be accounted for only by the ineffaceable trace in her heart of the injury inflicted on her at her start in life. She has been weakened gradually through the passing years by the remembrance of a slur. She would have confessed to Lord Wadham and poured out all her heart into his; but Lord Wadham has no such element as a heart in him, and Noëmie is thrown back upon herself, till, hypnotized by her fixed idea and unable to battle any more, she walks out of existence. "Morte pour rien" is the best epitome of the whole drama, — " died uselessly," as she had lived uselessly. More religious or more frivolous, Noëmie would have reconquered herself, as Henriette Scilly and Ely de Carlsberg did, — the one through the nobility of her unbending and rather childish dignity, the other through her love of the world.

Henriette Scilly, however, rises to the complete

sacrifice of self by intense religious feeling. She
has gone to Palermo with her mother and her future husband, Francis Nayrac, when, on an unlucky day, Pauline Raffraye projects herself on
Henriette's horizon. This lady is accompanied by
a little girl of about ten years, the daughter of
Francis Nayrac and Pauline in past years. Henriette speaks to the child ; and the guardedness
of the child's answers, as well as some secret instinct, prompts Henriette to guess that there exists
some bond between Nayrac and the child's mother.
Meanwhile Pauline dies. The old and much-used
system of hearing through open doors serves Henriette. She hears a prolonged explanation between her mother and Nayrac, and perceives that
the discussion turns upon the adoption by Nayrac
of the little girl. Henriette at once resolves upon
giving up her marriage ; thus sacrificing herself,
and leaving the father entirely to his duties. She
refuses to hear any of Nayrac's prayers. Occasions to express himself pessimistically about women are almost as dear to Bourget as to Dumas
fils. Traitresses and false women abound in his
books. However this may be, Henriette Scilly's
sacrifice is such that, though the reader is not led
to believe in any possibility of relenting on her
part, yet it may be inferred that as time passes
she will some day think of father and child, and,
perhaps, alter her decision.

"La Terre promise" is a mild book. It holds
in Bourget's works about the same place that "Le
Rêve" holds in Zola's. It is a book of courtship to the Académie, written in a widely different

order of thought from "Une Idylle tragique," for instance. The evolution from a Suzanne Moraines to the heroine of "Notre Cœur" is rich in varieties of types. At Bourget's starting-point his heroes are mostly pleasure-seeking men and women. Suzanne Moraines is a modern Manon Lescaut without the generous heart of her prototype.

His journey to America marked in Bourget a new era. Till then the saddest sides of the society of all great cities were exploited by our author: venality, adultery, lying, and dishonesty of every kind were his favorite themes. In Ely de Carlsberg, at least, we are brought face to face with a disinterested, but certainly very changeful, heart. At the beginning of the book she has already loved Olivier du Prat, married the Archduke, and begun her liaison with Pierre Hautefeuille. Ely is a victim to her tyrannic Archduke, — an archduke of the modern pattern, a scientist with a laboratory and a young secretary who receives for all his work nought but ill words and hard dealings. Ely has met Olivier du Prat at Rome, and Olivier has since married. Now he has come to Monte Carlo, where he meets Pierre Hautefeuille, his former college chum. Hearing of Hautefeuille's success with Madame de Carlsberg he grows restless, and, after various attempts at reinstating his friendship with Pierre, finally abandons himself to the return of his love for Ely, going so far as to introduce himself one night into the Archduke's garden. The Archduke, who is more despotic than jealous, discovers him, shoots at hap-hazard, and Olivier falls dead. Hencefor-

ward Hautefeuille and Madame de Carlsberg are
forever divided by Olivier's death. All around
Madame de Carlsberg in this book are grouped
most humoristic sketches, — Fregoso, the Genoese
owner of a beautiful gallery, for instance; Marsh,
the American, and his niece Flossie. Marsh is
a sentimental millionaire whose yacht contains a
chapel dedicated to the memory of a deceased
daughter of his, a girl of seventeen. Her marble
statue is the object on his part of a cult, and to
this holy room none are admitted save in the attitude of prayer. The amalgam in Richard Marsh
of money, love, generous chivalry, gaudiness, and
simplicity; the diverse moods in which he alternately treats those whom he helps as a tribe of
paupers, or with delicacy seeks the means of being
to them a providence, — these contradictions in
his character, the natural results of a lack of the
polish which education gives and which fails the
self-made nabob, are most carefully depicted by
Bourget; cosmopolitanism, as I have already said,
being his most distinctive feature.

The women of Bourget's novels are mostly cap-
tivating conversationalists, — because Bourget himself is the talker, — but their brains never react
upon their doings. All are as empty of purpose
as poor Noëmie Hurtrel, though all do not go to
the same extremes. A duplicate of Noëmie is to
be found in "Deuxième Amour," though this time
the victim, Claire, executes her heart, while remaining alive. Claire has been married very young to
a man whom she discovers to be a thief. Her
horror of him combined with her love for another

causes her to elope with Gerard. A short experience of Gerard, however, dispels all illusions from
Claire. This one is not a thief; but he lacks
delicacy of feeling, which she finds at last in a
friend of Gerard, whom she loves for himself, not
with the wish of getting away from such a low
character as her husband. This love, however, she
renounces, and Elie, receiving the letter in which
she announces that he will never see her again,
states that he now knows " ce que c'est qu'un
grand amour," — that great loves are great, fruitful tortures, through which souls rise to their
highest levels. Among "Profils perdus" let us
mark also the Russian doctress. " She would
accept my compliments and *empressements* with
her placid, masculine look; her speeches upon love,
death, maternity, and all other subjects were of the
coarsest materialism; and, as one listened to her,
one felt her very hand was virgin of a man's kiss."
In fact, a rather neurasthenic humanity in search
of duality of feeling, a humanity preoccupied with
the study of its soul through the medium of its
intellect, and in counting the pulsations of its
brain, — such is the humanity Bourget shows us.
It may well be said of our novelist that he is innocent of the creation of a single simple nature.

V

Whether sophisticated and complicated through
the multiplicity of their contradictory feelings or
through the pursuit of making apparent their inner
life, Bourget's creatures are never simple. They

are not simple because in them effects do not follow causes in a normal, natural way. Love, generous love, great love, is full blown in Bourget's heroines. Yet the heart, instead of following the bent of self-forgetfulness, which is the effect of real love, goes farther and farther on the road to selfishness; and the anomaly is seen throughout Bourget's books of a nature at once generous in its feelings and egotistical in its life. The men and women we read of in Bourget's novels are morally so deficient that their will never interferes to help them in the hour of need, — cold, reasoning, pleasure-seekers, snobs, creatures in whom even instinct seems a product of the brain, so factitious and unnatural are they.

As to Bourget's attempts at cynicism, they are very mild indeed. He seems, however, to believe no one ever tied together such astoundingly contradictory assertions as that, for instance, in "Cruelle Enigme," that the man who had worshiped a woman for her purity was held to her next by the lowest resources of sensuality! "The wildest physical desires may be felt simultaneously with the sincerest contempt." What is there so new in all this? Above all, what, critically speaking, is this method of approximating "physical desires" and "contempt"? Why this confusion of physiology and psychology? Most of Bourget's lovers fall under the description René Doumic gives of the modern young man. "They are mostly," writes Doumic, "poor attenuated creatures whom maternal spoiling and excessive university work have altogether destroyed." Zola has taken life in its whole. Maupassant has selected physiology and psychology. Bourget's principal merit is his sincerity about a certain world, — a world where moral nullity is the result of over-leisure.

Bourget is in the realm of romance what Frederick Amiel is in the realm of thinkers and philosophers, — a subtle, ingenious, highly gifted, but partial student of his time; rather prone, however, to what is easy and abnormal than to what is real and natural. With a wonderful dexterity of pen, a very acute, almost womanly intuition, and a rare morbidity of grace about all his writings, it is probable that Bourget will remain more known as a critic than as a romancer.

The personages he has created will be short-lived. De Quernes and Larchers will, necessarily, be replaced by the generations of athletic men whom modern sports are developing; and as to Mesdames Moraines, Chazel, and others, — these were, after all, but refashioned Marneffes and Nucingens out of Balzac's "Comédie humaine." It may be said of Bourget, as it was of Musset, that his glass is small; but, whereas Musset filled his glass with his own soul, Bourget has filled his with souls so artificial and so factitious that they will evaporate, and will leave certainly less of Bourget the novelist than of Bourget the critic.

EUGÈNE MELCHIOR DE VOGÜÉ

IF an Englishman of the great Carlylean epoch had heard MM. Villemain, Cousin, Naquet, Sainte-Beuve, or any other of that class, ask ingenuously, "Where, what, and who is Carlyle?" and glory in his ignorance, he would have assumed, perhaps rightly, the cause of such ignorance to be affectation; or would have attributed the remark to a desire of attracting notice; or, again, would have wondered what personal spite the questioner might be indulging. But all such moods are so fatal to the real conversationalist that he carefully leaves them at home whenever he sallies out upon the errand of talking.

An English critic was saying to me not long ago: "Talking (*causer*) is essentially a French occupation or acquisition, arising from the need to parade before the world the mental resources of the speaker. For *one* Shakespeare that we have you need half a dozen men of genius: a Pascal for the thought of Hamlet; a Descartes for the metaphysics of Lady Macbeth; a Corneille to recall the grandeur of Rome; a Racine to inspire 'Phèdre' with passion; a Molière to point the shaft of irony; and, after passing out of the seventeenth century, a Musset to sing the songs of fancy. Your Frenchman is an exclusive specialist and a classifier." All of which is quite true. At the same

time, this method or system of knowing one thing
only, but knowing it well, has its advantages, if
only in obviating the possibility of such surprises
as the one I instanced above ; for Frenchmen meet
in society on neutral ground, impersonally, not as
man to man, but as mind to mind. Personal vanity,
nervousness, or spite must be left at home : the
mind alone is invited out ; and thus we are spared
such amazing and pitiable confessions of ignorance
as that recently made to me by one of the most
deservedly popular English writers. "I do not
know Ferdinand Brunetière, because he writes in
the ' Revue des Deux Mondes,' which I never read,
and I do not know Vogüé, because his works have
not been translated." This latter misfortune
Vogüé, one of our greatest masters of style, shares
with Bossuet, whom, nevertheless, my witty friend
certainly has read. To be sure, the Bishop of
Meaux is dead, and, in the eyes of an ambitious
author, that is an immense advantage over a living
Vogüé. At the same time, the Englishman's natural aversion to a purely scientific, impersonal
treatment of the object or subject under discussion,
his preference for generalizing under the pronoun
"I," lead him into that most grievous of social
errors, an exhibition of self, — forgetting that a
bilious attack should be carefully wrapped up in a
dressing-gown. Where physical and mental individuality are too strongly welded together, conversation is allowed to recriminate : thus was I allowed
to perceive through my interlocutor's bitterness
his desire to make me believe Vogüé far more
ignored in England than he himself is in France !

When the bugle called, in 1870, the boy who was to become the youngest member of the French Academy (he was elected[1] in 1888), and who was then one of the youngest men in the army, followed his brother to the front. For centuries no Vogüé had awaited his coming of age to leave his eagle's nest in the mountains and sally forth for the king. The light-haired, clear, deep-eyed boy had inherited from his mother the stubborn Scottish perseverance in the path of duty, as he had imbibed the traditions that clung to the family name. The story of his younger years recalls that of Lamartine, for he lived among the same class of people, was one of them, and their ways were his. Like the "chatelain de Milly," he wandered about the fields with his friend Virgil, or pored over some ponderous quarto in the family library.[2] Lamartine, however, was obliged to defray the expenses of his first volume of poems, whereas the Vicomte de Vogüé entered at once upon a successful literary career. In 1873 he was introduced to M. Buloz, the founder of the "Revue des Deux Mondes," by one of the most eminent writers on its staff, and his manuscript "Voyage en Syrie et en Palestine" was immediately accepted. His success in the world of letters was as great as that of Lamartine's poems; and, indeed, the career of each of these authors sufficiently resembles that of the other to warrant a parallel. Again, a general election re-

[1] At the age of forty; he was born February 25, 1848.

[2] "Do you remember the quiet library in the old homestead, where, on rainy afternoons, you lived and read the hours away?"—*Heures d'Histoire.*

turned Vogüé, by an immense majority, as the representative for the district in which his name had been honored for centuries, as might have been the case with Lamartine before him. The new member said: "Whether as a man of letters or as a diplomat in the service of my country, I have lived my life loyally, openly, so that all may know it and scrutinize it in detail."

Throughout the campaign of 1870 Vogüé served in one of the very regiments described by M. Zola in "La Débâcle." His brother fell on the field of honor, and the disaster that overwhelmed his country, added to his own grief, stamped upon his brow the pale mark of melancholy reserved for the elect. When peace descended upon the land, Vogüé, again like Lamartine, chose a diplomatic career, in which, while serving his country, he could also study his fellow-men and follow the philosophical bent of his mind. His first post was Greece, where, under the shadow of the Acropolis, he read again Aristotle, Homer, and Plato ; at the bidding of Æschylus the terrible trilogy being once more enacted before him. Amid such surroundings the man who could grasp the vast dramas of history with such a master-hand as the author of "The Son of Peter the Great," and at the same time describe nature with the magic touch of Loti, was really in his element. Those who have kept the letters in which at that time Vogüé, with a pen worthy of Byron, described the soul-inspiring skies and seas of Hellas, can easily follow his early Turner stage into the stronger spheres of Decamps.

During what may be called the first stage of

Vogüé's life — that is, throughout the records of his impressions gathered in Egypt, Asia, the East, and at first even in Russia — the sun had been the pole-star of this child of Provence; but later the dreary sadness of the Russian steppe, the harsh lash of the Muscovite climate, the primitive fallow-ness of soul and soil, attracted him by their very repellency, and awakened within him the ambition of conquest, *coûte que coûte,* — the ambition so dear to the Scotchman's heart, who gauges the victory according to the obstacles he has overcome.

After Athens he was sent to Egypt. Isis and Cleopatra worked their spell. Before the Sphinx he dreamed of infinite horizons : no longer merely the infinity of space, but the infinity of thought. Before the colossal emblem of Egypt's past he in-voked the shade of Pascal ; and from the domain of physics into the wider realm of metaphysics he moved — from the real to the possible ; yet, not-withstanding their variety, their splendor, these single gems remained separate and unset, each per-fect in itself, but as yet only a part of an imperfect whole.

Governments change in France as they do else-where — perhaps even more often ; and a change of government may sometimes bring with it the golden opportunity to the coming man. It was thus in Vogüé's case. General Le Flô appointed him to St. Petersburg, where he was able to quarry in virgin ground.

It is the privilege of unprejudiced master-minds to see the thing to do, and do it. So Vogüé, ap-parently lost in the vast Russian desert, not only

found his way, but, in superb French, often finer
than even the firmest style of Chateaubriand, he
wrote of the soul of the steppes, and, in prose,
told us the poems of serf-life. In the cradle of the
East he had learned to understand the springs of
the great human drama, whence all that is good in
modern civilization has come; and in the wilder
country where he now worked the modern apostle
spoke clearly to him: Tolstoï of *Charity* because
of Christ, Sutaïeff of *Christ himself;* and in the
very language of the apostles Vogüé has repeated
what they told him. " You have taken my cloak;
now take my shirt also, and learn thereby to pile
sacks of corn on the thief's wagon, that he may
have the *given* grain as well as the stolen sacks."

But before considering Vogüé's Russian work,
his greatest at this time, we should examine his
first volume. It appeared in parts in the " Revue
des Deux Mondes," under the title " Voyage en
Syrie et en Palestine." Here, speaking of the
Holy Land anointed by the Saviour's blood, and
to him a perpetual source of inspiration to dream
or philosophize, he says : " It is not easy for the
modern mind, refined by incessant endeavor, detached from material considerations by the slow
processes of patient time, developed and purified
by centuries of evolution, to judge fairly the events
of such distant ages. The soul has lived and suffered much during this long rubbing of man against
mankind, and the rough outer shell has been worn
away. Among the men of old the tougher fibre
of material life bound the soul more closely, held
it more firmly, nearer to mother earth. Mankind

was young then, and the sun burned the new-born
earth, and the earth was drunken with the wine
of its own exuberance. Man — the man-child —
looked about him, .bewildered by the universal
bursting of the buds of spring life and crushed by
the passionate endeavor of nature. The gentler
weaknesses of to-day — the weaknesses of the flesh,
of the body-lord, the exalted refinement of modern
thought — he knew not; but he listened eagerly
to the voice of nature, and obeyed it. Life and
death really meant to him the beginning and the
end." And, as he stands in the land of Canaan,
looking backward through the long ages of its
desolation, the same heavy, passionate hand of nature fastens upon him with a stronger, more angry
grip. Vogüé goes on : " The landscape remains
unchanged, and in this frame we see the life that
was. The day is done, and the goddesses of the
night claim our worship. The virgin moon lingers
lovingly about Ghibal, and the passion-torn Astarte
casts dark mysterious shadows, — shadows preg-
nant with the secrets of the fates and with the fear
of death. Beyond, from the dimly glimmering
lake-sea of Aschera rises the breath of life, sen-
suous, uneven, powerful, yearning for the kiss of
the buried Tammouze, — Aschera, the irresistible
one, whose hot, thirsty breath has drunk in the cold
breezes of Lebanon, and now bids the grave yield
up its dead. Slowly, slowly the clamoring women
pass, — clamoring, clamoring for the soul of the
lost Tammouze. Watch them pass, — leading the
people of Byblos towards the empurpled waters,
where Christ bled to death, — watch them pass ! "

Later, in his " Images de Rome," his transitions
are more rapid — from gay to grave, from philosophy to irony, from the smile of sympathy to the
silence of meditation. In a single paragraph he
passes from the initial tumultuousness of the gen-
esis, when the world was "drunk with youth,"
to the plastic evolutions of classical mythology:
" Astarte, the sombre goddess of the uncontrolled,
unbridled powers of darkness, death, night, the
deep."

It was in 1875 that France sent the future academician and *député* to Russia, where, among the
yellow, waving wheat-fields, the prose poet studied
the simple soul of the Russian peasant, and learned
to understand how much of mystical dreaming, of
yearning for the Beyond, remains to-day, even
after all these centuries of sophistication, in that
primitive man. East, or west, or south, or north,
this man appears to Vogüé unconsciously nearer
to God than his educated brother. Vogüé was
liked in Russia deservedly, for he liked the people
about him. Eventually he married a daughter of
this new country, and through the prism of a
woman's soul, illumined by love, he saw Russia as
Byron through the same light had seen Italy, and
rejoiced in the sight thereof. His initiation into
Russia began with the revelations of Tolstoï, of
Dostoievsky, and he was the first to make the
French public understand the profound psychology,
as well as the human Christian side, of their apparent pessimism. Through them he learned to
understand what Tourguénieff's tales of Russian
rural life had failed to explain : he learned to

understand the fermentation of this multitude of
souls newly aware of the freedom of thought, but
just awakened to the possibility of individualism
of expansion — not realizable at once, to be sure,
but far beyond anything hitherto dreamed of in
their philosophy. Vogüé was the first to expound
before a French audience the colossal energy of
their endeavor, the passionate struggling toward
light and freedom of a vast congregation com-
pressed into narrow limits under an iron rule, to
whom straight paths were denied, and who must
fain expend the full intensity of its energy upon
the immediately surrounding mediums, like a mass
of germs fermenting in a barrel.

It is to Vogüé that France owes the discovery
of this undocumented human family, whose habits
and struggles would have delighted the pen of a
Balzac, and which both Gogol and Tourguénieff
omitted from their records of rural Russian life.

From this chapter of contemporary history Vogüé
read backward into the past. His first work relating to Russian history is an essay on Alexis, the
Don Carlos of the North; and the tragic ending
of the marriage of this son of Peter the Great with
"the daughter of a serf," an ignorant, prying little
savage, intensely fond of sweetmeats, moves him
deeply. There are few pages in history more dramatic than those in which he pictures the last act
of the imperial drama, where the Tsarewitch pays
for a mistaken love at the price of his honor and
his life. He had loved the peasant's daughter with
an unwise love, and to her ambition she sacrificed
the man for the sake of the willing tool. The goad

of love drove the blind Alexis to betray his father
and plot against his emperor. But the Christian
Euphrosyne, for whose sake he had thrown himself away, requited this devotion by revealing the
whole plot to the Tsar himself; and of the last
scene of this passion-play Vogüé writes: "Can
anything be more really tragic than this trial,
where, at the last moment, the credulous lover,
chained to the woman for whose sake and at whose
instigation he has trampled under foot every filial
duty and every human consideration, awakes from
his dream of love to hear from the beloved one his
condemnation and his shame? He loves her still,
and by the power of this love she wrings from his
own lips the final confession, and wrests from his
soul the last lingering illusions." The death of
the Tsarewitch followed close upon these revelations; and Vogüé maintains that, were a Shakespeare born to Russia, the story of the Tsarewitch
Alexis would be the theme of his greatest drama.

Immediately following the essay on the "Son of
Peter the Great," comes an admirable paper on
"Mazeppa" — not the Mazeppa of the common
prints, not the legendary martyr to a self-sought
fate, but the northern Macchiavelli, the prototype
of Talleyrand, deceiving in turn each one of his
employers, until, weary of perpetual deceit as the
price of their confidence, they cast him adrift.

To a certain extent Vogüé has followed the
Mazeppa of Pouchkine, careful, however, never to
leave the firm ground of history for the tempting
quicksand of legendary lore. His hero remains a
man, with a man's foibles, his tricks and short-

comings, his vices and weaknesses of the mind as
of the flesh. In the first pages of his work Vogüé
describes the prostrate hero pinioned to the ground
under his fallen horse, and half unconscious : —

" The eager, hungry crows are brushing past,
so close in their flight that their feathers fan the
fallen man; it is night, and Mazeppa quivers in
the last agony. The end is near when a young
maiden, Maria, the daughter of Kotchoubey, comes
to his rescue and offers help and shelter. A few
nights later the rumbling gallop of a flying horse
re-ëchoes through the darkness, and in the morning Maria's room is empty. Mazeppa has eloped
with her. It is the counterpart of a scene of his
youth, when a Polish lord, whose wife he had se-
duced, straps him naked to an unbroken horse and
drives them forth into the night. The wild horse-
man reaches the province of Ukraine, where his
ability is soon recognized by the title of Prince.
As his power grows, he is raised to the rank of
hetman, and Jean Casimir, King of Poland, in-
trusts him with the command of his army. Mazeppa espouses the cause of Charles XII., and
takes sides against the Tsar; but he is not quite
sure of his wife Maria, and asks her : ' Which is
the stronger, — your love for your father or your
love for me ? ' Fate answers for her ; Kotchoubey
is imprisoned and soon after executed."

For a man of Vogüé's imagination this was a
splendid foundation ; nevertheless, he preferred to
follow in the rut of history and leave aside the
legend with its locking charms. To be sure, history tells a different tale, more simply.

Mazeppa, a Polish lord, has been detected by his mistress's husband, who asks of one of his men, " How often has Mazeppa slept under my roof while I was abroad ? "   " As often," the peasant replies, " as I have hairs on my head." The outraged husband at once orders Mazeppa to be tied, naked, to a horse, and drives the wild steed across country. The man is saved. After many struggles, Mazeppa's superiority is acknowledged, and honors fall thick about him. Even the Patriarch of Constantinople feels it a duty to send him presents. The man is weary with wealth and honors; he is past sixty; he has had and enjoyed what man may have and enjoy, and he is gradually sinking into the slough of old age. Suddenly the girl Maria turns him back. He is smitten with an unreasonable love for the young thing, and the *blasé* old satrap, satiated with adulation, weary of swimming down the stream of undeserved honors, suddenly recovers his lost youth. He recalls the love-letters of many years ago, and imploringly writes to his loving heart, his blossoming rosebud; his heart aches, for she is near and he may not see her. " I may not look into your eyes nor gaze upon your dear little white face."

Such a master as Vogüé must perforce have been carried away by the dramatic possibilities of Mazeppa's story, — the Mazeppa bound to a wild horse and flung loose in the forest, to be miraculously saved and raised to the very highest posts of honor. And not less fascinating was the story of Alexis, the son of the great Peter, whose strange vicissitudes would fill a Shakespearean canvas.

Then Paul I., the son of the great Catherine, com-
pels his interest; for his is the life of Hamlet
lived over again two hundred years later than his
literary prototype. The unavenged shadow of
his father weighed heavily upon Paul, as it had
weighed upon the Prince of Denmark; and surely
the melancholy of the Tsarewitch, converted suddenly at his accession to the throne into the most
intolerant despotism, proves that in the mind of
one, as in the mind of the other Hamlet, the same
strange, interesting lack of balance, verging upon
insanity, was an equally powerful factor.

While yet Tsarewitch Paul wrote to his tutor
Sacken : " It is better to be hated for doing right
than adulated for doing wrong." On the morrow
of his coronation he forgot the God above, to remember only the ideal idol of his own setting up,
— a strange blending of Christ, Don Quixote, and
himself. Lost in the clouds, he cannot bear to
look down upon earthly interests, and, whenever
he catches a glimpse of them, he sees them wrong.
Fear fastens upon him. He mistrusts every member of his own family. Between fear and ambition he falls into melancholia, and there remains
not a vestige of trust or faith in those about him,
still less in himself. And wildly he seeks relief
from the impending madness in the most unwar-
rantable despotism.

The great work of modern Russia, the magnificent undertaking of the Transcaspian Railway,
suggested to Vogüé some of the finest pages he
has written. The man who could write poetry
even while grinding out a government report on

the machinery exhibit at the recent " Exposition "
was not to be hampered by the details of such
an enterprise. The mere suggestion was fine in
itself, the undertaking more so. To build a rail-
road fourteen hundred leagues long across the
Siberian wilderness, where mountains are high,
supplies are scant, and the ice king holds his sway
with a power second only to that of the Tsar, was
indeed a grand 'conception. Yet of this gigantic
undertaking he must speak modestly, for the
originator of this project, General Annenkoff, is
his brother-in-law. Nevertheless, and all his reserve notwithstanding, the poet is unable to resist
the charm of the wonderful country spread out before him; unable to resist the desire of comparing
the energy of the conquering worm — *man* — when
face to face with the ponderous, passive opposition
of nature ; unable to restrain his pen when obliged
to describe the gigantic struggle of Russian genius
and Russian patience on the one side, arrayed
against Russian space and Russian climate on the
other.

" To the north of the Caspian Sea the fire-king
holds his sway. Baku rises from a burnt beach
lapped by a flame-potent sea, black, smoke-encir-
cled, fire-plumed, like some Dantesque conception
of a modern Sodom deep down in hell. Fire has
made *this*, as fire destroyed *that ;* and the fire-
king, petroleum, reigns supreme. As the boat
leaves the wharf a rank odor of naphtha pursues
us, and writhing stringers of oil worm their way
across the quivering waves. The little steamer
that runs from Baku to Ouzoum Ada is densely

packed. Behind a crowd of Turkomans, scattered over the deck, a Persian hareem, draped in folds of pinkish cotton, lie or squat under the gaze of a pack of Jews, who are going out to see what there is to be done in the newly opened province of Armenia. Here a merchant of Kokand, able to stammer a few words of French, bears toward his distant country a seed or two gathered on French soil. Beyond again a group of emigrants — some thirty-five men, women and children, huddled together — are bound for Asia. They have left their country, sold their last parcel of land, and are prospecting for some place ' where life may be better worth the living.' Their leader, a bold, intelligent-looking man, answers my question : ' And do you leave no regret of home behind you ? ' ' Our home is where we are,' he says simply, stretching his arm toward the East. On the morning of the 22d, after eighteen hours' quiet steaming, we enter a narrow, shallow channel, dotted with little islands. The sea is blue, of a soft turquoise blue, inlaid with gold ; here and there a strip of yellow sand, and beyond it again blue streaks, fading, fading away into a distant quivering white under a hot, angry sky ; and still farther beyond a dimness that moves, yet is neither alive nor dead."

Truly we may say of Vogüé —

> " Many a land he has trodden,
> Many a hero sung."

For, besides —

> " The glory that was Greece,
> And the grandeur that was Rome,"

he has kissed the sand of the Holy Land, and sung of the aged waste of Egypt, and told us histories that happened in the vast domain that lies under the shadow of the white Tsar.

Yet modern life, and the achievements of modern industry, also possess some charm for him; and we feel the spell that the poet puts upon all things, great or trivial, while reading his amazing articles upon that apparently most prosaic and practical of subjects, "The Machinery Hall of the Exhibition of 1889." Even after this we must add to the table of contents; for, when Leo XIII. was elected Pope, Vogüé was sent to Rome as official chronicler. Victor Emmanuel, the father of modern Italy, was not so long dead that the tears of the nation had dried; and the country, *Italia una*, was yet stirred to emotion by the very mention of his name. Like Lamartine, like Chateaubriand, the diplomat Vogüé yielded before the poet. Listen to the diplomat's report: "Rome is still hearkening to the funeral bells of the dead king who had decreed her life. The city lends an inattentive ear to the little domestic festivity at the Vatican. An old man, whose discreet retirement the noisy horn of reputation had scarcely disturbed, is gently assisted by other old men to the *Sedia Gestatoria*. In the narrow Sixtine Chapel they cluster about him, as retiring and modest as the Pope himself, in dignified, unostentatious pomp. Here and there a thin ribbon of the faithful, edged by sightseers or reporters, notebook in hand, watches the quiet ceremony. From the vault above, the greater men of old look down, smiling at the smaller man of to-day. The Sibyls and Prophets, to whom the brush of the great Angelo lent something of his sombre dignity, frown down upon the trifling performers below, and it seems as though from above the solemn warning is wafted down: 'Human power is a fleeting glory;' and, indeed, what is human power before the clutch of Time? No bells are tolling, and it is better so; for were the brazen tongues to speak it must be for a dirge. Among this crowd of indifferent spectators many a one has said to himself: 'I must not miss this; . . . it is perhaps the last of the Pope.'"

Nine years later Vogüé, once again in Rome, no longer as a diplomat, writes thus:—

"One afternoon I stood watching the sun sink to sleep beyond the vast unrolled shroud of the Roman Campagna—fleeing, fleeting like a painted sea toward the real sea beyond. The red orb sank slowly toward Ostia, and was wetted by the pale waters. From the village of Palazzuola the quavering sound of quivering chimes was wafted tremblingly over my head, and from the distant villages that cling to the mountain-sides thin-voiced bells sent their answer. For nineteen hundred years they had sung the same song they attempted to sing to-day,—'The angel of the Lord;' and along the old worn roads wayfarers stopped as they listened to the bells, and once more they blessed the event. Ah, me, what event? The most trivial, the commonest of all! A woman, a woman of the lowest class, a Jewess of the conquered tribes of Syria, was delivered of a

son; in some unknown hamlet far away it happened quietly in those days long ago; and yet
to-day throughout what was once the Holy Roman
Empire the bells toll twice a day to tell the tale at
each rising and each setting of the sun. Other
events have passed unheeded, yet in their day they
seemed greater things, and in their day it seemed
to men that greater men were born to life. But
the birth of that child has changed the world. The
numbering of the years of our world-history
ceased to be begun anew, and this birth, this absolutely trivial event, is set above all other events.
Whence and wherefore this supremacy of nothing
over all things? so incontestable that even the
proudest say, 'I do not know; I cannot understand.' And is this confession of the mighty to
be lightly cast aside?"

Again, a little further, the suffering nothing-
ness, the thinking all-ness, that is man, suggests to
Vogüé one of the finest comparisons. A prince of
the Church is dead; a peasant child is born; those
are the bare facts of which Vogüé writes.

"Cardinal Armellini sleeps, the unfinished book
in his unclosed hand. The slackened muscles of
his neck yield to the weight of the passive head,
heavy with much thought. On the monument
erected by himself to mark the place where he
shall rest I read these words: 'Laden with honors,
bowed down under the favors and the gifts of man
and fortune, I have looked out upon the futility
of human life. I was afeard that the Lord might
call suddenly, in the night, and I made ready my
bed.' As I was reading these words on the car-

dinal's monument, a priest passed into a neighboring
chapel, and behind him followed a family clothed
in rags. It was a christening. I listened, and
behind them all it seemed to me that I saw the
mighty man of wealth, of worth and knowledge,
slowly closing his book; it seemed to me. that I
heard him say, ' Life is but a bubble,' — but then
a faint cry arrested my attention, and I saw that
it was the ' frail red thing' clamoring for life. I
did not hear the name as it fell from the lips of
the priest, and yet I knew it. I saw Dante approaching the city of Dis, and I saw a drowning
man clutch at the gunwale, and heard him answer,
as the poet asked his name: ' Vedi che son un che
piango.' So was the little newcomer christened,
and so he learned on the threshold of life the
password that was to guide him through its toils."

Vogüé, among all others, has the right to say,
" Shakespeare alone suggests more thoughts than
all the encyclopædias of the world, for he thrusts
man face to face with his own self." To him life
and thought are ever synonymous. The Angelus
suggests the whole history of Christianity. The
wail of a new-born babe awakens the infinite compassion of the Dante. Shall such a master-mind
remain unknown to the modern countrymen of
Shakespeare because he is not translated into
English ?

After Rome, Ravenna. Over the ancient city
of the Lombards, where Theodora reigned, Justinian lived and made laws; later, the modern
Victory, the Renaissance, held her sway. " The
great struggle of the Renaissance has left few scars

that may be recognized to-day; yet, as I passed under the gate of San Giovanni, I marked upon the very monument of Justinian these words: ' *En espoir Dieu*,' engraved thereon, no doubt, by some companion of Bayard when we Frenchmen held the town.   A solitary, simple inscription — no more; only one among some ten thousand pretentious or conceited ones that cover the stones of Ravenna, yet one that rings out clear and strong above the concert of all those pompous things — the clarion note of France: *En espoir Dieu!* "

While dreaming here under the shadows of Justinian and Dante in the cathedral of Ravenna (the poet's bones were deposited in the museum, contained in a simple box labeled "Ossa Dantis," and carefully guarded by Dante's daughter, who was brought up in Ravenna), — while dreaming under the poet's shadow, he was roused by a merry, whole-souled Italian woman, who mistook him for an Englishman, and broke in upon his meditations to inform him that Ravenna was the heart of Italy.

"And you may say the heart of humanity," he answered reverently; "for here the strongest, as also the gentlest soul may feel at home.   The worship of all Italians for the great man who was the creator of the language, of the spirit, of the whole political ideal of his race, is tendered here, and it is unequaled elsewhere."

The brief passages here quoted may, I trust, show my readers of what depths of pity, of what sublime flights, our prose poet is capable.   As the tale of life passes suddenly from the grave to the gay, from the gay to the grave, without apparent

transition ; so Vogüé often begins a page of pathos
to close it with a jest ; or, again, his smile is
blurred by a tear. From Tsarskeselo to Ravenna,
whether under the inspiration of Pouchkine or of
Dante, whether at Baku or in Rome listening to
the chimes of the Angelus, whether basking under
the relentlessly blue sky above the Acropolis or
among the ice-fields of Siberia, Vogüé seeks ever
the secret springs of life, and studies in mankind
the " fever called living." The everlasting human
tragedy, wherever it may be enacted, becomes the
story of his own life, and he feels, knows, suffers
the sufferings of the great human family as if
those sufferings were his own. The intense struggle upwards of the living thing called man — so
weak and yet so strong, so apparently impotent, so
really powerful, so cowardly and yet so brave —
fills him with pity, with awe, with sympathy, or
with enthusiasm, and his feelings are as over-
whelming as though he were himself the suffering
or conquering hero of whom he is writing. Like
Lamartine or Musset, he possesses the same profound appreciation, the same power of expression ;
and he is to the end of this nineteenth century
what they were to its beginning. Like them, he
has fired the enthusiasm of the youth of modern
France, and the rising generation has come to him
for help and hope and for the faith that man must
ever need. The old religious formulæ no longer
satisfy their craving; the so-called pseudo-realism
of the day has led them away from their ideals ;
and yet youth, looking forward, not back, needs
faith and ideals to feed upon. Alone in France

to-day he has had the courage to speak frankly as
a great-hearted lay preacher, leaving religion *as
religion* alone, but proving by the very sincerity of
his convictions, by the earnestness of his pleading,
by the logic of his arguments, by the limpidity of
his style, by the range of his experience and human
sympathies, that an ideal, a belief, a standard of
right and wrong are essential to man as is breath
to every living thing. The superb language of this
poet preacher, unequaled to-day in France, has
aroused the enthusiasm of the younger generation, as
well as the admiration of his older readers; for his
sincerity, his experience, his genuine Christianity,
are so far beyond discussion that the man is forgotten in the things he has written. It is a power,
not an individual, that speaks; and yet it is essentially a man speaking to a fellow-man, undeterred
by possible consequences to himself, so long as the
truth be known and understood. Without even
mentioning the Book, or any name that might
antagonize professed or professional skeptics, he
has contrived to evolve in the mind of all his
readers the conviction that faith, hope, and charity
sum up the primary duties of man toward himself
and toward his neighbor, and to these he has added
duty, the basis of all honor, teaching thereby that
love and cheerful resignation are really the essence
of all good; teaching besides, by implication, that
true beauty involves, demands an ideal, and thus
protesting against the worship of materialism.

The impulse once given, others were found to
direct it into special channels. Albert de Mun,
the impassioned orator, inspired by the doctrines

of Vogüé, applied them in a practical way to the advantage of the working-classes, for whom he claimed an increase of material comforts, more security, a better class-organization, and especially the lightening of the burden borne by woman. The "Pasteur" Wagner, author of two remarkable books, "Justice" and "Jeunesse," followed the same trend of thought, less as a preacher than as a philosopher. And yet Vogüé stands alone. He can be neither imitated nor copied. His disciples — perhaps it were wiser to say his active admirers — have understood the principles of his philosophy ; and each, according to his powers, has followed in the master's steps, in the attempt to revive a higher ideal among those whom, as legislators or churchmen, they are able to reach.

I

FROM the whole of a literary work may be gathered the surest glimpse of the author's personality. In the case of such a literary critic as Ferdinand Brunetière, the private idiosyncrasies of the writer constitute his best safeguard against any charges of injustice or partiality. If from the very writings of a man we can draw proofs of his literary austerity, of his sensibility, of his disinterestedness, of all, in a word, that liberates the pronouncements of his pen from the accusation of prejudice, we not only render homage to the personal merits of the man, but, above all, we sweep away any suspicion of injustice or arbitrary judgment in the writer.

The reader who has heard Brunetière saying of Lamartine,[1] "I lament with you, gentlemen, the poverty of Lamartine, because that poverty has injured his reputation as a poet, and because that poverty has the noblest origin, its source lying in greatness of soul and innate prodigality;" the reader who has heard him congratulate Alphonse Daudet on "never having had recourse to libertinism to excite interest;" has heard him as enthusiastic over Bossuet's tenderness as in revolt against

[1] *Lectures on the Lyric Poetry of the Nineteenth Century.*

the hardness of Fénelon, that false seraphic ; finally has heard him maintain that "sensibility is the supreme quality of man, because it alone contains the very essence of human beings," — the reader thus informed, who can appeal from Brunetière the writer to Brunetière the thinker, will be much less likely to believe that this critic expresses private rancor when he makes a stand against the monotonous lubricity of the Naturalists, or against the vulgarity of certain decrees of the crowd. Even if the private morality of a writer is no concern of the public, when it happens that this intimate morality modifies the quality of his work, it becomes necessary to speak of it. It is well that the reader should know that Brunetière's systematic attack on Zola has nothing to do with Zola himself, nor with the sale of his books ; but that this attack from the first has been prompted by disgust at seeing Zola pander to the basest appetites of the public. It is imperative that the reader be persuaded that Brunetière's indignation is not directed against the author of "Nana," nor against Hector Malot, or any other Naturalist; but that his vehement attacks are aimed at the filthy pictures Zola lingers over, and the newspaper gossip upon which Malot usually bases the plots of his plays, too frequently drawing them from the paragraphic reports of incidents of Parisian life.[1]

[1] "One of the reasons of the perishableness of novels based upon transient incidents," says Brunetière in his *Study of the Naturalists*, "is the ephemeral nature of the incidents they relate. Characters and not circumstances give durability to novels."

When the reader shall have formed an accurate idea of the delicacy of a mind which recognizes " the existence in the depth of souls of recesses where even the caress of the softest hand dare not venture ; " when he has a sure knowledge that in reading Brunetière he is face to face with a nature which revolts against interested adulation, and whose whole activities, of pen and speech, are solely vowed to vindicate respect for the dignity of life, and, above all, to the elevation of the moral plane of the literature of fiction, he will be still farther from injustice to one of the most militant and eminent of our thinkers.   More than any other critic, Brunetière has enemies, because he heeds them not.   In his quality of autocrat of triumphant convictions, he disdains and ignores them.   To enter the Sorbonne through the Academy[1] as professor, at the request of the most reactionary and conventional body of France, without any of the hierarchical degrees exacted, but upon the sole authority of talent, was enough to excite the anger of officialism ; how much more when the professorship is followed by triumph?

During the three winter months of 1894, the most fashionable public of Paris was seen to forfeit its hour in the Bois, and crowd into the corridors of the Sorbonne, at the risk of life (the crush was such that it was nothing less), as in 1891, 1892, and

---

[1] A professor of the Sorbonne must be a Doctor. Brunetière is only a Bachelor. But this law does not apply to members of the Academy. Thus Brunetière became a professor on entering the Academy, instead of becoming an Academician because he was a professor.

1893 that same public had rushed to the Odéon. Since the famous "crushes" of the "Mariage de Figaro," nothing had ever been seen to be compared with the course of lectures on Bossuet in 1894. Such sights formed big grievances in the envious mind against their hero. The climax of these public tributes of admiration was the direction of the "Revue des Deux Mondes," which a committee of the most prominent men of Paris unanimously offered Brunetière in that same year of 1894. The writer had engendered the orator, I might even say the preacher, for his method as a lecturer was destined to introduce considerable innovations into this art.

The reform was accomplished the day Brunetière summoned before his judgment-bar all the creations of Corneille and Racine, and, lending life to platonic causes, convicted, vehemently and without compromise, the superhuman heroism of the one in the name of the impassioned sensibility of the other ; when, with the inspiration of a convinced advocate, he contrasted the complex tenderness of Phèdre with the simple impulse of Camilla and Pauline. Above all was this accomplished by our critic the day he, untrammeled thinker, if not freethinker, raised a moral statue to Bossuet before a numerous ecclesiastical audience, the audience of the Bossuet course being one third composed of priests. He had substituted an animated and impassioned debate for a mild lesson.

Later on I will describe the development of this work, which is certainly his special achievement. I refer to the "free and gratuitous lesson," where the audience is equally free from "subscription" and from "inscription." It is this innovation precisely that may be regarded as his work. To it is due the fact that he is now illustrious, discussed, admired, abhorred, and famed, — the last state, as Madame du Deffand said, being the immediate and necessary result of being famous.

However, if the Conférence-Oratoire, in which Brunetière shines alone, is his most individual work — since it required his eloquence and the clearness of his style, as well as that of his mind — if this is his work above all, it is not the only one of a life yet young and already so filled with labor.[1]

There is Brunetière the orator, but there was Brunetière the critic before, and since the appearance of the articles of January and May, 1895, we have Brunetière the philosopher, without forgetting that before, since, and along with the orator, there was Brunetière the eminent contributor to the review which to-day he directs. A subtle, profound writer, without pedantry, who for more than twenty-five years has had something fresh to say upon the worn-out themes of Sainte-Beuve, flashing his own peculiar clarity of interpretation over the seventeenth century, which he adores, over the eighteenth, which he execrates (this passion, for or against, is the vivifying element of Brunetière's talent), over all these vanished ages. His eclectic mind retreats before neither national myths nor the severe limits of Chauvinism. His admira-

[1] He was born July 19, 1849 : on my table, for consultation in writing these pages, are eighteen volumes, and he has at least another eight in preparation.

tion for George Eliot makes him place this foreign
lady above Flaubert. "In her writings George
Eliot has the advantage over Flaubert of not resort-
ing to adultery. The observation of simple facts
suffices her without the aid of crime." Careless
of the epoch as well as of the writers, he gives the
Middle Ages their share of blame. "Our rhymed
tales of the eleventh and twelfth centuries are ignoble agglomerations of indecency and filth."

I purposely insist on Brunetière's antipathy for
the unclean, before examining him as a critic, so
that the reader may have a clear notion of how
much the decisions of the writer are influenced by
the conscience of the man.

II

Towards 1870 Ferdinand Brunetière first appeared in the "Revue des Deux Mondes," not
only as contributor, but as secretary of editorial
departments, a mission already sanctified by a mar-
tyrology whose chief figure was Victor de Mars, a
true character of Dickens, killed by scruples and
by "proofs." The deity of the place was rather of
the thundering than of the effusive kind, but a Ju-
piter Tonans that beholds the flashes of alien genius
without anger. This perhaps was the cause of the
excellent understanding between the brilliant newcomer and his director. This same period saw the
rise of another star in the review, Vogüé, whose
"Voyage en Palestine" announced a picturesque
and fantastic course, interrupted by the Exhibition
of 1889, which became the occasion for a most pro-
ductive pause. The admirable pages in which this

modern Chateaubriand was inspired by the iron
structure of the Eiffel Tower to "Thousand-and-
One-Nights" suggestions will long be remembered.
In the Rue Bonaparte, in 1872, Brunetière and
Vogüé met daily in the editor's room, and talked
for hours, both by the clearness of their teachings
destined to react so effectively against the graceful
dilettantism of Renan, both to prove such militant
enemies of "Perhaps" and "What matter?"
The two minds supplemented each other, Brunetière all logic, and Vogüé all poetry and fancy.

Brunetière began his campaign against naturalism in 1875 by an article on "La Faute de l'Abbé
Mouret." Here his attack is not solely against the
young novelist "because his book is full of revolting pictures, of indecency, of gross impiety, and of
repulsive cynicism, but also because," adds Brunetière, "one asks one's self first, what has become of
the honest clarity of the French tongue; afterwards, if the last term of art is to lead to the persistent degradation of man, is to paint man laughing
the laugh of shameless brute, or panting like a
snared animal under suffering, or repenting 'as if
monsters were fighting in his entrails.'" Such an
art, continues the critic, is not realistic, because
the truth of characters alone constitutes the realism
of a study, and where everything is forced, the result is caricature. If Zola, he adds, sometimes
succeeds in breathing a momentary life into his
characters, Hector Malot and his other imitators
hardly succeed in making manikins. "There is
no heart that has never been moved," cries Brunetière, "no mind that has never thought, no imagi-

nation that has never dreamed, as Malot would have us believe in the 'Mariage de Juliette,' the 'Mari de Charlotte,' the 'Héritage d'Arthur.' " Here he breaks off to tell the naturalists that indecency and low descriptions are so perfectly useless to the *vraisemblance* of the experimental novel that Chateaubriand was able to write " René " and Goethe " Werther," these two masters in their books giving the most precise and circumstantial "minutes " of passion without ever offending the reader's delicacy. In " Manon Lescaut," even truth itself, even the " lived " does not fall into the ignoble; and as for Richardson and Rousseau, who, above all others, had the art of making the hearts of their heroines throb, neither one nor the other found it necessary to be gross in order to be true.

Flaubert is the only Naturalist who finds mercy at the critic's hands. Flaubert's supreme artistic virtue, in Brunetière's eyes, is his impersonality, the fact that he never makes a tool of his characters for the expression of his own sentiments. " Above all, Flaubert knows his trade. Such is his marvelous knowledge of it that he extended it," and the reserve with which Brunetière follows such warmth of praise is prompted by George Eliot. " Flaubert creates life from the quality of dullness, with a Homais, a *curé* Bournisieu, but George Eliot has done better. She found the means of creating nobility from the commonplace and vulgar in 'Adam Bede,' and in 'The Mill on the Floss.' " [1] In our critic's opinion, Flaubert's

[1] Perhaps we should plead for the alteration of the words " vulgar " and " commonplace ": Adam Bede bears no vulgar or commonplace character.

irresistible gift is his art of "inserting the appropriate word in the frame of a phrase." It needed nothing less than these special literary gifts to make him forgive Flaubert the free candor, for example, of some of his letters to Madame Sand : " At the last Magny [1] the talk fell to that of *hall-porters.* They spoke of nothing but Bismarck and the Luxembourg." The question of the urgent need for impassibility in the writer preoccupies Flaubert. He holds that no writing should contain a vestige of individuality, and Madame Sand replies, " On the contrary, one should only write with the heart, and not for a restricted number of persons. We should write for all who may profit by good reading. Besides," she adds, making an open allusion to the failure of " L'Education sentimentale," which had cost Flaubert seven years of labor, " if you were sincere in your assertion of having only written for twelve persons capable of understanding you, you would laugh at your unsuccess, instead of being affected by it." To which Flaubert, no doubt irritated, replied, continuing to unfold his theory on impersonality : " I am convinced that a novelist should not let his opinion be known, God himself never having given his on creation. That is why there are things I would like to spit out, which I swallow back, because, after all, the first-comer is more likely to resemble the rest of his fellows than Gustave Flaubert."

It is certainly out of regard for this impersonality that Brunetière finally consents to declare " Madame Bovary " a masterpiece, but an incom-

---

[1] A monthly dinner of men of letters.

plete one, through its "lack of elevation." Equally lacking in elevation are "Azyadée," the "Mariage de Loti," "Mon Frère Yves;" the plot of the last being nothing but the narration of the intoxication of yesterday and the intoxication of to-day. With the exception of "Pêcheur d'Islande," Loti's works only excite Brunetière to controversy. Daudet's hardly please him more, save "L'Evangéliste," which, being less encumbered with characters and of more chastened style, wins his approval.

Maupassant holds the first place after Flaubert in the critic's esteem. He allows him clarity, finish, rapidity; he even recognizes in him a more natural "gift of style" than Flaubert's. "We do not see him torturing himself to find a phrase or avoid a repetition." Let us remember that this praise implies, on Brunetière's part, forgetfulness of the fact that Flaubert was Maupassant's master. In Maupassant's work the short tales win Brunetière's approval, and these little *nouvelles*, masterpieces, indeed, of brevity and subtle psychology, owe their value to Flaubert's teachings, so that justly all the praise reverts to the master.

I shall return presently to Brunetière the lecturer, to complete his criticisms of his times. In the series of lectures on the "Lyrics of the Nineteenth Century" he travels from Chenier to Leconte de Lisle, and from Chateaubriand to Bourget. But before returning to these subjects of the day, the English reader should get a glimpse of Brunetière in the society of Louis Quatorze's century, wherein he has won, by election, a retrospective place. I wish to show for an instant his tender-

ness for Bossuet, which reserved for the audience
of the lecturer in 1894 the revelation of certain
aspects, till now unrecognized, in the great bishop.

Brunetière loves the seventeenth century as
Sainte-Beuve and Cousin loved it. He loves this
century through his passion for Bossuet, but he
loves it above all through an innate tendency toward an outward show of decorum very much in
keeping with that period; as Sainte-Beuve loved
it through his passion for Jansenism, as Cousin
loved it through his passion for the fair " Fron-
deuses." The society in which Bossuet lived is
Brunetière's own intimate society. He breathes its
very air in thought. He is so imbued with it that
he gives us to-day in his own person an excellent
presentment of the man of the world of Madame
de Sévigné's time, better known as "l'honnête
homme."

If he has not, like Sainte-Beuve and Cousin,
written big volumes on this period of his predilection, he is still young enough to write them, and
his life, now flooded with articles and lectures,
leaves him no leisure at present. A few quotations, gathered haphazard from his works on this
epoch, will suffice to show how vividly he lives by
the passions of the heart, with Bossuet against
Fénelon, with Madame de la Vallière against the
Favorites, with the public against Fouquet; in a
word, how intimate he is with the persons and
events of that period, hardly less so than with
those of his own time. In his study of Bossuet's
philosophy, he declares Bossuet the greatest of
orators, because the interests treated of in his ser-

mons are above those which prompted the speeches
of Cicero, Demosthenes, and Mirabeau. "But
this is not all; I wish to prove that the eloquence
of Bossuet is humbler, milder, more persuasive
than imperious, and that his soul reveals the treasures of native simplicity." If the Bishop of
Meaux's ingenuousness excites our writer's enthusiasm, his faith, which makes him assert "the here-
tic is he who holds an opinion," — that "faith in
Providence, which is one of the stepping-stones of
Bossuet's soul," — seems to delight Brunetière still
more. "He is the inventor of Providence," . . .
he corrects himself; "I do not precisely say that
he *invented* it; if I dared to say so he would shudder with anger and indignation."

"The Stoics had already accepted Providence;
Lucretius admitted it in 'Nature;' Boëthius, Chry-
sostom, and Gregory of Nyssa had also hymned
its praises. But Bossuet in his books," continues
Brunetière, "has made it the basis of his entire
teaching. He brings all his learning to bear
upon Divine Action among humanity."

"L'Histoire des Variations des Eglises protes-
tantes," above all, calls up the critic's liveliest
admiration. "This work is not only one of the
most formidable machines directed against Protes-
tantism, but it is also the finest book in the French
language, and adds to all its other merits that of
being a work as impassioned as it is sincere." A
less superficial knowledge of Brunetière's sentiments in literature and sociology leads us to conclude that his profound passion for Bossuet is as
much inspired by his admiration of the great

bishop as by the uncompromising spirit the two
men have in common. Bossuet does not veil the
expression of his thought even when he speaks of
princes. He dares to say in the funeral oration
on Anne de Gonzague, "She rose from intemperance of the senses to intemperance of the mind."
The same audacity encourages him to attack intellectual pride, without any indirectness : "Erudite
and learned men, why make such an ado about
your reason, so constantly astray and ever limited?"
It is this freedom of attitude that charms Brunetière quite as much as Bossuet's genius.

Speaking of Mademoiselle la Vallière's retreat,
our critic goes still further in his partiality, for he
actually explains the favorite's sentiments by his
own, and supposes gratitude in La Vallière toward
Bossuet for a proceeding that forever removed her
from all that was dearest to her. "One of Madame la Vallière's principal reasons for being
attached to Bossuet," writes Brunetière, "was
that the friendship of such a courageous man prevented her from growing old among the basenesses
of the Court." True, Mademoiselle la Vallière
deserves that we should credit her with much generosity, but here Brunetière, substituting himself
for her, perhaps goes rather far ; it is hardly probable that, at the time Bossuet was directing her
toward the religious life, she had the strength to
bless him, though she had sufficient force to obey
him, which is quite another moral process.

This attraction, by reason of an analogous temperament in Bossuet and Brunetière, becomes still
more evident when, in treating of the preachers of

the eighteenth century, Brunetière quotes Bourdaloue in preference to Massillon, and even selects
from Bourdaloue's sermons such aggressive passages as: "The reason why men are unjust,
haughty, and sensual is because they are rich, or
they have the passion for becoming rich." Brunetière's preference for attack to the satyr's caress,
to flattery, is one of the characteristics of his temper, felt through all his work; one of those features
which I pointed out in the beginning as the stamp
of his personality above everything else. With
the same easy grace, Brunetière says again, speaking of the *surintendant* Fouquet, "Fouquet was
only a cheat; he simply represents the passion of
money in all its grossness." Rapine in palaces or
genius in misfortune, it is all one in Brunetière's
eyes. He sees only the fact; and if he declares
Fouquet a culprit, he recognizes a victim of generosity in Lamartine, utterly indifferent to the
partisans for or against his statement.

I have been particular in exposing those features in Brunetière's work which underlie his own
individuality: his worship of human dignity, his
contempt for money, his disdain for flattery — all
idiosyncrasies which strongly influence the critic's
severity toward the demoralizing literature of the
Naturalists; a literature that is generally little else
but excitement of the least noble instincts in humanity. In a word, he is chiefly concerned in
literature with its ethical purport.

It is this preponderance of the moralist in his
critical judgments that explains Brunetière's severity toward Baudelaire, for example, and the

"Fleurs du Mal," which he qualifies as "a scandal." "One of the grave errors of this unhealthy literature," he writes, "is its insistence on an artificial art, — on an art which, instead of imitating nature, pursues and finds its inspiration in everything that is anti-natural, reaching, as result, the three conditions of exhaustion, — brutality, the state of seeming, and the candor of the idiot." Yet another of Brunetière's delicacies of feeling is his horror of a writer's occupying the public with his personal sufferings. Thus he reproaches Lamartine with having presented Elvire to his readers, thereby exposing her to the blame of a few and to the jeers of all. "The writer should not solicit for himself a sympathy that only his works or his actions should win him."

Through more than twenty-five years of labor Brunetière, whose criticism has been besought for every kind of work, has written in his fortnightly pages of the "Revue des Deux Mondes" criticisms of every modern literary work except the contemporary drama, which, after all, was outside his domain. In this broadly limned sketch, where I have shown him, first in French Naturalist literature of the day, then in the seventeenth century familiar and sympathetic among his retrospective friends of predilection, — through all these varied evolutions it has been my aim to show him giving *himself* in his writings, and, above all, eager for every occasion of enunciating his moral appreciations ; we ever find him homogeneous, always true to his line of conduct. He lashes the grossness of the primitive rhymed tales just as insistently as he does the most accomplished description of the modern realistic novelist. I have striven to point out the lofty severity of soul the critic always maintains, and to what degree his mind is ever concerned for the elevation of thought in the reader.

Now let us consider him as a lecturer, so that, uniting the thinker with the man of action, the reader may have a more precise conception of the militant character of the most "acting" of our men of letters, of a man of letters who is the apostle of intellectual elevation in France.

III

In November, 1891, the Odéon theatre engaged Ferdinand Brunetière to give a series of fifteen lectures on the Classic Drama. Since 1889 he had been master of the lecture-hall at the Ecole Normale. He was asked to explain to the public the pieces about to be acted, from the critical and æsthetic point of view; to make a fashionable Parisian audience understand the whole evolution of the French theatre, from Corneille to Emile Augier. One should have heard Brunetière throw light on the plastic "hits" of Racine in "Phèdre," those lines where the heroine's attitude is dictated by the words: "Je ne me *soutiens* plus, Enone;" "Que ces vains ornemens me lassent et me pèsent;" where Phèdre leaning upon the nurse disturbs her headdress. No less vivid, though much more partial, was his comparative study of Corneille and Racine, all his sympathies being enlisted on the side of Racine, "the man of feeling," against Corneille, the superhuman.

Nothing escapes the "professor-lecturer," and those who have not heard his classic lessons will miss the entire synthesis that a single verse of Racine often contains; as, for instance, when Pyrrhus rests the whole evolution of the play on these few words: "Madame, en l'embrassant, songez à le sauver;" or when Phèdre gives voice to all her perplexities in one sole line: "Hippolyte est sensible, il ne sent rien pour moi." Brunetière is essentially "modern." We cannot complain that the absolutism of Corneille repels him, and certainly no one can deny the advantage to Racine's plays — which our modern romantic needs in spite of ourselves force us to qualify as conventional — of the rays of such an intellect directed upon his theatre. Corneille's work has a formal movement of passion; the lines have the sweep of an eagle's wing, but this flight is always toward eternal spheres. Racine's more psychological drama guards at least externally against anything like realism, and here it is that such a penetration as Brunetière's renders service to the audience by lifting the veil of formula and revealing the touches of nature beneath, by bringing before it the profoundly modern note of these psychological plays. Brunetière traces all the stages through which French tragedy is led, from the Æschylean region of the abstract passions in Theophilus, Hardy and Rotron to Corneille, and thence to Racine, with their counterpart in the evolution of comedy. He shows how the satyr of the fifteenth century formed with Molière, in the "Ecole des Femmes" and "Tartufe," the basis of a new comedy of observation, falling first upon Marivaux to end the old method, and beginning the new with Beaumarchais; how with Beaumarchais and the flagellations of the " Mariage de Figaro," comedy makes a fresh start upon lines which lead Alexandre Dumas to convert the stage into a pulpit. These are the transformations, the *avatars*, the evolutions through which Brunetière conducts his audience along the most escarped meanderings of his theatrical conferences with an incomparable dexterity. These lectures appeared in the " Revue Bleue " the day after their delivery. The demand for them was incredible, especially by those who had heard them, no orator having ever put more of himself into all he does than Brunetière, so that, when reading him, you see him again as you heard him, and his very gestures seem to accentuate the written thought.

This series of lectures at the Odéon, in 1891 and 1892, was a triumph; still they did not suffice the lecturer, since he had not fully accomplished his work, the lectures being paid and a theatre being the place of meeting. However successful this first campaign was, Brunetière had not yet founded the " free and gratuitous lesson." This he accomplished only in 1893, when the Sorbonne yielded, and engaged him to speak in its great amphitheatre on the " Evolution of Lyric Poetry in the Nineteenth Century." This was a subject suitable to expose his strong likes and dislikes, a subject affording the author of that excellent article on the " Question of Latin "[1] a sufficient occasion

[1] *Revue des Deux Mondes,* 1885.

to uphold classicism at the expense of the follies
of exaggerated romanticism.

The basis of this new series was that "art is
necessarily the reproduction of life." This is one
of the points on which art differs from science,
based rather on speculation than on observation.
However, art is not a copy, but an adaptation of
the facts of life. In fiction and in poetry this
adaptation must be sustained by the noblest inspiration, if it is to be preserved above the servile
level of photography. Whence, according to
Brunetière, the unreality of unmixed Naturalism.
The fact of its being natural does not constitute
its truthfulness, for the natural is true only when
it is wedded to the ideal; the human soul being
never quite exempt from the upper influence even
in its most complete yielding to the lower instincts,
and some divine ray mingling at times with the
basest manifestations. In Brunetière's eye, Naturalism and individualism are one and the same
thing; and the father of "individualism" in literature, in his opinion, is Jean Jacques Rousseau.
According to this view Saint-Preux is the origin
of Manfred, Lara, René, Hernani, Ruy Blas, and
their like, — in a word, of all those beings of the
lowest rank in this society of recriminators, who
are dominated by the "Prometheus" of Æschylus;
creatures of suffering and revolt, who believe themselves to be heroes because they suffer, instead of
concluding, with Tasso, that "the most manly man
is he who suffers most."

Placed by his study of the lyrics in an atmosphere where sensibility triumphs over reason,

Brunetière could not escape its influence. He pronounces in favor of sensibility by saying: "Sensibility, after all, is, of all faculties, that which makes us *ourselves*. It distinguishes us above all others; it is the very essence of our individuality." One of Rousseau's principal virtues for Brunetière is precisely that of having turned public interest back to the inward life, at a time when Montesquieu and Voltaire had monopolized literature for the sole profit of history, politics, and sociology. "False human respect and false modesty," says our critic, "not only prevented writers from painting, but men from recognizing in themselves, these sentiments." In teaching man again what he no longer knew, that social and political questions are not the only ones, nor yet the most urgent; in restoring to us this possibility of the inner life, of which the worldly and busy existence of the eighteenth century was the negation, "The Profession of Faith of the Vicar of Savoy" sowed the seeds of religion and poetry which Chateaubriand reaped afterwards in his "Génie du Christianisme." Bernardin de Saint-Pierre, also one of the fathers of lyrism and romanticism, interests Brunetière less, since he is but a "landscape-painter," and fails to link the feelings of his characters with exterior beauties, but allows the latter to usurp the interest that should belong to the former, and makes the personage the accessory, instead of the landscape.

The following, according to Brunetière, is the genealogical order of the literary filiation of lyrism and romanticism: Chateaubriand proceeds from Rousseau, only modified by the note of Christian-

ity. In his turn, Lamartine takes his inspiration
from Chateaubriand, and in Hugo more than once
the manner, the form, — for example, that of
enumeration, which recalls the enumerations of
the "Martyrs," and certain passages of the "Lé-
gende des Siècles" — evoke vivid gleams of the
life of Eudore and of Cymodocée. All — Chateaubriand, as well as Rousseau and Lamartine — are
"individualists." All hymn their *moi* through
the intermediary of their characters. The transition toward the impersonal, toward the abstract,
in modern poetry, is brought about by Alfred de
Vigny, who leads, by this new poetic departure, to
Leconte de Lisle and Sully Prudhomme, the very
essence of impersonality. Brunetière's criticism
of Alfred de Vigny is too characteristic to be
omitted here, especially because of the critic's
congratulation to the poet on his pessimistic humor.
"If life is evil," cries Brunetière, "it is all the
better. Men approach and gather closer together
in the interests of mutuality. They call to their
assistance religion, art, science, good deeds, and
the private misery of each one becomes responsible
for the effort of all toward freedom and the lessen-
ing of the cruelty of life on earth. If life is good,
on the contrary, there is no need of any effort to
improve it, and this means the fatal fall into
elementary and inferior existence." But it is not
only the pessimistic mood that pleases Brunetière
in Alfred de Vigny. The refinement of feeling,
with which he is in sympathy, touches him to the
core. He quotes admiringly the poet's lines: "Je
me tourmente des jours et des nuits entières par

la souffrance d'autrui. Un instinct involontaire me force même à me laisser connaître. J'ai l'enthusiasme de la pitié, c'est la passion de la bonté que je sens dans mon cœur." (Day and night I am tormented by the sufferings of others. An involuntary instinct forces me even to let myself be known. I have the enthusiasm of pity, and it is the passion of kindness that I feel in my heart.)

In the eyes of Brunetière, one of de Vigny's greatest merits is the fact that he does not discuss himself in his writings, and this distinction he also allows Théophile Gautier, with the addition of color and warmth of imagination, which are his particular qualities.

Always following this order of moral ideas (for I insist upon this, which the reader must see, that the study of Brunetière is more that of souls than that of forms or schools; or rather, that of schools evolving themselves from moral tendencies) we find Leconte de Lisle one of Brunetière's favorite masters of modern lyrism. Of him he says: "He has never indulged in an unworthy trading upon his own afflictions; he has never invited the public to examine his wounds; he has never solicited commonplace commiseration through means of his writings; he has never prostituted his heart." There is nothing to wonder at if, following the logic of tendencies, the reader has recognized from the opening lines of this study that Brunetière displays for the symbolists a sympathy as lively as that which the lyric and romantic writers inspire in him. His partiality for the symbolists is the

sufficiently indicated counteraction of his aversion
for the Naturalist. " Happily, fifteen years after
his death, at the moment when Baudelaire became
one of the educators of youth, two other influences,
which at first seemed coadjutors of his, interfered,
and prevented him from working all the ill he
might have done. I refer to the influence of the
English Pre-Raphaelites and of the Russian novelists." Lyric poetry, according to Brunetière, is
that which waves to the surface the emotions of
the inner life and of circumstances. Its seat is in
the private feelings of the soul, as in Lamartine's
Jocelyn, and Alfred de Vigny's Eloa.

But while Brunetière recognizes only the expression of the soul's best forces in lyrism, — those
forces gathered from suffering and painful experience, — so in romanticism he recognizes above all
the manifestation of force in revolt, of the soul's
rebellion. "Romanticism is the expression of the
writer's own changes of soul, of his soul's tumult,
of its storms, but not of its succeeding calm.
Whence the lyrism of Lamartine and the romanticism of Hugo. The first chanting the triumph,
of the victorious soul, the subdued feelings of
Jocelyn. Hugo, on the contrary, thundering,
through Ruy Blas and Hernani, all the revolt of
life. Lyrism, romanticism, symbolism! After
the inner battles, after excelsior, the symbol! It
is the ascending march steadfastly traced. The
romantic school," continues Brunetière, "is the
school of sensation. Wê desire, and we rhyme
our desire: it is a madrigal. We regret, and we
rhyme our regret: it is an elegy." In lyrism it is

the panting soul aflame with life that "describes" itself. On the contrary, symbolism is the reign of the abstract. It is the image of man's ultimate destiny, inspired by an actual picture : —

" Tu les feras pleurer, enfant belle et chérie,
    Tous ces enfants, hommes futurs."

This is the symbolist suggestion upon sight of a child at play in the garden of the Tuileries. It completely distinguishes symbolism from allegory, for symbolism is the figure of a moral condition, abstract and future, whereas allegory is the figure of facts existing or already past. In Parsifal and the Wagnerian legend we are in full symbolism ; in Tasso and Ariosto in full allegory. From one end to the other of these pages examples are not lacking to prove what I suggest in my sketch of the moral character of Brunetière's critique, a critique so imperturbably drawn to the intimate tendencies of the work he judges. Still the literary apostolate of Brunetière can never be so direct, so immediate with youth as that of Vogüé, since his moralizing pursuit of the elevation of the mind through literature is but a feature of his mission as critic, criticism being the protest of Brunetière's lofty developments; while Vogüé and Desjardins only sought to exalt the inner consciousness of those they addressed, and for whose sake they labored.

Having shown himself somewhat of a controversialist in his discourses on Bossuet, Brunetière, who had won the nickname of " the Young Inquisitor " by his rigorous defense of dogmas, set himself the task of fighting science in the name of

faith in an article of January 1, 1895. This was
an event. Polemics rained. Professor Charles
Richet, in the " Revue Scientifique," wrote in a
strain of direct fencing; other answers were wordy
and insignificant. But Brunetière's work had
been the big gun; it roused every one, though it
concluded nothing, because in such questions decision must always be a matter of individual ultima-
tum. But to rouse minds to dispute and argue
upon questions of belief, to call forth discussions
among men of learning upon problems that thirty
years ago were regarded as beneath the consideration of the superior mind, was a result! This article of January was followed by another in May on
" La Morale évolutive." These two philosophic
manifestoes of Brunetière opened the door to the
literary lame and halt to prove by attacking the
author that he had not yet taken his place beside
those whom none dare discuss more. It was a
rare occasion for all those who had failed in the
higher literature to fling sprays of bile in the face
of the director of the " Revue des Deux Mondes,"
of the Academician, of the triumphant lecturer of
the Sorbonne.

Had this conqueror, on the other hand, striven
to win pardon for his good fortune by that precise
amount of suavity and graciousness with which the
cautious politician covers his success? Had he
endeavored to win over those he defeated? Did
he foresee calumny beneath each approval, menace
under each caress? The penetration which we
may believe kept him alive to every vengeful back-
stroke that the mediocre and envious hold in

reserve for those who outrun them, had not dictated
to him the false humility which the clever man
offers in atonement to his jealous enemies.

I have already said that Brunetière is a man of
courage, one of the strong and disdainful. Do
not, however, class him with the unfeeling, for this
he is not, by any means.[1] We must not forget
that he won where so many perish, — won without
sycophancy, without baseness, by emphasizing his
contempt and proclaiming his admiration. The
envious who attack him have at least this point in
favor of their shabby feeling, that jealousy may
imply, in those who have paid for success by the
sacrifice of dignity, a private regret for the loss in
the struggle of that which the object of their envy
has been able to preserve.

However, this very dignity, which has never had
to pay so much as a stumble in a career so brilliant
and rapid, ran fewer risks with Brunetière than
with any other, because his aggressive temper carries him so forcibly to attack that he has less to
fear than any one else from temptation to flexi-
bility. This pugnacious mood is his standard,
which he flings into the fight with the air of Henri
IV. at Arques.

He casts his paradoxes like flaming torches at
his audience, then jumps into the arena, gathers
them in handfuls, throws them back again, one by
one, burning, vivid, flaming, in the teeth of the

---

[1] If I were not afraid of being accused of panegyric I
could accumulate proofs of Brunetière's faculty for pity, and
of generous replies received by more than one of his detrac-
tors.

shaken and electrified audience. It is the fire of
Brunetière's own individuality that gives his eloquence its particular convincing character.

This vivid way of speaking of ideas is the cause
of the rumors that Brunetière's real tribune is
the parliamentary one. We need not insist on
this last supposition. Brunetière is young, and
chance is his friend ; and then Providence, in whose
favor, apropos of Bossuet, he has said so many
fine things, will perhaps not prove ungrateful. But
so far nothing whatever justifies the notion that
Brunetière has the smallest political ambition. It
is not improbable that the eminent Academician
may entertain on these questions the conclusions
of Frederick Lemaître on Tartufe's rôle. One of
the most brilliant contributors of the " Revue des
Deux Mondes " tells the story that, one day meeting Frederick, he asked him if he had never
thought of playing Tartufe.

" *Mon Dieu,* yes," replied the artist. " But I
have made up my mind. I won't play it."

" Why ? "

" Because I prefer that minds like yours should
continue to think, ' What an admirable Tartufe .
Frederick would have made had he wished ! ' "

Perhaps Brunetière may prefer that we should
continue to say, " What an admirable deputy he
might have made had he but wished it ! "

JULES LEMAÎTRE

I

ON the 17th of February, 1896, Monsieur Gréard, Vice-recteur of the University of France, received Jules Lemaître at the French Academy —
the schoolmaster-general of his country receiving
the most sparkling of reviewers, the bold Lundiste [1]
who pulls Ninus' beard!

The Rector of the University of France and the
critic of the "Débats" are not so far apart, however, as they may seem at first. The gap between
them is filled by two most touching figures, — Bérénice and Héloïse. A spirit of courtesy moved
each of the two men to show his appreciation of
what the other admires, leading them on this occasion to mutual concessions: Lemaître launched
forth into classical dissertations about Duruy;
Gréard slipped into the tone of the dashing *chroni-
queur*, applying the term *boite* (den) to the school
in which Lemaître was brought up, and alluding
to the tricks of the stage as *ficelles* (wires)! The
grace of these mutual salaams was welcome to the
select assembly.

Lemaître is a living proof of Darwin's demon-

[1] " Lundiste," or Mondayist, is the name given to French
weekly critics whose articles generally appear in the Monday
papers.

stration that the creation of an organ springs from
the want of it. A Lundiste is a necessity in Paris,
and Lemaître is a Parisian, although a native of
Beaugency. Lemaître is a Parisian like Renan,
who was a Breton, and like Weiss, who was an
Alsatian. They all claim one fatherland, the
"Journal des Débats," the right-honored country
of Saint-Marc Girardin and Sainte-Beuve! Only
Saint-Marc Girardin belonged to the north of the
journal, whereas Lemaître is a meridional of the
same. Thus it is that Lemaître executes the wildest fantasias on tragic themes, from Æschylus to
Bornier and from Sophocles to Parodi, without
ever losing the measure, and with the spirit and
skill of a Mozart playing variations on his "Don
Giovanni." How can one explain to a foreign
public the ever-renewed pleasure French society
feels in being told that the "Cid" is a noble work,
"Phèdre" a play of passion, and "Bérénice" a
work of sentiment, and in hearing this repeated for
a whole century, too, alternately by Sainte-Beuve,
by Jules Janin, by Weiss, and by Lemaître?
How can we explain the delicious titillation produced in the mind of the Parisian on reading
the impressions of his favorite critic upon a new
work? How describe the delight of a lettered
Parisienne giving out on her reception days little
slices of her favorite Mondayist? These things
are more difficult to understand than the quarrel
about the Investitures or the Spanish Marriages!
Why do Parisians prefer listening to what they
know, to being taught what they ignore? Why
are Lemaître's articles never more successful than

when they treat of the "Misanthrope" or of
"Andromaque"? Whether it be vanity on the
reader's part to prefer knowing beforehand what
the author is treating of, or whether he would
rather repeat the ideas of others when these ideas
spring from the same source as his own, I will not
attempt to decide. I simply establish the fact,
that Lemaître is the chosen one, the favorite, the
deity of all the reading society of Paris, and that
he owes his popularity in great measure to his
consummate art, thanks to which he never lavishes greater learning than when appearing most
simple.

His way of writing being entirely the result of
his own individuality, Lemaître's talent is many-
sided, bold, ironical, poetical, at times almost religious, and always proud and lofty. As Monsieur
Gréard said at his reception: "Carefully attentive
to the duties of life, shunning nothing which might
contribute to enlighten it, you rally round your
undefined belief, to use the expression you yourself invented for Lamartine, the noblest dreams
that suffering and thinking humanity, whether
pagan or Christian, has been able to conceive.
Marcus Aurelius and the 'Imitation' stand side
by side in your private library on the shelf reserved
for those you call the sages and the comforters,
your Lares. This fusion of the two great souls
of the world, is it not what you represent in the
person of Serenus, the unbelieving martyr, whose
pagan relics work miracles? By the side of the
exaltations of Faith and above the weakness of
Reason, you place the universal and eternal reli-

gion of the propositions you spoke of just now.
You would scruple to sound their metaphysics too
deeply, but you love to comment upon their moral,
to bring it down to the rules of existence. You
surround and imbue your philosophy with goodness. If it is sad to know, because knowledge only
serves to remove a little further off the boundary
of what we can never know, one thing at least does
not deceive us. That is the gift of sympathy and
pity. Tolstoï had not yet preached his gospel in
the West, and you had scarcely risen to the observation of the world when you wrote those touching
lines : —

'Heureux qui sur le mal se penche, et souffre, et pleure!
  Car la compassion refleurit en vertus,
Et sur l'humanité, pour la rendre meilleure,
  Nos pleurs n'ont qu'à tomber, n'étant jamais perdus.'

"Maturity of thought has not yet made you re-
ject those accents of a mind early moved by the
sight of human misery. Among the many pages
on which you show what you feel, I should like to
quote the speech you made a year ago to the youth
of the schools!"

We find the noble sentiments of Lemaître thus
alluded to by M. Gréard in his reception speech
to the new member, when, mentioning the charming poet, Auguste Dorchain, speaking of a star,
Lemaître says: "Once it gave birth to love, to
thought, to life, then its songs were hushed; its
light grew dim and died. Having wasted its
strength in idle pleasure, it wanders silent and
dark through space."

Also about Sully Prudhomme he follows in the

same vein. "All the delicate shades of suffering, of pride and ambition which modern souls contain, form the precious elixir which Sully Prudhomme enshrines in vases of pure gold." No less exquisite is his allusion to Paul Desjardins. "There is a deep and touching good nature in Paul Desjardins,[1] and a great thirst after charity and pureness." As to the persistent sarcasm which Lemaître is accused of, and his total incapacity to become imaginative, we may remind the reader that his first passion was poetry, and that he has shown us how perfectly able he is to escape from the realities of life in his essay on hypnotism. "We live in mystery," he writes; "we find everywhere that mystery of the senses — suggestion. Poetry is but suggestion; so are eloquence and authority and love, by which one individual being is completely subjugated and absorbed in another being." Lemaître, however, descends from Parnassus to attack the tiresome pedants who reproach Renan for his gayety. "Is he such a great culprit? You are very innocent! You might as well say, 'This man is human and dares to be gay.' Renan is gay because he keeps up his gayety by watching men and things as they pass before his eyes."

Lemaître is himself the Renan of reviewers, very learned (we need only read his works to perceive this); he draws from the absurdities of men and fate that delicate irony, too, in which he is unri-

---

[1] Paul Desjardins founded some years ago a society, the annals of which are contained in a *Bulletin pour l'Action morale*. This moral activity, though rather vague in theory, proved useful in practice and did a great deal of good.

valed; his knowledge of people and of life gives
him pity and emotion, when moved by true pathos.

Lemaître was born April 27, 1853. After having followed the career of a professor at Havre, at
Algiers, and at Tours, he began in 1884 to write
for the "Revue Bleue," where he won a marked
success. He joined the staff of the "Journal des
Débats" in 1888. His fame as a reviewer rose
long before his first victories as a playwright. An
amusing peculiarity about this critic is, that he
always reviews his own pieces just as he would the
plays of any other author.

II

I have described the "Journal des Débats" as
a fatherland for reviewers, because that newspaper
has really been the conservatorium of French critical art. This art is so inherent in our race that,
from Rabelais to Weiss, including Montaigne and
Diderot, French wits have never ceased to comment, discuss, develop, and correct, in a word, to
do the work of the critic as it were spontaneously.
The chit-chat of our literary *salons*, indeed, is but a
succession of fugues and flourishes executed upon
a given theme of art or literature by the visitors, a
sort of "Monday" paper in dialogue to which every
one contributes his note of admiration or candid
calculated admiration.

Acquired cleverness is not everything. It is the
natural gift of writing which gives the stamp, as
well as the characteristic qualities. A bold as well
as skillful command of language goes far towards
forming a Jules Lemaître; of that we may be con-

vinced when we find him using the current slang
expressions of *tombeurs* (wrestlers), *arrivistes*
(men who succeed *per fas* or *per nefas*), and similar words in speaking of the long-robed, tunic-
draped heroes of Corneille and Racine. Lemaître
dashes in these bits of color ; they cling to the picture and catch the eye for the effect. It is consummate skill. He sometimes changes his tone, too,
without ever losing his attractive personality. In
the volume before me, he speaks at the same time
of "Les Horaces" and "Le Chat noir," of Leconte
de Lisle and the "Cirque d'Eté," — in each of
these different atmospheres remaining himself, as-
suming neither the disguise of a pedant nor that
of a "decadent," playing nowhere the unworthy
part of an old-school pedant with the young, or a
young-school pedant with the classics.

His theatrical essays are divisible into four
parts : the "ancients," the French classic tragedy,
the comedy, and lastly, "foreign drama," that is,
Shakespeare, Ibsen, and Björnson. The opinion
of a Frenchman, a Parisian like Jules Lemaître,
on Shakespeare's plays, on "Hamlet," "Macbeth,"
and the "Midsummer Night's Dream," cannot fail
to open new vistas to English eyes. Lemaître
very sincerely calls Shakespeare the "sovereign
poet;" which does not prevent his exclaiming,
however, no less sincerely, in the face of some obscure passage : "Voltaire was not far wrong when
he called him a drunken savage." Lemaître is
not one to be duped in any way. Hence his admiration for Euripides, which leads him to speak
slightingly of Racine himself. "When we con-

sider that Racine thought he was producing works
at least resembling the tragedies of Euripides (see
the Série d'Euripide), we are struck by the strange
influence that education and tradition bring to
bear upon our way of thought, and we feel how
hard it is to discern in the works of the past and,
I believe, in those of the present, what is really
there.   You would not speak like Admetus or
Pheres in ' Alcestis,' though you would, I think,
feel as they do.

"Euripides seizes and brings to light those
secret feelings, as yet unstrung chords of instinct,
which move in the inner depths of our being, which
we never speak of, and even scarcely own to ourselves.   And I fancy he finds in this betrayal of
our hearts a kind of satirical pleasure, not always
harsh, but rather tempered by the thought that we
must take life as it is with its unavoidable instinct
of self-preservation and selfishness."

Lemaître considers Greek drama especially naturalistic and simple.   Not content with blaming
Racine he attacks Molière.   While recognizing
Terence's " Phormio " in the " Fourberies de
Scapin," he says : " Terence contrived, I know
not how, to express the most delicate sentiments,
and to utter the most touching words of love ;
whereas Molière, in taking his ' Fourberies de
Scapin ' from ' Phormio,' does not attain that
poetic elevation by which Terence made the spec-
tator forget the huge brazen mouth, and the un-
movable mask worn by actors among the ancients."
In the " Fourberies de Scapin," Molière not only
copied most of the incidents from Terence, but the

scene of the sack from Tabarin, and the opening
dialogue from Rotrou. What then ? " Molière
lent these borrowed scenes the light of his own
genius, the superiority of his simple, lively, lifelike
language, and we love Scapin in spite of all because he is the first, the most important of comic
personages, produced by popular imagination at
the very origin of comedy, and *because he represents in the eyes of common people what they
always love to see, that is, the triumph of the
weak over the strong.*"

Jules Lemaître's wit is in very special accord
with his style. He is as bold and fearless as a
merry street Arab; nothing stops him, he bows to
no idols. If Voltaire falls under his scourge, so
much the worse for Voltaire. " What does Voltaire do but make the characters of the classic
drama go through the commonest stage tricks ?
Zaïre and Lusignan, Merope and Ægisthus, Arsace
and Semiramis figure, reduced and diminished, in
performances where the whole plot consists in the
finding and recognizing of lost relationships, just
like one of Ducange's melodramas. It is pitiable
to see what a mess he makes of Æschylus, of
Sophocles, and of Shakespeare, while pretending
to ' strengthen ' them ; for instance, he makes
Shakespeare's Julius Cæsar the father of Brutus.
It is no longer a legend, but a fact ; not a mere
on dit, but a proved thing [*un fait documenté*].
He makes a mess of the entire drama. Suppose
Hamlet ignorant of his birth ; suppose Gertrude,
instead of marrying her accomplice, wanted to
marry Hamlet, as Jocasta marries Œdipus ; make

the Ghost appear to prevent the incest; take away from the part of Hamlet his sufferings, his internal struggles, his pretense of madness, everything, in a word, that makes the beauty of the part, and then put mysteries and silly complications in their place, and there you have 'Semiramis.' Nor should we forget what Voltaire made of Sophocles' 'Electra,' or of the 'Choephori' of Æschylus in his 'Orestes.'"

The English reader who sees Lemaître speak so freely of Voltaire, one of the deities of our classic drama, will perhaps forgive him his opinions on the Shakespeare tragedies. To Shakespeare's comedies he gives his entire approbation. The poesy of the "Midsummer Night's Dream," the hidden meaning of the part of Titania, and the clown-like presumption of Bottom — all this delights Lemaître. But Hamlet is another thing. "Who are you, Hamlet, Prince of Denmark? Weak, headstrong, melancholy, yet violent youth! Dreamy and brutal, superstitious yet philosophical, sensible yet insane, by turns an exquisite poet and an insipid punster, strangely fantastic yet genial personage! You who appear to Shakespeare in the shape of a stout, asthmatic fellow; whom we always see as a pale, elegant figure in a black velvet cap and doublet, like an elder brother of Faust; whom we consider as the personification of modern romanticism, of the pessimism and nihilism, of the nervousness of our day. We have ascribed to you so many thoughts and feelings, poor Hamlet, that you have become unrecognizable. In order to see you as you really

are, we should have to efface the layers of paint
laid on by commentators and interpreters. What
would we not give to see you with unprejudiced
eyes, to see you as you came from the hands of
Shakespeare ?" And he adds, "However obscure,
however full of contradiction a dramatic character
may seem, a great actor can always illustrate and
explain certain passages in the part. Mounet Sully
does so in Hamlet." We cannot fail to see that
Lemaître confesses himself lost in the whirl. The
gloomy workings of the Dane's mind are too foreign
to his race ; he takes refuge in the "Midsummer
Night's Dream."

"What a difference there is," he exclaims,
"between the forest of the dream and the sacred
grove where Œdipus loses his way. How unlike is the spirit of Shakespeare to that of Sophocles ! Instead of evergreen oaks and laurels,
with their leaves standing sharply out upon the
blue sky, we have great waving trees with moon-
beams filtering through their quivering branches,
and the rustling flight of invisible beings. A whole
swarm of hidden life pervades the piece. Titania
calls, and the sylphs appear, wreathe roses about
the head of the beloved donkey, and dance around.
The contrast is so great, the symbol so plain, the
whole scene so bold and so gracefully fantastic,
that it is painful and comical at the same time.
We seem to move in a dream, and scarcely know
whether our heart is most troubled or our fancy
most amused." This description of Titania is in
one of Lemaître's best "notes of fantasy," but in
the name of logic what has Œdipus' sacred grove

to do with it? Where was the necessity of bringing in Sophocles, and what could Titania's pretty
little fairies and the dark Erinyes have to say to
one another? There is certainly no palpable reason for so far-fetched a comparison.

I must return for a moment to the comments of
Lemaître on French classic authors, and in particular to the most religious of Corneille's tragedies, because these essays contain the very essence
of Lemaître's mind; that eclecticism of education
which drove him from the seminary, where he was
preparing to take orders, to the university, whence
he rose to fame. This piety, strained through the
sieve of philosophy, is peculiar to Lemaître. What
he says of Polyeucte, though in a way absolutely
critical, proceeds from a mind sufficiently open to
receive all dogmas and yet closed enough to refuse
every kind of relief through logical deductions —
to be, in fact, what Lemaître says of himself:
"Prince ne puis, Bourgeois ne veux, curieux
suis!"

"The public of to-day," says Lemaître, "appreciates Polyeucte much more than did the public of
two hundred and fifty years ago." This play, so
full of religious feeling, pleases us more than it
pleased the men of the seventeenth century, because we are not such good Christians, nor are we
suspicious of it as were the men of the eighteenth
century; we are more philosophical. For the austere believers of the seventeenth century this martyr, who talks more of the delights of Paradise than
of the grace of God, is but a "mystical glutton."
This audacious expression none but a Lemaître

dare use. But how picturesque under his pen!
Such is the opinion of Arnaud's contemporaries
upon Polyeucte. We, on the contrary, look upon
him as one of those sincere enthusiasts, those apostles militant, who are the salt of the earth. Pauline
and Severus were always favorites in the two preceding centuries, and opinions have not changed
concerning them, as Voltaire says in the following
well-known lines : —

> " De Polyeucte la belle âme
> Aurait faiblement attendri,
> Et les vers chrétiens qu'il déclame
> Seraient tombés dans le décri,
> N'eut été l'amour de sa femme
> Pour ce païen favori,
> Qui méritait bien mieux sa flamme
> Que son devôt de mari."

Lemaître concludes Corneille's tragedy in the
best possible way, — he makes Pauline marry Severus. The latter, he says, " will make her perfectly
happy and not interfere with her religion ; "
irrespective of the period in which Severus lives
Lemaître proclaims him to belong to the Renaissance. As Lemaître wishes every one to be
happy, he writes codas and epilogues to divers
plays, makes Pauline marry Severus, as he makes
Alceste marry Célimène.

" Alceste, like Hamlet," says our critic, " is so
disfigured by commentators that he has become
incomprehensible. What with René, Lara, and
Rousseau, we have formed a painful and melancholy Alceste, quite different from the honest,
plain-spoken gentleman Molière introduced to us.
If Molière could hear us now ! He would cer-

tainly opine that we have altered the 'man with
the green ribbons to a man in mourning.'"

Lemaître is exceedingly severe, too, upon Célimène's salon; he calls it coarse. "We are told,"
he says, "that this is the drawing-room of a court
lady, and the talk is that of the servants' hall.
It is stiff and odd, and we turn with delight to
the polite conversation of our day, carried on discreetly and familiarly in low, broken tones. What
shall we say," continues the critic, "of the scene
where Arsinoé, instead of gently hinting what she
has on her mind, informs Célimène that she has
come to tell her unpleasant truths? What modern society of plain citizens (and we are supposed
to be at court!) would stand the behavior of such
cads as the men who show Célimène's letters one
to another? Can one imagine worse manners
than those of Eliante and Philinte? 'If Alceste
does not marry Célimène, I shall be delighted to
get him myself,' thinks Eliante. 'You know,'
says Philinte to Eliante, 'you need not mind; if
nobody else will have you I'll marry you myself.'" Lemaître thinks the behavior of these
so-called noblemen towards Célimène outrageous.
"Any gentleman would be ready to offer his arm
to Célimène and lead her out of the room, when
these ponderous scandal-mongers commence attacking her." What must be Sarcey's anger at
the liberties Lemaître takes with Molière!

Apropos of the "Malade imaginaire," our critic's satire thunders at Molière's *morale* "that the
children should see their father made fun of, and
Thomas Diafoirus turned into ridicule *because he*

is a good pupil. Argan is laughed at by his entire household; his wife, his daughter, Louison, all poke fun at him. Children leave this play bursting with mutinous laughter and vaguely inclined to open revolt. Is it not very serious to make them rebel so young, when we know the greatest blessings of life are innocent credulity and resignation?" Begging Lemaître's pardon, in this case he greatly overestimates the critical faculties of a schoolboy audience. Children mostly laugh without knowing why; it is only toward the age of fifteen that they begin to understand and to draw conclusions from the causes of their mirth.

Neither do plays chosen especially for the young win Lemaître's approbation. He attacks "Andromaque," repeating in other words Madame de Maintenon's censure upon the part of Hermione. "The part was so well acted at St. Cyr *that none of the girls shall ever play it again.*" Hermione's outbursts of passion are certainly rather vehement, but it is only later in life that girls can share the sentiments of women under any costume. Up to the age of twenty no girl would think of fancying herself a Hermione, or of assimilating Hermione's passions to her own feelings, unless some one else put the idea into her head.

When we consider Lemaître's bold nature, his frankness, and his freedom of thought, we are not surprised at his aversion to Marivaux. The latter makes him laugh nervously as if some one tickled him. "I always feel inclined to plunge into Rabelais when I have been reading Marivaux." Among modern authors his preferences lie with

Alexandre Dumas fils, whose precise logic, sharp
and prodigious eloquence, daring wit, he naturally
appreciates. " When writing of one of Alexandre
Dumas' plays I feel an intense desire to discuss it
with some one before even reviewing it for the
public ; this shows plainly enough how these
dramas take hold of one's whole mind." "'The
Ideas of Madame Aubray,'" he continues, "is the
work of a man of great courage and of prodigious
talent. All Dumas' great and despotic qualities
appear fully in Denise also. But, in most of Dumas' works the great interest lies in the *cas de
conscience*, as it does in Shakespeare's plays and
in those of the ancients. Dumas is a prophet of
Israel, who condescends to be witty, a Jeremiah of
the Boulevards, a misogynist like Euripides, who
scolds women while dreading their influence. In
his plays the critical person possessed with Satan's
witticisms whilst at the same time he seems in
the secrets of the Almighty's wisdom is a notable
figure." The admiration for Dumas' despotism is
characteristic of Lemaître's talent, vigorous and
supple as steel, quick, penetrating and powerful.
"The great and despotic qualities of Dumas!"
One sentence rarely gives, as this one does, the
very essence of an author's talent, and I know no
words better calculated to convey to the mind of
the English reader a true notion of Jules Lemaître
as a critic. He admires Dumas' despotism because
despotism implies strength of belief, and because
Dumas is a man of great courage and prodigious
talent. Lemaître steadfastly keeps away from forcible epithets unless he is excited, and he is never

excited but by transcendent talent! The enthusiasm falls, when he comes to Sardou, "who in 'Patrie' rises not above a simile — 'Corneille minus genius!' ever pursued by the unique research of theatrical combinations."

"In 'La Tosca,'" writes Lemaître, "it is difficult for me to be at all impartial, as the sight of physical suffering has always been so unbearable that in childhood, whilst reading the 'Vie des Saints,' the details of martyrdoms were so repulsive to my feelings that I dreaded the very sight of the book. Whenever, to this day, extreme physical suffering is imposed upon me it stuns me, and entirely destroys any feeling whatsoever except horror and a wish to rush from it; though it has to be admitted that bodily pain, being the basis of much in our lives, is necessarily also a component element in art. The Tosca, however, shows very unlike real life in this, that no living woman could silently withstand the sufferings of the man she adores. Words were not perhaps indispensable, but screams and writhings must have happened. In the scene with Scarpia also, no speech was required, tragical pantomime was the essence of the action." "Cet académicien est un décadent," declares Lemaître; "he is bringing the French stage back to the Roman circus."

Before coming to Lemaître's appreciation of the foreign stage, I will show him meeting, strange to say, in his appreciation of actresses, with two men as different from himself as they are different from each other, namely, Dumas and Brunetière. As to the artificiality of actresses in general, Brune-

tière says : " Illumined by footlights in all their
doings they never cease ' acting ' in the most commonplace deeds of their daily lives." Dumas, in
the " Comtesse Romani," takes up the same theme.
About to step on the " boards " the Romani meets
her husband, who has suddenly found out the scan-
dals of her early life, and threatens to kill himself
before her eyes. The audience is waiting.

" I am an actress above all," says Dumas' heroine. " My mother sold me at the age of fifteen
to a man I never loved any more than I loved you ;
my only real lover is my Audience ; all actresses
are the same. Kill me at once or let me pass ; the
house is waiting." The substance of this speech
amply displays the contempt Dumas entertains
toward actresses. Lemaître's comment upon Dumas' conclusions, if a little less definitive, is not
much more cordial to the parties concerned.

Dumas makes the Romani draw the frank brutality of her speech from her own stage reminiscences ; but the idea that a child picked up in
Bohemia goes logically from the sale of her innocence to the stage, and from the stage to courtesan-
ship, — the idea of sporting such discourses at such
a moment is essentially " stagy." " The Romani,"
goes on Lemaître, " might have flung herself at
her husband's feet ; she might have said, ' Save me
from myself ! ' But . . . she is wearing her stage
costume — the stiff gold brocaded dress of the
' Fornarina,' . . . very inconvenient for kneeling ;
she has just put on her rouge, darkened her eyebrows and lashes, and whitened her arms. If the
Romani believed her husband was going to kill

himself, she would not pass by him; but she believes
he is only talking as she does, for the sake of hearing her own voice ring. Besides, she has confessed
to the count, and 'confession' in theatrical life is
ever 'the scene.' Repentance means platitude; no
'effect' in repentance. Expiation is a phenomenon of inner life; comedians possess no inner life.
The Romani," ends Lemaître, "is merely playing
a 'fifth act' to her own self, and working herself
up to factitious feeling, which is the essence of
'stagery.' "

If Lemaître despises hyperboles when speaking
of Sophocles and Æschylus; if even when expa-
tiating on the literary cults of our public, Racine
and Voltaire, his undaunted humor cuts its freest
capers, how can one expect him to lie prostrate at
first sight before Björnson and Ibsen? To spring
at once from the bowers of "La Baronne d'Ange"
into the abstract spheres of "Brand," or of
"Higher than Nature," is no easy gymnastic feat
for a thoroughly French mind, trained especially
to French feeling and to French philosophy; to a
bent of feeling which leads our stage to study the
results of conjugal infidelity far more narrowly
than the evolutions of faith. This does not at all
mean, as too often is believed in England, that we
do not care about this last evolution, but simply
that we are a nation particularly fond of classi-
fications, since St. François de Sales himself
thought so much of the diversity of souls as to
declare: "La religion du soldat ne doit pas être
la religion du capucin!" I would almost say that
our austerity is at the bottom of our apparent flip-

pancy, as the greatest secrecy lies often in the depths of the most apparently jocose personalities. According to our one-sided views religious questions belong to the church. Questions of feeling belong to the stage. Reasoning and arguing belong to philosophy.

Until Dumas came, a theatre with us had sometimes been a school, it had never been a pulpit. The great difference, however, to be observed between Lemaître's critique of the northern dramatists and the critique of his fellows in the press is this: that no ill-will, no short-sighted patriotism, hinders or hampers Lemaître. On the contrary he goes to this entirely new form of drama with a wish to appreciate it.

" Why, after all," writes he, apropos of " Higher than Nature," — " why should we not feel as great an interest in a soul which is undergoing the tragical loss of its faith, as in a heart which is tearing itself away from human love?" Setting aside the abstract tendencies of some of Ibsen's pieces and symbols, which ever will remain adverse to the Gallic genius; setting aside the mystic tendencies of certain of these pieces (not because they are mystical, but because northern mysticism is not congenial to us), — setting aside this note of the Ibsen literary temperament, the other dramas, the social dramas, for instance, or the pathological ones, such as " Ghosts," might find an echo in the author of " Les Rois " and in the " Lemaître du théâtre." I name " Ghosts " on purpose, because the freeness of the physiological consequences of a vice would at once predispose the English reader

to name that piece among all Ibsen's repertory
as one of the most agreeable to our public. In
the point of view of the science-loving auditor, the
English reader will be right : " Ghosts " effectively
won Ibsen among French scientists his first vein
of popularity. We are fond of truth to nature,
and this piece, above all others, was true in its
sequences. But scientists are scarce, a theatre is
not a laboratory, and Lemaître being a French
man of letters, trained to French ideals, has necessarily and paramount not only the religion of the
mother, but also the impossibility of admitting
that out of a mother's weakness there can ever
come any good.

Now what of Madame Alving, with her compro-
mises and her connivances at her husband's private pleasures ? What of a mother — according to
the French ideal of the family — what of a mother
who, for fear of losing hold of her husband, puts
up with his lowest tastes, and, in order to keep a
hearth for her son, brings down her own motherly
dignity ? Lemaître, being French among French,
and writing principally for the French reader, must
necessarily rebuke Madame Alving, — rebuke her
far more energetically than any of Madame Sand's
révoltées, because these last are only *révoltées*
through the momentary ascendency of passionate
love in their souls ; whereas Madame Alving
speaks never the language of rash and violent impulse, but preaches, and tires with her eternal
" brain arguings." " If she has no faith," concludes Lemaître, " no faith in God, she should at
least have that other faith which teaches us that

sacrifice and resignation are far above empty
revolt."

There ever remain in a cultivated French mind
slight reminiscences of Port-Royal, if only to be
applied to the moral standard of his time as with
Sainte-Beuve, to the appreciation of foreign liter-
atures as with Lemaître. "If Ibsen's continual
moral insurrections were not helped on by genius,
I should not bear with them a moment."

A Lemaître after all cannot be expected to slip
on a cowl, and, taper in hand, follow the pilgrims
to Denmark or Baireuth, Ibsenism being akin to
Wagnerism ! Certain of Ibsen's works are sincerely displeasing to him. "'The Wild Duck'
is the most flagrant contradiction to all of Ibsen's
work," writes Lemaître, "since Grege's truth-tell-
ing is accompanied for all the truth receivers by
most cruel catastrophes. 'The Wild Duck' appears as though it were the apology of insincerity,
whilst till then Ibsen seemed to have set his whole
belief on truth *à outrance!*" Pasteur Sang, in
"Higher than Nature," is less antipathetic to our
critic, because his natural tendency towards cate-
gorization finds its vent in a piece so neatly and
uniquely in the abstract. No interference of
human passions brings in any complication of elements. Pasteur Sang has lost his faith. Upon
that one tragic evolution stands the whole drama,
and none will think it strange in a compatriot of
Pascal to sympathize with Sang, who dies of the
loss of a belief, the mere transient fluctuation of
which in the end caused Pascal's death.

III

As a dramatist Lemaître was only revealed to the public in 1891 by a political piece, " Le Député Leveau." Since then he has often appeared on the stage twice in the same year. " The Pardon " was a great success, acknowledged by Lemaître himself in his following " Lundi."

He is as impartial to his own pieces as he might be to any other reviewed writer. Still he defends his own work when attacked. Such was the case of " Mariage blanc " (Platonic marriage), the story of a young consumptive who meets a generous-minded "viveur" possessed with the desire of giving happiness. Simone Aubert is dying. Her greatest sorrow is not to leave life, but to leave it unloved. Jacques de Thièvre, a man of five-and-forty, sobered down by a very fast life, goes through the form of marriage with Simone, and Simone's innocence leaves her convinced that she is Jacques' wife. Simone, however, has a sister Marthe, a half sister, a strong and vigorous young woman, who, before Simone married Jacques, already loved him. Marthe pursues Jacques. At last one evening Simone perceives Marthe in the arms of Jacques. She says not a word, but silently drops dead. Jacques never loved in reality either Simone or Marthe. The æsthetic wish for a noble deed to end his life with prompted him to marry this poor child and give her the illusion of love! The abnormality of his situation and the untiring persecution of Marthe lead him to what happens. " I have myself expe-

rienced what I have depicted," writes Jules Lemaître on the Monday following the presentation
of "Mariage blanc." "'Une Mourante' once inspired me with the sentiments I have put into my
play. My mistake is this. A 'viveur' is not
placed in a way to act the St. Vincent de Paul;
my hero undertakes deeds much above his moral
means. Charity leads to self-forgetfulness, whereas
my hero's mood is but that of an observer, of a
kind, good, amiable observer, for whom the world
is nought but a pantomime in which he merely
watches the actors." The reader is moved above
all when poor little Simone, half guessing at
Jacques' motives, says to him, "How you lived
before we met I ignore, but what I feel is, that I
am the noblest deed in your life. To remember
me, mon Jacques, will be to remember the moment
when you were best and kindest. That will support you. Thus my life will have been of use to
you!"

In "Révoltée" the situations are coarser, but
more natural. Hélène Rousseau is a kind of
Emma Bovary, introduced to a society superior to
her own (Rousseau is a professor) by Madame
de Voves, the old friend; in reality the mother of
Hélène. (Atavism here explains Madame Rousseau's taste for another sphere than her husband's.) Introduced to the "world," properly so
called, Hélène meets Bretigny, the commonplace
stage-lover. She opposes him with irony. "You
wish for me as a mistress; this does not suit me."
Still poor Rousseau is "too resigned." He has a
way, says Hélène, of submitting to fate, of persist-

ently doing his duty through all, which means a
disapproval of her own views of life. One day
events bring Rousseau and Bretigny together, —
the brave, noble, plodding husband and the " thief "
lover. The duel in which Rousseau fights Bretigny
for his wife wins him back this wife's love, — the
eternal truism, that love only goes toward visible
strength, and that few women are able to depict
courage under the steadfast, monotonous accom-
plishment of daily duties. André de Voves, who
feels toward Rousseau a deep and devoted friendship, acting unknowingly thus as the brother of
Hélène, whose brother he really is, — André de
Voves is the only very interesting character in the
play.

Whether in " Mariage blanc," or in " Révoltée,"
or in " Les Rois," or in " Le Pardon," the evidence
of Lemaître's effort to arrive at Dumas' strength
of dialogue is striking. That, however, is not
reached. The sphere where Lemaître *is* a Dumas
is criticism. There, in that field, lives a Lemaître
unequaled by any writer of his period. In " Les
Rois," which he dedicated to Dumas, the effort
(very possibly unconscious) toward imitation is
very striking. " Les Rois " is a subtle satire of
the modern social status — where kings are borne
with only when they take good care to obey the
public tendencies. Hermann, however, the liberal " kronprinz," ends by being obliged to resign.
He flies with the socialistic Lady Frida, and both
disappear in death, whilst Sarah Bernhardt, who
represents " divine right " and frantic jealousy, has
not remained platonic in the mystery of Frida's

mortal disappearance. Wilhelmine is avenging,
soi-disant, her son's rights, in reality her own
heart-sores. This part of haughty autocratism and
desperate passion, conducive to displays of great
caresses and great outbursts of fury, was written
expressly for Sarah and formed the success of
"Les Rois."

"Le Pardon" brought up strong recrimina-
tions on the stiff side of society. To see in the
space of two hours the very dolorous and very
true drama of definite reconciliation between husband and wife because both have been untrue to
each other; to establish a new start in life for a
ménage on the fact of both being faithless, is, of
course, very true as to naturalistic observation,
but, because true, rather unpalatable to the hearer.
Suzanne comes home in the first act, after having fled with a lover. She is brought back to
Georges, her husband, by Thérèse, her dear friend.
And poor Suzanne's heart has risen now to a real
cult for Georges after comparing his nobility of
character to the poor personage she had given him
for rival. But circumstances and mutual confi-
dences have brought Thérèse and Georges so near
that now Suzanne knows her husband has done
unto her as she did unto him. The repeated
phrase, "I know that," which comes mechanically
to the lips of each whenever they rise to *épanche-
ments,* shows this, and "pardon" comes all the
more thoroughly between this couple, because they
are thoroughly acquainted with the distastes of
deceit and falsehood!

Those are the truths that the public does not

always wish to hear. " Le Pardon " at first gave
that impression, but time wore on, and Mme.
Bartet's wonderful acting won favor for it. The
very rigorous *morale* Lemaître invokes when he
condemns Madame Alving *au nom de la famille*,
might perhaps stand in the way of " Le Pardon "
as fairly conceived after the fashion of Georges
and Suzanne; the *ménage* is not exactly the type
of what children would wish to honor in the persons of father and mother. Is Lemaître's *morale*,
then, of the double nature of the Marquise de
Sévigné's chocolate, at once "aperiative and di-
gestive " ? " Je prends du chocolat également
pour me mettre en appétit et pour m'alimenter ! "

Is Lemaître's critic severe or indulgent toward
the same failings according as these failings will
produce themselves in or out of his own country?
That we will not admit. Lemaître is no narrow
" Chauvin." His foremost feature is impartiality,
— the impartiality of curiosity, the impartiality of
a *dilettante*, who wishes not by any useless display
of severity to put boundaries to his investigations.
In a vivid sketch of a " Prince," written *apropos*
of the Duc d'Aumale, where Lemaître alternately
shows, with great equality of justice, all the advantages of being a prince and all the disadvan-
tages as well, he ends with the typical word, pic-
turing his own personality, — a word so thoroughly
comprehensive of Lemaître's whole being that we
will let this word be the signature of these pages:
" Prince ne puis, Bourgeois ne veux, curieux suis,"
says Lemaître. And curious indeed may well be
said to be the man whose critical appreciations

from Æschylus to Renan, and from Ibsen to
Scribe, are awaited by the men of letters of Paris
with the same unswerving anxiety; the man before whom all "délicats" suspend their judgment,
saying, "Attendons Lundi pour voir ce que dit
Lemaître."

ANATOLE FRANCE

I

"If the oak," I suggested to Professor Daren, "were not disposed to grow, no power on earth could make it do so!" Professor Daren said I was mistaken, — which confirms me in the belief that Academicians certainly differ from oaks, as most of them settle into their seats only after long series of willful efforts, directed uniquely towards the result finally obtained.

Innumerable cups of tea handed round and unctuously swallowed by candidates, in the euphemistic atmosphere of the pompous Cathos and Madelons so wittily sketched by Pailleron,[1] old mistresses worshiped and young ones discarded, professions of faith about "no woman being worth looking at till past fifty," and "l'age de l'esprit," extolled far above all else (whatever the unexpressed and effective worship of the "hopeful" may be) — those are the unmistakable signs of will on the part of candidates which essentially differentiate them from the oak.

If towards the age of forty a man has managed to write a few volumes, he begins to ask himself why he should not become one of those who in company with a prince of the blood (Monsieur le

---

[1] *Le Monde où l'on s'ennuie.*

Duc d'Aumale), debarred from other government,
go and rule over the destinies of a dictionary.[1]
The forty-year-old individual in question, who
has written these few volumes, does not further
ask himself whether, endowed with the pen of a
Renan, he is really sufficiently master of the language he himself uses to decide upon the language
of others. Our forty-year-old individual concludes, if he be a naturalist writer, that he will
become an idealist, in order to please the dukes.[2]
He abandons his own racy atmosphere, and falls
into the puerile style, writing " Le Rêve " [3] in vain,
since " La Débâcle " is to follow.

Whatever, indeed, be the work by which the
aspirant recommends himself to the select company of the Immortals, it is generally a book
written *ad hoc*, a book showing a distinct design,
a work aiming at a particular object, rather than
the inspired creation of the man's own brain.
There are Academicians who are so by vocation.
These are born old. At an age when their fellows
delight in suppers and amusement, they read for
the dowagers, and coddle the lady-electors. They
are bald at thirty, speak in a whisper, have no
other ideas than what are allowed them, no mistresses except those "prescribed." Such are sure

[1] The proper function of the Academy is the classifying of
the words in the French language.

[2] The duke's party at the Academy is that which votes
with the Duke de Broglie, Pasquier, etc.

[3] *Le Rêve* was written by Zola with a view to entering the
Academy, and *La Débâcle*, which followed, was a return to
naturalism, which sufficiently indicated that the object of
his dream had not been attained.

to succeed, for their success, utterly regardless of talent or worth, depends only on forbearance, patience, intrigue, and suppleness. There are, also, Academicians who are so by right. These naturally form a minority, as they owe their election only to their talent. Last of all, there are Academicians whose title is their wit, and these are the exceptions; exceptions because wit, properly so called, implies spontaneity, both in a person's writings and in his character. Spontaneity is rarely an ally with strategy, and, to enter the Academy, strategy is necessary; plans and measures make up the enterprise. Wit, on the contrary, is essentially composed of unpremeditated sallies; wit spends more than he gets back in return! I repeat that an *Académicien d'esprit* is an exception.

Such a title is the one to characterize Anatole France. His wit is so abundant that one forgets there were "father wits" in times bygone; and the comparison arises in the mind between him and Voltaire, Henri, Heine, Renan, and others, — a comparison referring, of course, more to the Voltaire of the "Contes ; " to the Renan of the "Abbesse de Jouarre ; " to the Heine of the "Mémoires." It is in reading such sentences as these : "When God created the world, it was a great crisis in his existence ; " or again : " A God being everything, He cannot stir in space without risking the overthrow of the world," that we are compelled to think of "Candide," or the "Mémoires " of Heine. Similarly Frère Ange, one of the characters of " La Reine Pédauque," evokes

at once the image of Rabelais' Frère Jean or the
Neveu de Rameau.

This mention of Voltaire and Rabelais, however,
is in no way intended to suggest that Anatole
France is an atheist. True, in one sense, he is
almost worse, since, instead of denying, he smiles;
but then he smiles at the philosopher no less than
at the devout, while dogmatists of all sects seem
to him equally absurd; and as he makes fun of
savants and monks indifferently, of mummy-admir-
ing Egyptologists together with the venerators of
relics, he is, in fact, completely devoid of the aggressive characteristics of the real atheist. Anatole
France would more correctly be called a *fantaisiste*.
The lechery of ecclesiastics elicits his humor, because it is engendered by abstinence; and this
virtue, producing its contrary, is eminently funny
to a mind like his. Moreover in his satires there
is no fury. He does not wage war like Voltaire;
the needful conviction and resentment are both
wanting in him. An exquisite humanist, passionately fond of literature, he delights in such re-
vivals as "Thaïs" and "Marie Madeline." The
highborn Roman lady who says to the exalted penitent, "Go, thy Jesus and the virtues he reveals have
troubled my horizon," — this daughter of Cæsar,
so deeply moved by her chance glimpse of the
inner life, is a complex figure whose contrasted
moral callings naturally interest Anatole France. ·
If the beautiful Roman lady does not become a
saint of the calendar like Thaïs, at any rate we
are not sure but like Paula and Eustochium she
may follow St. Jerome some day.

Does this mean that Anatole France sees in Christianity merely a subject for satire? Far from it. Indeed, whatever he has to say on Christianity itself expresses rather his admiration. His raillery is reserved for theology and theologians, whereas, on the other hand, speaking of the gospel, he observes that "a finer policy might be drawn from its precepts than that derived from them by the harsh Monsieur Bossuet." The question might very well be asked of a man so learned in the worth of words as our author, with what application he uses the word "harsh" here, whether to Bossuet himself or to his style. The latter hypothesis would seem to be hardly tenable, grandiloquence, rather than harshness, being the ordinary mark of Bossuet's writing.

Anatole France is one of those diversely gifted minds to whom it is almost impossible to assign any one characteristic epithet. He is not properly a satirist, since, in contrast with Thaïs, he has written "Le Livre de mon Ami." Even the epithet *fantaisiste* will be found inadequate; for after having written "Balthasar," "Lilith," and "Le Réséda du Curé," he wrote weekly, and still writes, in the "Temps"[1] subtle, discriminating criticisms, in which his "judgment" shows itself as penetrating as his fancy is brilliant and his imagination fertile. In the four volumes which constitute his "Vie littéraire," and are made up of his articles, it is not a matter of rarity at all to see

[1] Monsieur France has written in the *Temps* for many years imaginative sketches every week, as well as critical studies of new books.

Monsieur France succeed in characterizing a work
or an individual by a single phrase. Of the " Me-
moirs of Marie Bashkirtseff " he says, " Their chief
merit is the death of their author ; " of Madame
Ackermann, the pessimist poet, " She was a Puritan
atheist ; " of " Sérénus " (one of Jules Lemaître's
tales), " It is the history of a saint, whose tomb-
stone inscription is his greatest virtue." The difference between Leconte de Lisle and Lamartine
he defines thus : " Leconte de Lisle is determined
to owe everything to talent, Lamartine to accept
nothing but from genius." According to him,
Balzac is " the historian and not the novelist of his
epoch." Zola, he declares, " does not know how
to make his peasants talk in ' La Terre,' since he
gives them the violent loquacity of townspeople."

In particular, therefore, Anatole France is the
man of wit. This in itself is no small praise, as
the quality is sufficiently rare.

His " writing," what the French call *sa forme*,
is exquisite. To be at once a critic, a novelist, a
fantaisiste, according to occasion or circumstance,
is thrice to merit the honors he has reaped. When
France became an academician he had no easy task
to perform in the way of a " discourse," having
to pronounce the eulogium on the standing ruins
of Panama, of the vanquisher of Suez.[1] Anatole
France is known in England only to a minority
of delicately critical minds.

---

[1] Anatole France took the place of the deceased Ferdinand
de Lesseps. It cannot be denied that the eulogium of Lesseps at that time was an undertaking as delicate as would
have been the eulogium of Law at the time of Voltaire.

The writings which maintain a line of literary inspiration between Voltaire and Mérimée can appeal abroad only to those who know our language enough not to lose the faintest meanings of it. Men whose works excel in fineness of literary execution always take longer to cross the frontiers than do inferior authors; and mediocre novelists especially find more readers in foreign countries than the critic does. In order to be interested in critics and criticism one must know the writers who are discussed. The railway novel, or the shilling shocker, which is not a work of literature, — quite the reverse, — will travel much farther outside a country's boundaries than the delicately composed novel, which, in the real sense of the word, is *written*. For instance, where four or five copies of a book of Edouard Rod's are sold, a thousand will be asked for of Georges Ohnet's. The literary critic stands somewhat in the same relation as the friend in life. Between friends one hardly ever speaks of people one does not know. So a critic is rarely read unless he happens to treat of works or men well known already and familiar to the public. Moreover, the novel interests every one as being a sort of introduction to the manners and customs of a country, or, at least, readers persist in believing so. Three fourths of the French novels read abroad owe their success to the fact that they are considered as guides to society. " Pot-Bouille " is supposed to be the exact type of the flat system in Paris; thus people imagine that in this town the tenants of every story think of nothing the livelong day but of grati-

fying their lust. This error arises more through
the reader's fault, however, than through that of
the novelist. The author engraves on his pages
one of the many traits that life has delivered to
his observation. If the reader willfully takes this
trait for a generalized truth, he deceives himself.
The unfortunate thing is, however, that those who
suffer from the error are the novelist and the people he describes, not the reading public. It is
another form of the idiotic traveler asserting, "In
that country all women have red hair." The real
culprit is the title, "Roman de Mœurs," since
from a book being called a novel of manners, the
foreigner infers that the manners described are
characteristic of the nation. Be this as it may,
one thing is certain, namely, that in our time,
initiation into a knowledge of foreign society is
obtained through the novel, with the result, as we
have already said, that the inferior novelist is
infinitely better known abroad than even the finest
critic. Thus in Paris we may hail the reception
of Anatole France among the academy forty as an
act of simple justice, whereas abroad, except for
the few who have read "Sylvestre Bonnard," our
author's name may be yet unknown. Monsieur
France's *nouvelles* are not studies of manners,
unless, indeed, an exception is made of "Le Lys
rouge." The majority of these novels are due
solely to the author's need of developing or creating ideas. Hypnotism and soul evolution have
furnished him with the chief scientific and mystical notions on which he has based his stories.
"Thaïs," in particular, is a true page of the Golden

Legend, interpreted in a contrary sense; in reality
one of the subtlest lessons of skepticism amid the
display of Christian scenery.

II

"In a purified atmosphere, where the savor of
the good hermits' virtues ascends toward heaven,
a reformed rake, the young Paphnutius, was doing
penance in company with the monks of the
Thebaïd. Notwithstanding the severity of the
penance, the thorns of the flesh forced him to cry
out. But however keèn these assaults were, '*as
the sign of the cross was on him, Paphnutius
triumphed.*'" It is by such small phrases, apparently harmless, that "Mephistopheles-France"
shows the reader his claw. A little further on, it
is an Abyssinian cook on whom the "Lord had
conferred the gift of tears;" an intimate confusion between the humility, of the personage and
the greatness of the gift, which once more reveals
the smile of the author. "One day Paphnutius
was meditating on the too numerous hours of his
early youth that he had spent far from God. He
remembered that at that time he had seen an
Alexandrian actress, named Thaïs, who was ador-
ably beautiful. He had gone to her door with
intent to hang there the famous garland, the peti-
tion of pleasure. But his parents had refused the
money, and . . . Paphnutius had given up his
project. . . . Behold, the flower of Thaïs's nude
breast appears to him; . . . he feels Thaïs's loving arms lavishing caresses on his neck; . . . and
the more he feels ànd sees these things, the more

he is overwhelmed by the horror of sin. . . .
Thaïs must *not* continue to sin, because she is the
breath of God! And the devil," adds Monsieur
France, "thereupon installed himself in Paphnutius's cell, under the form of a little jackal,"
prompting Paphnutius to Thaïs's conversion.

"Thaïs must not continue to sin, because she is
the breath of God;" that is to say, Paphnutius is
carried away by his own jealousy, which disguises
itself under the cloak of devout zeal. Paphnutius
no longer hesitates: he proceeds to Alexandria.
The advice he receives from the old monk, Palemon, would enlighten him were he open to be
enlightened. "Often, at your age," said Palemon,
"what seems to be religious zeal is mere pride and
concupiscence. Take care, Paphnutius; the virtues that anchorites embroider on the tissue of
faith are often as frail as they are magnificent."
However, nothing stops Paphnutius, who, on reaching Alexandria, goes to a former friend's house.
This friend, Nicias, a philosopher, receives him
and lends him the necessary clothing for his enterprise, as his own is in tatters after the long
journey through sun and rain. Thaïs had been
baptized, when a child, by Saint Theodorus.
Paphnutius therefore goes to Thaïs, and comes
on the scene at the critical moment when she is
tired of her life of pleasure, so that she offers but
faint resistance. Before following him into the
desert, however, she gets him to accompany her to
a banquet of philosophers at the house of Nicias.
There each has his say: Epicureans, Platonists, all
express their opinions; Nicias alone is taken to

task by Paphnutius, who considers his eclectic indifferentism as the greatest of all crimes. "You
are going back to your cell to wear out your knees
and mortify yourself," says Nicias to him; "I am
going to take my perfumed bath, and be dressed
by my two lovely slaves, Myrtale and Crotyle.
Then I shall eat a pheasant's wing, and read a tale
of Apuleius. You see, my dear Paphnutius, however opposed we may seem to be, we each seek
happiness; differently, it is true, but happiness is
the sole object of our search." Paphnutius, who
has quietly listened to the speeches of all the other
philosophers, grows so wroth with Nicias that he
tries to tear out his eyes. As a matter of fact,
Nicias is the owner of Thaïs, her lessor, in a word,
and Paphnutius is unconsciously actuated by jealousy and the other feelings which Thaïs inspires
in him. Nicias replies to the petulant outbursts
of the latter by expressing a wish "that he may
keep faithful to the strength of his convictions as
long as he lives!" and Paphnutius leads Thaïs
away through the desert. The rough road causing
the feet of the courtesan to bleed, her guide kneels
down and kisses this martyr-blood. They arrive
at their journey's end; Paphnutius has triumphed
over the devil, and Thaïs is confided to the care of
the Abbess Albina, the converted daughter of one
of the Cæsars.

Alas! when the penitent gets back into his cell,
after accomplishing his task, he fails to find there
the peace he had hoped for; he meets instead with
temptations and moments of madness more desperate than ever. This Thaïs, whom he has placed

under God's care, becomes an obsession to him!
When he prays, meditates, scourges himself, everywhere and at all times, it is she who is before his
eyes. His cell, instead of being inhabited by one
jackal, is now filled with troops of them. He
mounts on the top of a pillar, like the Stylite,
and exposes himself to the sun and wind until his
whole body is covered with ulcers. Yet the Lord
does not hear him, and his soul remains a prey to
the sharpest attacks of the Evil One. One night,
when at last his head grows bewildered, his conscience cries out to him, "Cease this obstinate
persistence. Jehovah does not hear thee! Moreover, as God fills everything, He cannot move for
want of space; if, which is impossible, He were to
make the least movement, He would overthrow
creation!" So, then, Paphnutius thinks, he has
supported the tortures of the body, the revolt of
the flesh, ills, maladies, leprosies, ulcers; he has
held out against all, but now, — and here comes in
the irony, — now it is ended; he yields! Paphnutius sets off, and reaches the convent just as Thaïs,
at the end of her penance, is going to die, and the
sisters are singing her glory, which is about to begin. Maddened, Paphnutius throws himself on
her, and presses her to his heart. "I lied to you,
Thaïs; live, let us be happy; there is no Paradise;
let us make haste and enjoy the earth; all the rest
is deception." But he comes too late; Thaïs ex-
pires, and Paphnutius leaves the convent in despair. The reader is left free to arrange the
future destiny of the monk, henceforth disillu-
sioned, according to the inclination of his faith

or incredulity. The author does not determine it.
Throughout the temptations and victories of
Paphnutius, Anatole France lavishes as much wit
as Voltaire in his tales, maintaining at the same
time the perspective due to the environment of
the author, and to an epoch in which the monk is
no longer anything but an archæological document,
having no longer any political or social influence!
M. France makes use of lightning flashes to com-
bat a clerical fortress which in France at the
present time possesses little but the consistence of
a cloud!

With "La Rôtisserie de la Reine Pédauque"
we change both environment and epoch, but the
moral outlook is the same. In taking from Nicias
the high philosophic culture which he has in
"Thaïs," and in making him descend the rounds
of the social ladder, our author displays the same
humor, the same verve, in the character of "le
Tournebroche" as in that of Nicias. If you have
present before your minds "L'Embarquement pour
Cythère" of Watteau, with its nymphs, prelates,
bird-cages, comedians, princesses, and astrologers,
arranged in a fairy-like scene, you will have an
idea of the medley of burgesses, soothsayers, savants, courtesans, abbots, monks, attorneys, and
populace, placed by Anatole France before our
eyes in the "Reine Pédauque."

Jacques Ménétrier (whose name and ideas recall
Jacques le Fataliste of Diderot) is the Paphnutius
of this book, as d'Astarac, the alchemist, is its
Nicias. As for the Abbé Coignard, he expresses
the author's own thoughts, with explosions of mirth

that find their justification in the period and circumstances wherein Monsieur France has set his
story. Jacques Ménétrier, who acts as turnspit to
his father the cook, is intrusted when quite a child
to the care of the Abbé Jérôme Coignard, himself
the secretary of the astrologer d'Astarac. What
with the Abbé, who rails more at theology than at
the Scriptures, and is yet a much better satirist
than a fervent Christian, and with d'Astarac, who
believes in salamanders and mandragore, Ménétrier furnishes a soil sufficiently neutralized to receive all paradoxes. Amid the enchantments which
are the atmosphere of d'Astarac's mind, and the
scientific teachings of the Abbé Coignard, embel-
lished also with the help of Demoiselle Catherine,
the mistress of each in general, and of the rich old
La Guéritaude in particular, all sorts of astragals
are embroidered: whilst Jacques Ménétrier carries
on an adventure with d'Astarac's Jewish mistress,
which ends in the death of the good Coignard.
The beautiful Jahel is the niece of Mosaïde, an old
Jew, whom d'Astarac keeps in his pay from year
to year to explain to him Hebrew texts. This
Jahel is d'Astarac's Salamander; but as there
would be little utility in being Salamander only
in name, the beautiful Jahel gradually involves
herself in numerous intrigues, which she endea-
vors to carry out simultaneously. Meanwhile her
uncle, Mosaïde, who is jealous of her, gives information to the Abbé Coignard as being the lover
in-chief, and afterward, mistaking his man, kills
him.

All these intrigues and confusions of person-

ages, in which we see a revival of the amalgams
whose secret belonged to the eighteenth century
novels, all this chaos and these imbroglios, have
no other object than to call forth the discourses
of Coignard, discourses in which the good Abbé
takes care that the merits of temporal things
shall have the precedence over the spiritual in the
ecclesiastic state. Indeed, he has no great opinion of things spiritual, and does not hesitate to
say so. "The Bible in the hands of theologians,"
says Jérôme Coignard, "has become a manual of
errors, a library of absurdities, a storehouse of
stupidities, a cabinet of lies, a gallery of follies,
a grammar school of ignorance, a museum of
nonsense, and the furniture depository of human
wickedness and imbecility. They have made Jehovah an ingenious potter, who works in clay instead of in fire. We men are nothing but animated
bits of pottery, and to tell the truth, if Jehovah,
on looking at his work, could declare himself content, He was not very hard to please." Here, indeed, the attack is an open one, and the worst
strokes are not those we see approaching. The
following is a subtler one, and more after our
author's manner. "Since it is overcoming which
constitutes merit, we must recognize that it is concupiscence which makes saints. Without it there
is no repentance, and it is repentance which makes
the Christian. If the blessed Pelagia, for instance,
had not practiced prostitution, she would never
have had the opportunity to practice such copious
penitence ; whence it would seem to follow that in
order to make a saint a foundation of very big sins

is necessary." Here we have something like the
Renan of the "Abbesse de Jouarre," and the Voltaire of the "Contes." Next, however, to so much
impulsive wit come such expressions as this : " We
must possess riches without riches possessing us."
The scene in which the Abbé Coignard on his
death-bed is awaiting the visit of the village curé,
who is much more anxious to see to his vine than
to look after his sick parishioner, rather resembles
one taken from Balzac's repertory, and is all the
more excellent therefor. "The barber doctor shook
his head, and pronounced that the case of the
Abbé Coignard was hopeless. The curé gave a
glance, then bethinking himself, remarked, 'There
is still time to go to my vineyard. It might rain ;
let us get in the grapes ; we will see the patient
after.' " In connection with this book I have
spoken of the "Embarquement pour Cythère" as
illustrating the grouping of characters and the
framework of the story. Wilhelm Meister and
Gil Blas will serve to give an idea of the tangled
melody of marvels and mysticisms, of religion and
absurdity, which so eminently characterizes our
author's work, "La Rôtisserie de la Reine Pédauque."

"La Fille de Lilith" is a strange story of beyond
the grave. A soul from hell has come back to
earth, and a new Tannhaüser has attached himself
to her. It needs all the exorcisms of the Curé Sa-
frac to purify this penitent from his intercourse with
the new Venus. In the collection entitled "Balthasar," Anatole France has put together various
fanciful narrations, of which one of the most dain-

tily told is this tale of "Balthasar," where we see
the magician king pass through all the phases of
the most passionate love for the Queen of Sheba ;
then tired out, and finding he did not get the better
of this passion she inspired in him, we see him
devote himself to science and astronomy, even to
the point of entirely forgetting the queen. When,
piqued by the disdain of her former lover, she
comes at last to try to win him back again, he
is absorbed and only quits his scientific preoccupations to follow the shepherds to the cradle at
Bethlehem. In the "Œuf rouge" the marvelous
is replaced by suggestion. An unfortunate man
having read that, at the birth of the Emperor
Severus, a red egg was found in a nest, fancies he
is an emperor because a similar egg has been
found in his farmyard. With the exception, however, of the "Œuf rouge," in which the melancholy of the story belongs rather to the subject,
the phantoms, ghosts, and wandering spirits of
Anatole France have more of the sarcastic about
them, and nothing of the ghastly. They are phantoms treated after the manner of Mérimée.

Contrasts in the quality of the inspiration are,
moreover, one of the particular features of France's
writing. For instance, there is nothing more unlike, in the work of our author, than "Le Crime
de Sylvestre Bonnard" and "Le Livre de mon
Ami," compared with "La Reine Pédauque" and
"Thaïs." "Le Livre de mon Ami" is the very
essence of moral grace, with sallies of irony absolutely free from bitterness. Sylvestre Bonnard
is the simple *savant*, the being whose superior cul-

ture has rendered him affectionate, whose heart has been enlarged by literature, whose feelings have been softened by it. He is the ideal of the man of science. The diversity of France's talent is one of its charms. When we see him as critic, for instance, cut up Georges Ohnet, or some other contemporary, with the spirit and verve we know so well, an amazement seizes us as we remember that this same brain has written "Thaïs" as well as the sweet, delightful pages of "Sylvestre Bonnard." The literary criticism of our author possesses another merit, and that a rare one; it is impartial, so far that it lashes and strikes only mediocrity. A proof of this is seen in the appreciations and judgments he passes on Villiers de l'Isle Adam, and on other of the "irregulars" of modern French literature, whom he certainly does not praise through inclination, but because their talent impresses him, and because he is, above all, too much of an artist not to celebrate talent, even though it be not just of the kind he cultivates himself.

III

"Le Crime de Sylvestre Bonnard" is not a novel. Can a book be called thus, in which love plays no part, and in which the gamut of the heart's feeling and passion is replaced by the story of the forgetfulnesses, omissions, and childishnesses of a *savant*, who is the most learned of archæologists, and the most affectionate of men? Amidst all rivalries and the struggles necessary to a career, as also in the enjoyment of satisfied ambition, Syl-

vestre Bonnard has kept green the remembrance
of Clémentine, the woman he once adored, and
who preferred to him a husband of larger fortune.
Fifteen years after Clémentine's death, a chance
encounter brings Bonnard face to face with her
daughter in Monsieur de Gabry's library, whither
he has been summoned to classify the books. The
savant at once conceives a fatherly attachment for
Jeanne Alexandre, — such is the girl's name, —
and wishes to adopt her. But Jeanne already has
a guardian in the person of a *maître*, Mouche, who
opposes the plan. Bonnard possesses a marvelous
collection of old books and extraordinary missals,
which he has sought out far and wide, even to
Naples. All these marvels he intends to bequeath
to this child, and henceforth his only thought is to
devote himself to her. His heart, which has remained young and loving, concentrates itself on
Jeanne, whom he looks upon as his daughter ; but
all he can obtain from the guardian is that Jeanne
shall come to see him from time to time, accompanied by Mademoiselle Préfère, her schoolmistress.

The entry of this latter lady into the life of Bonnard is an unlucky event. " Mademoiselle Préfère
walked on the polished floor with clasped hands,
like the saints of the Golden Legend on the crys-
tal water ; her face reminded one of a preserved
rennet apple ; round her shoulders was a fringed
cape, which she wore as if it were a sacerdotal
vestment, or the insignia of some high civic function. She walked without moving her legs ; spoke
without opening her lips." Mademoiselle Préfère
takes in the situation, and makes up her mind to

marry Monsieur Bonnard. One day while Jeanne
is busied in the examination of an old colored
missal, Mademoiselle Préfère, who is seated near
the *savant*, opens her batteries. " You need some
one to take care of you, Monsieur Bonnard. There
is no woman who would not be proud to bear your
name and share your fortune. I am a woman,
Monsieur Bonnard, and my instinct does not deceive me. I feel that you would find happiness in
marriage. Your health, you see, needs some one
to be always at hand to look after it. The health
of a Member of the Institute! Why, I would
give my life to preserve the life of a *savant;* and
I should despise any woman who would not do the
same!" As Bonnard is a patient man he does
not like to hurt her feelings, and allows matters to
reach a crisis. One day Mademoiselle Préfère
secures Bonnard to dinner, taking the precaution
also to get Monsieur Mouche as witness of what
happens. No sooner is the dinner over than the
lady exclaims, with a glance toward Mouche, " Monsieur Bonnard is so noble! so generous! so admirable! . . . a simple woman like me dare not repeat
the words I have heard from him!" Thereupon,
Mouche congratulates Bonnard . . . and the *savant*, who is at his wits' end, sees himself obliged,
under penalty of being married in spite of himself,
to make an energetic defense. "Terror lent me
courage," cried Bonnard, when relating his history:
" I flatly declared to Mademoiselle Préfère that
my intention not to marry was unalterable ; and
with that I fled into the street."

The poor little Jeanne is the one to suffer for

her friend's rejection of the schoolmistress. She is hidden away by the latter, and for long months all Bonnard's efforts to see her fail. Like Oliver Twist and Nicholas Nickleby, her literary companions in misfortune, the unhappy Jeanne is reduced to sweep the passages and do the cooking. At last, Bonnard, whose anxiety can no longer contain itself, pays a visit to Mademoiselle Préfère's servant, and bribes her to bring Jeanne to him, and this constitutes the Crime of Sylvestre Bonnard, a crime falling under the application of the criminal code, to wit, the abduction of a minor. Fortunately, the dishonest guardian, Mouche, has absconded, and Bonnard becomes Jeanne's guardian and adoptive father, which latter title, owing to Jeanne's marriage, he soon after exchanges for that of grandfather. Such is the issue of his crime.

In this book, where none but the most delicate sentiments are expressed, France's humor, nevertheless, crops out occasionally. "Thérèse, my cravat! [It is one of the days when Bonnard is going to see Jeanne.] Thérèse, my cravat! You are forgetting it is the first Thursday in June, and Mademoiselle Jeanne will be expecting me. The mistress has, no doubt, had the floor waxed: I am sure they look at their faces in it; one of these days I shall break my legs on it. Just see the beautiful sun, Thérèse! The quays are all gilded by it; the Seine smiles in a thousand sparkling ripples; the town itself seems of gold. . . . Thérèse, my cravat! Ah! I can understand now the good man Chrysal putting his neck-bands in a big Plutarch. . . . Henceforth I will put my cravat

in the *Acta Sanctorum !* " This torrent of words,
this flow of youth which the old man feels in the
joy of his anticipated visit to Jeanne, is at once
charming and true to life. Another time it is a
lucky find in a library which calls forth the joy of
the *savant.* " After having read fourteen pages
of my *Cartulary*," writes Bonnard, " I plunged
my hand into my gaping pocket and drew forth
my snuff-box, a movement which cost me some effort. I extracted a few grains from the silver box,
grains whereat my nose manifested its joy. I had
just discovered, under the very eyes of my colleague
Brioux, the *Cartulary* of Notre Dame des Anges,
which he had allowed to escape him ! "

The perusal of " Sylvestre Bonnard," of " Le
Livre de mon Ami," and of " Thaïs " will readily
convince the reader that in Anatole France there
are two distinct natures, one of which draws its
inspiration from the ironies of its verve, while the
other, which remains affectionate and mildly philosophic, regards with gracious eyes the passage of
men and things without either embellishing or dis-
figuring them, albeit with a good humor that indicates the perfect equilibrium of the writer. There
are whiffs of Montaigne, also, in France's talent.
" Le Livre de mon Ami " might as well be called
an autobiography, for one feels it is the childhood
and youth of the author as related by himself. " I
am halfway along the road of life," says the author at the outset of his book ; " ' nel mezzo del
cammin di nostra vita.' On the hypothesis that
the way was equal for all and led towards old age, I
knew twenty years ago that I should have to reach

this point; I knew it, but I did not feel it. Now
that I have climbed the hill, I turn my head in
order to get a view of all the distance I have come,
and I would willingly pass the night so, in calling
up phantoms. I no longer have confidence in my
friend, life, but I love her still."

The very first years of existence, the years in
which the intelligence can scarcely be said to be
awake, are evoked by France in this book, in such
a way that we are astonished at the vigor and vivacity, revealed at a time when, as a rule, all is obli-
vion. "My going to bed," he tells us, "was quite
an undertaking; it needed supplications, tears,
kisses, without yet the object being achieved. I
would escape on the way, and begin jumping about
like a rabbit; my mother then caught me again
under some piece of furniture and put me in bed.
It was very amusing. I was no sooner lain down
than I found before my eyes numbers of people I
had never met with in my family. They had noses
like a stork's beak, bristling mustaches, pointed
bellies, and legs like those of a cock. They showed
themselves sideface with a round eye in the middle
of their cheeks; and along they passed one after
another, carrying brooms, spits, syringes, and gui-
tars. Being so ugly, they ought not to have shown
themselves at all; but I will do them the justice
to say that they glided silently along the wall, and
that none of them, not even the last, ever came near
my bed." It will be understood that these personages were no other than the *figures de callot*,
which the child saw during his walks with his
nurse, and which with their grotesque forms had
engraved themselves on his mind.

A little later on, the puppets of the fancy vanish and give place to living physiognomies: "the black lady," "the white lady,"—thus had the child named the tenants of the same house, who used to make a great deal of him each in her own way. "As soon as I arrived," writes France, "I fell into ecstasy in presence of two Chinese idols placed on either side of the clock on the chimney-piece. They wagged their heads and put out their tongues in a most marvelous manner, and when I heard that they came from China I resolved to go there. I was sure that it was somewhere behind the Arc de Triomphe, and determined to make my *bonne* take me; but my project failed." Farther on: "I could not suffer to meet other people where I was admitted as a privileged person. I wanted to be alone received in the drawing-room, where the 'magots' were. One day I saw there a gentleman sitting on my small couch, which displeased and irritated me, so that in my vexation, being determined to draw attention to myself, I asked for some sugar and water, and grew ferociously angry on hearing the gentleman remark, 'He must be an only child. He seems so much spoiled.' That day I left without kissing the white lady, as a punishment for her. Another time, the white lady desiring to remain alone with the same gentleman, I was sent into the dining-room, where I had for amusement nothing but a picture clock, which struck only the hours. It was a long hour. The cook came and gave me some jam, which for a moment relieved the grief of my heart. But when the jam was all gone, my grief returned. . . . I flattened my nose against the window, I pulled the horsehair out of the chairs, I made the holes in the wall-paper larger, I plucked out the fringe of the curtain; and at last, when I was bored to death, I raised myself to the knob of the door. I knew I was doing an indiscreet, a bad action, but I opened the door, and there I found the white lady standing against the chimney-piece, while the gentleman, on his knees at her feet, was opening his arms wide to embrace her. He was redder than a cockscomb, and his eyes seemed starting out of their sockets. The lady said : ' Let there be an end of this, sir.' He rose when he saw me, and I think he wanted to throw me out of the window. When the lady in black came in, the white lady said, ' Monsieur Arnoux called, but only stayed a second.' The lady's good genius inspired me to hold my tongue, for I was going to cry out ' What a lie ! the gentleman stayed a very long time.'"

The author adds this profoundly human reflection : " I was astonished when a child at the absurdity of grown-up people. My mother said to me that she had cried as she listened to the ' Enfants d'Edouard.' I replied that Casimir Delavigne must be very wicked to make her cry, whereupon she answered that it was all a matter of *feeling* and *talent*. . . . I failed to understand what she meant; . . . at four years of age it is difficult to comprehend the sweetness of tears." When he was a little older, his school-mistress, Mademoiselle Lefort, equally failed to understand him. " Mademoiselle Lefort," he says, " was giving us, as dictation, a story of her own invention, entitled ' Jane,

the Scotchwoman.' Jane died the day of her marriage. The emotion from which I saw Mademoiselle Lefort suffering affected me in turn and I
began to cry. ' You are a very intelligent child,'
she said to me, ' and you shall have the cross of
honor.' Unfortunately I added : ' I am pleased,
mademoiselle, to know you are sad on account of
Jane's fate, and that *that* is why you don't pay attention to the class in dictating to us.' . . . ' Jane
is only a story,' answered Mademoiselle Lefort,
curtly, ' and you are a fool ; give me back your
cross.' " This eight-year-old *naïveté* is not the only
instance of its kind. Here is a piquant incident
of his boyhood. Madame Gance, a pianist, whose
artistic power was equaled only by her beauty, had
been playing before the young collegian, and had
thrown him into raptures. She addressed the young
man and asked him if he would like to hear her
again ; but Anatole's emotion was so great that he
completely lost his head and answered, " Yes, *sir.*"
This anecdote has an epilogue. Long years after,
the whilom collegian met the heroine of this incident, and spoke to her of her successes as an *artiste*
and as a woman. She said, " No success has ever
been so dear to me as the homage of a collegian,
whose confusion was so real that he replied to a
question of mine with a ' yes, sir.' " This is a story
which, adorned as it is by the merits of France's
pen, is really dangerous for timid people. It is so
daintily related that even the most awkward would
derive from it an excuse for, and almost an encour-
agement to, their weakness.

I cannot quote all the " Livre de mon Ami," and

I regret it, for this book is the reader's friend. It is a living book made out of the human impulses of the heart, just at the moment when the heart is the most worthy of interest, because policy and compromise have not yet enslaved it to villainous artifices. Anatole France, the critic, is perceptible beneath the ironist of " Thaïs " and the " Rôtisserie." His smile glances, indeed, from time to time athwart the web of the " Livre de mon Ami," also, but veiled and softened. It is in " La Vie littéraire " that this smile asserts itself, and that our author, with a something that distinguishes him from the indifferentism of Montaigne, and with a touch that recalls Beaumarchais, allows his titillating pen to pass backward and forward beneath the nostrils of his victims in a manner unrivaled for its dexterity.

IV

For many years now, Anatole France has contributed weekly to the " Temps," a literary chronicle of men and books. In these articles some of his epithets are most happily conceived; as, for instance, where he calls Villiers de l'Isle Adam [1] " the dilettante of mysticism; " Barbey d'Aurevilly " the confessor by impiety; " Edouard Rod "an intuitivist; " Jean Moréas " the Ronsard of the Chat Noir." All these men are equally unknown to the English reader, but they are requisite here as indicating the open-mindedness of Anatole

[1] Villiers de l'Isle Adam, who wrote *Contes Cruels*, was one of the leaders of the " Jeunes," and remains the idol of this school.

France's judgments, his good will in appreciating
even those who are not academicians, even those
who are the sharpshooters of modern literature.
Our author's verve is boundless, and, once fairly
started, he has everything his own way.   He knows
how to put into the movement of his story as much
art as he puts into the arrangement of the various
tones and the weighing of epithets.   In the case of
Anatole France, when speaking to a foreign audience it is an effort to limit one's quotations, every
line of his is so thoroughly French.   The sixteenth
and eighteenth centuries gave our country the most
French of our writers, Rabelais and Montaigne,
who are much more the ancestors of Diderot and
Voltaire than are Descartes or Pascal, especially
the latter.   In like manner, Anatole France is in-
tellectually a child of the eighteenth century, and
traces back his origin through the Abbé Prévost
and Lesage to Montaigne and Rabelais.

If it may be said of Brunetière that he is the
Bonaparte of our criticism, of Lemaître that he is its
Mazarin for penetration and subtlety, one may say
of Anatole France, neglecting examples of states-
men in the comparison, that he is the Voltaire of his
epoch, a Voltaire whose philosophy is to be felt in
his fanciful writings, a Voltaire whose verve breaks
out in his nouvelles and criticisms, a Voltaire without a Frederick; and yet who knows?   Perhaps
one would not have to seek far among the corre-
spondents of our author in order to find the intellectual small-change of the King of Prussia.

MADAME BLANC BENTZON AS A ROMANCE WRITER

I

IF woman, equally with man, has not always the temperament of her talent, it may so happen that she has the talent of her temperament. Such is the case with Madame Blanc Bentzon. The heroines of her novels possess for the most part, as their share, an energy and a courage which they seem to hold from the woman who, by the effective exploration of America two years ago, closed a parenthesis she had opened with reference to the genius of the American nation, when first she began to write.

Madame Blanc has had the rare courage to earn a place for herself in the literary world with no other aid than her own merit. Her writings are both numerous and important, and contain as large a proportion of critical work as of fiction. To her the French owe their acquaintance with Bret Harte, Aldrich, Hawthorne, in short, with all America's interesting writers during the last twenty-five years. It will not be one of her least merits in the eyes of foreigners, who are pleased to reproach us with the immorality of our novels, —it will not be one of her least merits that she has but rarely introduced adultery into her books,

and that she has made use of it, for instance, in
" La Vocation de Louise " and in " Jacqueline "
only as the agent of all the catastrophes which follow.　One of Madame Blanc's chief charms, too,
in our eyes, is that her literary children are her
own likeness, and that Constance, Louise, Juliette
evince and assert the same energy of will at the
dawn of their troubles as their author herself
showed when she started in life, fronting, while
still almost a child, though married, struggles
from which men oft come back defeated.

If Madame de Lafayette, in the " Princesse de
Clèves," and Madame de Staël, in " Delphine,"
gave their own souls to their heroines, the author
of " Jacqueline " will be easily recognized by her
friends at certain outbursts of Jacqueline on freedom and self-assertion.　It is evidently the author
who speaks when Jacqueline at her first contact
with difficulties exclaims, " People in society who
pity me are strangely mistaken ; in their empty
frivolity they have no notion of the joy experienced by a valiant young heart in trying its own
strength."　In Tony, in Jacqueline, and in other of
her types of character, Madame Blanc has exposed
her love for the industrious girl, the heroine of
work, who turns her back on luxury, and prefers
the bread she has earned to any gilded cage.

The material energy we see displayed by Lucette
and by Jacqueline, in their efforts to escape from
the tyranny of facts, shows itself again in the moral
sphere in other daughters of our author's brain.
In Constance, in Juliette, in Elsbeth, in Rosine,
we see minds that no inward torture has power

to turn back from the path leading them to the achievement of their duty's fair ideal. Elsbeth does not recoil even from suicide. Feeling unable to tear herself alive from the man she adores, she kills herself in order to restore to him his first wife; for, friend and admirer of George Sand [1] though she was, Madame Blanc does not approve of divorce. She is silent as to its legal advantages, and persistently dwells on its inconveniences. Energy and force, such are the individual elements of our author's mind, which stand out most prominently in her creations and show themselves especially by the exuberance and vitality of her heroines.

In his discriminating and subtle study on Madame Sand, Professor Marillier says with justice: "She had, above all, from childhood an imperious need of loving." We may add, if tenderness is the imperative of Madame Sand, action is the imperative of Madame Blanc. "To act," "to affirm herself," "to live her own life," at ten years of age to make the nuns of St. Odile understand that she has a heart which cherishes certain sentiments and rejects certain others, — these are the qualities in Juliette de Brévent, the heroine of "Vie manquée," which indicate to the reader the tendencies of the writer's mind. Again, also, when from Marguerite de Valouze's lips comes the generous avowal of the superiority of Zina's love over her own, it is somewhat of the author's own

---

[1] Madame Blanc used to visit Nohant, and, when still quite young, received the baptism of letters from the hands of Madame Sand herself.

heart which is delivered to the public. Such literary treatment is, in fine, real woman's work ; it is
to write out of the fullness of her experiences, sufferings, and struggles ; it is to write with the intent of applying to the hearts of her creations the
benefit of the teaching she has herself received
from life. Hence it comes that Madame Blanc's
novels, into which psychology enters largely, are
more especially " moralist " novels, the moral life
in them having a marked preponderance, and the
soul's aspirations toward a higher plane being
strongly maintained. The conflicts in Rosine's
mind and in Juliette's assume an intensity that
make them resemble some of Corneille's heroes and
heroines, all the more so that such conflicts always
end in the confusion of interest and the triumph
of the higher call.

Another of our author's characteristics is that she
avoids fitting her novels to a theory, and does not
mistake the novel for the pamphlet, as Zola does,
for instance, in " Rome," which has liberal Catho-
licism as its subject, and in " L'Argent," which
treats of the seamy side of the Bourse. It is right
to add, moreover, that in this order of ideas, if it
were a question of procuring information with regard to the " bête humaine " or the " ventre de
Paris," woman novelists would be always inferior
to men. It needs a Rosa Bonheur to plunge into
the mire up to the ankles.

Psychology has its place in Madame Blanc's
novels, but it is not aggressive, a result, we believe,
ensuing from the author's most philosophic conclusion of the inanity of human deductions, and

also from the conviction that it is the unforeseen which is paramount in the world. Of what use, then, are schools of psychology, tables of mental atavism, and the whole arsenal of moral and other heredities, since it is nearly always the unexpected contingency which decides? Now, oddly enough, these atavisms, to which she attributes so little importance in her writing, have imposed themselves, so to speak, upon her without her knowledge. The divers currents of foreign races that meet in her have produced in her a faculty of cosmopolitanism rare in France. Owing to this intuition she has been able to depict Russian and German women with greater truth than any other writer; moreover, socially speaking, she is acquainted with every kind of society, a circumstance which places her beyond the risk of committing solecisms.

Allied by her family to the old French aristocracy,[1] she grew up amid the relics of the ancient order of things, and came thus to know and describe provincial and rural forms of life that will definitely disappear with those who already speak of them as antiquities. In " Parrain d'Annette " and in " Tony," the descriptions of Madame de Kernor's house and Lucette d'Armançon's home are stamped with an exceptional truthfulness, which, indeed, cannot be attained, or, if attained, is exaggerated, by a writer who describes such things without an intimate personal knowledge of them.

Although Madame Sand's literary career, which began in moral revolt against society, ended in the

---

[1] The Count d'Aure, squire to the Duchess de Berry, was her father-in-law.

far-fetched dissertations of Mademoiselle de la
Quintinie, the lyrical novel was not yet entirely
dethroned by the novel based on statistics when
Madame Blanc began writing. As late as 1872
Octave Feuillet possessed the monopoly of the
novel of society psychology, and the place Madame Blanc was going to take was beside Feuillet;
being, however, more eclectic, perhaps, for the
reasons I have pointed out above, reasons which
show her to be a unique writer among her contemporaries.

Gifted with all the personal attractions which,
without making any real addition to a woman's wit
and intelligence, show off her merit to advantage,
Madame Blanc, from her first appearance in society, received the worship and homage of the most
eminent artists. Amaury Duval and Henri Ré-
gnault sketched fine portraits of her, and her *salon*
was no sooner formed than it became what it has
since remained, — the rendezvous for all those who
possess true worth in the domain of thought and
art.

The individual and the author are always two
distinct beings, more especially so when the author
is a woman. Any disclosure relating to private
life is an indiscretion; and yet how is it possible
to pass by such an example of labor and courage
without at least saying to the public : "The author
indeed has talent; but the woman has not been
wanting in aught of the grandeur of mind one
meets with in her books."

Put into a single heart the motherly self-denial
of Madame de Brévent, the daughter's affection of

Juliette, the youthful energy in the struggle for life of Jacqueline, and add to these qualities the generosity of Jacques and Rosine in "Grande Saulière," and you will have estimated in the heart of the woman the capital which the author has rendered current coin among her characters.

A long study of America and its literature necessarily led Madame Blanc to make a practical acquaintance with the United States, in a visit which she paid in 1893. Leaving France in October of that year, she traversed alone this country, which she already knew so well. A series of articles that appeared in the "Revue des Deux Mondes," in 1894 and 1895, since published in separate volumes, have informed our reading public what were the impressions of a Frenchwoman with reference to American activity. Art, manufactures, pedagogy, prison-life, commerce, have all found their appropriate place in the lines traced by her dexterous and vivid pen. Later Madame Blanc Bentzon took up the novel again, and "La Double Epreuve" shows her once more as a lofty moralist and delicate psychologist. The following pages are especially devoted to her works of fiction. Her critical writings, though of great importance on account of the new horizons they have opened up for our benefit, are perhaps neither so individual nor so original as her novels. In the classification of these I will give precedence to such as may be called psychological, the novels of country life will come next, and the novels of passion will close the list.

II

From a religious point of view in " Constance,"
from the family and maternal point of view in
" Un Divorce," the question of the woman's remar-
rying, and of the reconstruction of the family out
of the ruins of the past, has seriously occupied
Madame Blanc. In " Un Divorce," Elsbeth, who,
being a Protestant, has no scruples in the matter,
comes to a conclusion quite as unfavorable as that
of Constance ; and, to judge by these two cases,
it would seem that our author does not consider
divorce likely to result in much good.   The back-
ground of the story in " Un Divorce " is picturesque, and the whole of the small society of
the town of Goslar, in Bavaria, is marvelously
described.

Dr. Klaus, the heroine Elsbeth's father, would
have been a good father if the children's noise had
not made him take a dislike to them.   Science was
the culprit !   This it was which had rendered him
incapable of paying attention to his wife, of even
mourning her loss.   He had married her without
reflecting, and five or six years later had found
out that she was not a suitable wife for him.   As
for Elsbeth, her father's bird-like profile and his
blue spectacles were objects of dread in childhood ;
on growing up, however, Elsbeth, learning to look
deeper than the blue spectacles, and discovering
that the savant possessed a good heart, begins to
love him.   Among Elsbeth's friends and companions, Rosa Meyer, the queen of Goslar's professional beauties, furnishes us with another charming

portrait. " Rosa Meyer was short and stout, with
hair as fine as gossamer-threads and as yellow as a
child's ; her lips were cherry-red, her eyes shone
with smiles, and her dimpled cheeks were perpet-
ually twitching with merriment." The Hofrath
plays the part of Talleyrand in this small town,
where the Count de Waldheim, an officer in the
army, plays that of Don Juan. In vain Waldheim
offers his hand and title to Elsbeth ; father Klaus
refuses to sanction their marriage until the young
man has chosen a profession. Waldheim's promises not being kept, father Klaus breaks off the
engagement, and the rejected suitor goes to America, where he marries some one else, yet without
forgetting Elsbeth. The latter does not die of
despair ; her life, however, becomes solitary, as now
she has become fatherless. Ten or twelve years
elapse, and one day Waldheim appears at Elsbeth's
home, accompanied by his daughter Betsy. From
the first, Elsbeth and Betsy see each other constantly ; then, after another lapse of years, Waldheim, who had married a woman unworthy of him,
and obtained a divorce, asks Elsbeth to become
Betsy's mother. There comes a day, however,
when Betsy's true mother, who, in spite of her
fallen character, has always been kind to her child,
makes her appearance on the scene, and claims her
daughter ; Betsy, who at heart hates Elsbeth,
hastens to obey the call, whilst the latter realizes
that her duty is not to usurp the rightful mother's
place.

During her husband's absence, Elsbeth decides
the question by committing suicide ; she writes to

Pastor Uandel, her lifelong friend : " I am guilty
toward this woman ; Karl's daughter is more necessary to him than anything else in the world,
and Betsy will be able to reconcile her father and
mother ; indeed, Betsy said to me one day : ' My
duty is to be with my mother, because she is unhappy ! ' When she comes to feel her father's misfortune, she will love him enough for both. I am
more than in despair, I am undeceived. I send
you my last thought because you understand my
heart. I ask you to speak to God for me, so that
I may find in Him a God of pity." Then she
throws herself into the lake, at the same time
freeing her husband's conscience from all remorse
by giving to her death the appearance of an acci-
dent.

The real reason of Elsbeth's death is that she
lacks courage to tear herself away alive from the
husband she adores. Actual death or moral death,
such so far are the consequences of divorce, according to our author. Elsbeth, who has accepted
marriage after divorce, is compelled by her conscience to renounce it. As for Constance, she rejects it, without hesitation, and to the end of the
chapter. The " unexpected, which always happens in life," is that contingency among all upon
which Madame Blanc lays most stress.

The unexpected it is which in " Tony " transforms Lucette's malignant heart into a tabernacle
of gentleness. The Count d'Armançon has fallen
under the influence of a " dryad." This wood-
cutter's daughter has a son Tony, whom he prefers
to Lucette. Claudine Forgeot, Tony's mother,

obliged as she is to yield in presence of the " young lady," revenges herself by ruling more despotically over the father, and, although Tony is a good boy, exuberant and affectionate, Lucette, who suffers from the yoke of her father's mistress, has taken such a dislike to the boy that one day in an unreasoning fit of anger she pushes him into the pond. It is this flash of madness which becomes in Lucette the origin of her moral regeneration. She saves her victim by immediately plunging into the water after him, and she expiates her crimes by the tenderness she afterwards shows to Tony, the child never suspecting his sister's sentiments, and seeing in her only the saint he venerates and cherishes.

This book, in which Tony's affection restores his sister's strength, and Lucette's tenderness finally revives the hardened and embittered heart of Mademoiselle Arnet, is a touching paraphrase of the gospel triumph of the meek. All hearts are modified under the influence of love, and the inward conflicts of Lucette's mind supply the author with pages of subtle study of human nature equal in interest to the successful psychological study entitled, " Un Remords."

A beautiful Mexican girl who suddenly finds herself in the thoroughly Parisian home of her aunt, Madame de Clairac ; an impetuous character whose unconscious charms are the envy of all the women who surround her ; an ardent passion for a novelist of the experimentalist school, who out of gallantry offers adultery to Manuela as an excuse for his fear of marriage ; and, last of all,

the death of the husband, — such is the canvas on
which Madame Blanc has skillfully traced the inmost movements of Manuela's heart. These emotions of remorse and grief so deeply undermine
Manuela's health that, like a strong and fruitful
plant which has exhausted itself in flowering, she
withers and dies. Unfortunately, while in her
aunt Clairac's house, where everything tells her
she remains only till an opportunity for marriage
offers, Manuela consents to marry Walrey, a rich
manufacturer of the north, possessed of a noble
heart into the bargain, since he attaches himself to
Manuela all the more because she is poor. This
marriage, instead of extinguishing, serves but to
inflame the love she cherishes for the Parisian
novelist ; and, through the agency of a wretched
fellow employed in her husband's works, who is in
love with Madame Walrey, her husband is informed of the real state of his wife's sentiments.
This same informer is a man fallen in the world,
who, brooding over his wrongs as a victim of society, at last attempts to assassinate his employer
by stabbing him with a knife. Walrey survives
for a month, and Manuela employs this time in
proving to her husband that he is at last understood and loved. Under the influence of the conviction that his wife has come to love him, Walrey
experiences a soothing calm which relieves and
consoles the reader. After her husband's death,
Manuela is preyed upon by remorse as much as
by grief. The fact of having failed to appreciate
so noble a heart torments her, and she dies, ful-
filling the curé's saying that " the soul which no

longer has strength for its task receives in due course its deliverance from God." The author's idealism appears in this book no less than in " Vie manquée ; " it is Manuela's moral defeat which kills her.

The same thing is true of Juliette, married against her will, by a father whom she adores, to the "Boursier" Daverne, whom she despises. Juliette resists the promptings of her heart, and refuses to become the mistress of George Owald, whom she passionately loved before her marriage. But though she does not indulge herself in such feelings, more than once a resentful wish crosses her heart against this husband, who, indeed, was depraved and unworthy. When he is smitten with smallpox, she remains constantly by his bedside, and nurses him tenderly, as much to pacify her own conscience as in performance of her duty. Free at last, she consents to marry George, but only after three months' probation, to be passed by her in the Convent of St. Odile, where she spent her childhood. Before going to St. Odile's, however, she is herself attacked and disfigured by smallpox, and so changed, that Sister Aldegonde, her favorite nun, does not recognize her. When George comes to claim her hand, he receives the packet of letters he has addressed to her, and which have remained unanswered. Juliette, who entered St. Odile's under an assumed name, witnesses the despair of the man she loves, she hears the door of the convent close behind him, her sacrifice is complete. To George's mother she writes that her son will never see her, Juliette,

again, and explains the reasons for this separation.
Thenceforth she devotes her life to the unfortunate.
Many years afterward, in the Luxembourg Gardens, she sees George and his wife pass before
her; George's eyes turn from his wife and gaze
lingeringly towards a path where Juliette and he
used to meet. " I saw at a glance," Juliette writes
afterwards, " that the wife who was of one flesh
with him had not gained and never would gain
possession of his heart; I saw that the remembrance of me bound George more closely than all
chains, being more precious than all present ties,
superior to that which passes away and grows old;
for him I felt I was still Juliette; and I envied
nothing and no one in the world; I had my share of
happiness!" Here once more it is an unexpected
manifestation of artistic treatment, a somewhat
Racinian solution, which consoles the reader, heart-
broken over Juliette's sacrifice, and carries him
into a loftier region, after the manner of Bérénice.

> "Be we three an example to the universe
> Of the tenderest and most unfortunate love
> It has ever recorded in its painful annals."

What Juliette does not say, nor Bérénice either,
is that she tore herself away from the affection of
him she loves, only in order to remain forever the
same image in the recesses of George's heart; she
thus avoids the waning of passion which comes
with age and custom.

Juliette's and Manuela's conflicts are purely
and simply of the moral order. In the case of Constance the conflict is a religious one. The mother
of Constance Vidal is the first Catholic of a long

line of Protestants living at Nérac; and it is the neophyte's fervor of her Catholic faith which justifies her excessive zeal and uncompromising conduct. One night Dr. Vidal, Constance's father, is summoned to the bedside of a woman who has made a pretended attempt to cut her throat. This lady, who has recently come to the " Parc," the residence of a new landowner, freshly arrived from Paris, the Count de Glenne, suddenly departs, and people's tongues begin to stir. The Parisian is a savant, and an intimacy naturally springs up between him and Dr. Vidal. But the doctor's eyes, absorbed by his crucibles, forget to warn him of the sentimental " combination " between Raoul de Glenne and his daughter Constance, a regrettable combination too, since Raoul is the husband of the pretended suicide, and Constance is inflexible in her refusal to marry one divorced. There is a rupture, and Constance, who is left alone in the world by her father's death, gives way beneath the burden of her mind's agony. When Raoul makes a final effort to change her mind, she says to him: " I yield ; take me far, far away! " Yet Raoul is not the dupe of his own desire: " You have never refused me more rigorously than in these words of consent! " he exclaims, and they separate with this other cry uttered by Constance : " It is now that I am forever yours." There is a striking resemblance, it will be owned, between Juliette, who declares she possesses her lover *because* she recognizes that her image is still in his heart, and Constance, who in leaving Raoul feels that he is hers " more than ever and for-

ever." Such conclusions are all to the advantage
of the inner and moral possession, and rank Madame Blanc Bentzon's writings in a category by
themselves as regards their idealism. The reader
clings passionately to this idealism; especially in
the case of Constance, its manifestation, however,
produces a conception of God which would be
hatefully severe, if it were not connected with the
last outburst of passionate tenderness that makes
Constance appropriate to herself the heart of him
he has chosen for her master.

III

Psychology pure and simple, and psychology of
the passions, such are the two "genres" adopted by
Madame Blanc Bentzon. "La Grande Saulière"
and "L'Obstacle" give us passion carried to the
extreme of sacrifice and immolation. Rosine and
Zina, the first among haystacks, the second on her
death-bed, are lovers to the full extent of what
the word implies, of self-annihilation, — lovers to
the extent of St. Thérèse's word: "It is not I
who live, but him whom I love who lives in me!"
or, again, to the extent of Héloïse's letter to
Abélard after fourteen years' separation from him:
"To be thy concubine is a more envied title to
my heart than that of queen!"

Thus all self-consideration is withdrawn from
their hearts, and they give or refuse themselves
to the lover only in accordance to what happiness he may derive from the gift. Zina kills herself in order to secure her lover's happiness with
another woman. It is the constantly heroic at-

mosphere of their passions which maintains the
loftiness of Madame Blanc's characters. They are
always ready for sacrifice.

Rosine, the chief character of "La Grande
Saulière," marries the man she loves, but only to
discover, when she is about to lose' him, that he
really never loved her, and that the one to whom
she has sacrificed herself has always possessed
her husband's heart. The Doyens have lived
for generations on the farm La Grande Saulière;
neither peasants nor gentlemen, they are yet
proud of their origin, and through this pride
Jacques, the heir, cultivates with equal care his
mind, his heart, and his fields. The Latin Jacques
learned from the curé has made no pedagogue
of him, rather the reverse. Marie, a cousin of
the Doyens, governess in a boarding-school, visits
them during a period of convalescence. For this
refined town girl, Jacques soon neglects Rosine,
Madame Doyen's adopted child, to whom he was
affianced. Next to the farm lives a pseudo-chate-
lain, who calls himself in Paris Vicomte de Charvieux, and is really the son of the money-lending
peasant Charvieux. He carries away Marie to
Paris as his mistress. Jacques takes back his
homage to Rosine, and marries her; but ten years
later the delirium of a sunstroke makes him confess to Rosine, whom he momentarily mistakes for
Marie, the secret of his long half-stifled love of
her rival. Generously, at the beginning of the
Empire, she saw Marie gaining upon her husband; generously she said to him, " You are free,
Jacques; follow your feelings; you did your best

to be loyal, but your love is stronger." The story ends with the return of Marie, dying, whilst Rosine gives her the welcome of the prodigal.

Strong souls, capable of rising up to reach moral resurrection after the first defeat, natures nobly excessive in heroism or in despair, full of heart rather than of reason, such are, for the most part, the women set before us by our author. Zina in " L'Obstacle " is another one of the same family. Born on the highroad, Zina has entered into a convent, under the protection of a Russian lady. Countess Lavinoff prefers fortune-tellers to the decalogue, and magnetism to liturgies, " as in the way of material alimentation caviar and tea please her better than beef or Burgundy." One unlucky day for Zina, the countess loses her money and her life. Zina has now to choose between becoming a nun and following Mademoiselle Chauveau, the companion of the countess, to a clerkship in the post-office at Nivernais, of which Mademoiselle Chauveau is chief.

The post-office becomes a magnet, with such eyes as Zina's behind the *guichet*, and Zina elopes with the Marquis de Valouze, whose mistress she becomes.

Zina is a Georgian ; for her love means slavery. Valouze having deserted her, she takes refuge in Paris, and kills herself, meanwhile accusing herself of every ignominy, in order to exonerate the conscience of the loved one ; her capacity for loving exceeds that of Juliette or of Rosine, for Juliette kept the heart of her lover, and Rosine the worship of hers, whereas Zina keeps but contempt, as this contempt is for her the principal means of insuring to her faithless lover the peaceful enjoyment of his venal marriage with Marguerite de Selve, the one convent friend of Zina.

However, Valouze is not entirely base. On reading Zina's last letter before dying, he avows to Marguerite his whole conduct, thus revealing Zina's heroic courage in trying to give this man's conscience peace at the cost of her own name. Before such abnegation as Zina's, Marguerite cannot refrain from saying to Roger, "She loved you more at the last moment of her life than I shall be able to love you in the whole course of mine!"

Psychology and passion are not, however, the only two elements of the modern novel. *Le monde* is a third one, and *le monde* may be likened to the Salon Carré in the Louvre : it is a synoptic table of all excellences. In England politics, with us letters, give it its dominant tone. The "world," however, in every capital, is but a first selection, the second and refined selection being expressed by "society."

IV

Between society, properly so called, and *le monde* there is the same distance as between the aristocracy of the Empire and that of *l'ancien régime.*

A woman of *le monde* in France does not in any way necessarily belong to society. Should it be asked where this society resides, what it does, by what right it arrogates to itself the supremacy it claims, the answer is ambiguous, in spite of the fact that its rôle may be clearly enough defined.

The reason of the strength of society is precisely
its occultness; it is a force in the abstract, possessing no stronghold, therefore escaping attacks.
Neither the Marais of bygone fame nor the classic
Faubourg St.-Germain was, or is, its peculiar abode.
Some of the women members of society bear about
them traces of the Ghetto, — beet root, wool, or
plaster, according as the money that has purchased
their titles has been gained in sugar, sheep-farm-
ing, or building. But the titles thus bought are
authentic, and when once the bargain is struck,
the person sold so effectually changes into the
owner that, by means of intermarriage and maternity, nearly all these products of wool, beet root,
or plaster truly become after a very few years
veritable women of society. Society, having thus
sold itself, amicably adopts the newcomer, and the
buyer obtains incorporation by virtue of the hard
cash paid for the right to class all the historic
names in France among her aunts and cousins.
Thenceforth society gathers into its fold celebrities
of arts and letters, and by so doing bestows upon
them a seal of official consecration. However absurd may be the whims of a Bohemian of talent,
every Verlaine is pretty sure of finding his Montesquiou-Fezensac.

The novelists of the day touch but slightly
upon the characteristics of this society. Their private intercourse scarcely carries them further than
the elegant plutocracy; the *monde* in which the
women of fashion copy the *demi-monde*, and display in their boudoirs a luxury of furniture that
the old French society always repudiated on prin-

ciple. The society in which (whatever its real
morals, outward manners keep their traditional
austerity) grandmothers dress in woolen gowns —
this real French society figures but slightly even
in the writings of Guy de Maupassant; never in
those of Bourget. It is, consequently, one of
Madame Blanc's merits to have utilized her acquaintance with society and to have portrayed it
excellently, whether in the country in "La Vocation de Louise" and in "Tony," or in "Jacqueline," where it is represented by Giselle and her
mother, as Marguerite de Selve represents it in
her turn in "L'Obstacle."

It so happens that in "Jacqueline" the *monde*
and society are closely entangled and interwo-
ven, yet without loss of identity, wherein is revealed Madame Blanc's intimate knowledge of
each. The Marchioness de Valouze, Marguerite
de Selve's mother-in-law, in "L'Obstacle," is the
perfect model of the woman of society; Madame
de Nailles, in "Jacqueline," is an excellent prototype of the woman of the *monde*. In Madame de
Nailles' drawing-room, on a flower-bed of celebrities, exotic beauties, and people of every class, appear a fair number of three-halfpenny peaches,[1] together with one or two women of society who do not
remain, but seem to make only a fugitive appearance in this heteroclite environment. Jacqueline
de Nailles, who has been spoilt by a stepmother
who lets her have her own way in everything, in
order to get rid of her, will manifest a noble

[1] An expression borrowed from *Le Demi-Monde*, in which
Dumas thus characterizes *déclassées*.

courage when the time comes, but meanwhile shows much of a child's rebelliousness. "It is really vexing," she says, "to be present at mamma's 'at homes,' without understanding a word of all the scandal they talk, for, I must confess, I could make nothing of all the ambiguities every one, except me, seems to relish."

From the moment when Jacqueline discovers that Marien, the artist to whom she has given her fresh young heart of sixteen, is in reality her mother's lover, the deep affection she cherishes for her father is mingled with a touch of pity. "My poor father," is the burden of her thought. Her father dies, and, being ruined, Jacqueline seeks for work. It is then that Madame Blanc shows us the world pitiless even in its beneficence. It grants Jacqueline a share of its charity while persistently refusing her its confidence. Jacqueline being a good musician, the former friends of her family use her for their own advantage, but hesitate to intrust to her the education of their children. Worldlings look upon amateurs with the utmost contempt; they will give their support to the most mediocre professional rather than to one of themselves. Amid the various attempts to gain independence by her work, in which Jacqueline becomes in turn music-mistress, lady companion, singing pupil in order to go on the stage, the poor girl is forced to recognize that the only career which invites her is that of becoming the mistress of some one of her father's friends.

Great fertility of production, a marked preference for strong-willed heroines, such are some of

our author's characteristics. Psychologically she
ranges next to Octave Feuillet. In one point of
view, however, she is above him, namely, in her
perception of other horizons than those exclusively
French. She possesses an intuitive insight into
foreign races, which classes her apart in our country. In certain sketches of rural life, for example,
in "Désiré Turpin," Madame Blanc almost equals
George Eliot and Charlotte Brontë in country
savor and coloring. Applying Alfred de Vigny's
just remark that "sorrow is never a unit of feeling," we may assert that talent is likewise never
found in the unit state. It is a compound made
up of diverse elements, that of Madame Blanc being more complex and varied than that of any of
her writing compatriots, at any rate, as far as the
comprehension of foreign countries is concerned.
Without belittling her by calling her talent "vi-
rile," which is as unbecoming in a woman as the
contrary in a man, I must conclude by once more
pointing out Madame Blanc's preference for minds
that act, over natures that are passive, and her
taste for women who make even the greatest love-
passion only a chapter of their lives and not its
whole sum and substance. An imperturbable
equilibrium of soul is allied in her to the most
vivid flights of imagination, — imagination that
keeps pace with such continual wholesomeness of
purpose that she might well say of herself in beginning a new book what Madame de Sévigné
wrote to her daughter, on coming home from
Vichy: "Je vais reprendre le cours de ma belle
santé."

Such a healthy brain in our days of neurasthenic pathology applied to novel-writing is in itself an enviable merit, and in these few pages we have seen enough of Madame Blanc's writings to conclude that it is neither the only nor the major merit of a mind so variously gifted and so rich in ideas and in plots.

PAUL VERLAINE [1]

Supercilious and solitary in the esteem of some, a Bohemian in that of others, Verlaine has had his fanatic disciples, his merciless traducers, — a Grand Seigneur for friend, the Philistines for executioners !

A Montesquiou-Fezensac, a descendant of Henri IV.'s comrade at Coutras, it was who draped the fold of his shroud to the music of the poet's own verses, dropped like flowers upon the bier. At the very moment the subscribers of the " Temps " (most of them shareholders) were falling foul of " society " for making the funeral of an " old offender " almost a matter of public sensation. As soon as spoken, the words " old offender " brought upon Verlaine a shower of inappropriate comparisons with Villon. I say "inappropriate " advisedly, for in their use of the dagger there is no possible link between the work of these poets ; the fact that a poet of the nineteenth century, like a poet of the fifteenth, once knifed a rival, forms no logical reason for proclaiming a resemblance between their verses.

The dagger still not sufficing, there remained the disorderliness of his life, and so La Fontaine was called on the scene. Thus the most delicate of the soul's poets, Verlaine, is compared with Villon, one of the most sombre thinkers of French poe-

[1] Born March 30, 1844 ; died January 8, 1896.

try; because, like Villon, Verlaine did not call
in the police to avenge the blows of the heart.
And then, again, Verlaine, the subtle sentimental-
ist, is compared with the sanest of reasoners, the
protagonist of common sense, simply because neither one nor the other had any tendency to domestic life. What a singular method of criticism!
Because a man whose worldly wisdom and absence
of enthusiasm wrap the gems of his work in the
moral of an old man, as Lamartine said; because
such a one forgot his landlord, — the truth being
that he had no lodging whatever, living as he did
on the hospitality of two of the most excellent women of his time, — is this a reason for hazarding a
comparison between Verlaine and La Fontaine, or
between their works?

What similarity can be established between a
writer who thus sums up his philosophy: "I owe
all to myself, to my own care, to my talent for
placing my money,"[1] and the sensitive writer of
"Bon pauvre, ton vêtement est léger"? What
relation is there between the ant who jeers at the
good-natured grasshopper with her dry "chantez,
maintenant" — or him who prompts the ant's harsh
speech — and the apologist of the beggar?

> "Ton boire et ton manger sont, je le crains,
>   Tristes et mornes;
>   Seulement, ton corps faible a, dans ses reins,
>   Sans fin ni bornes,
>   Des forces d'abstinence et de refus
>   Très glorieuses,
>   Et des ailes vers les cieux entrevus
>   Impérieuses."

[1] *L'Ingratitude et l'Injustice des Hommes envers la Fortune.*

Who ever saw or felt "imperious" wings float from the verses of La Fontaine to the reader, and bear him and the poet away, and above life?

These absurd comparisons, however, have their excuse. They furnish copy. On the very day a contemporary of mark is carried off from the ranks of human society, the public, excited by the hunt for news, must find a full account of his life in the daily paper. The journalist, inadequately supplied with documents, is compelled to fill up his pages as best he can at a moment's notice. He makes fuel of every kind of wood, and hence such conjunctions and pell-mell parallels, — comparisons between talents so foreign, often based on the fact that there was a single point of resemblance between the men. Thus is the person classified by the exterior side of his life, while here, on the contrary, a close glance reveals above all the essential difference between Verlaine and La Fontaine.

Married to a woman whom he worshiped all his life, — those who were with him in his last moments heard his appeal to her, and to her alone, — Verlaine, who was not haunted by fantasies in verse only, sank a part of his wife's fortune in a speculation with a circus of merry-go-rounds. He himself had yielded to the childish fascination : —

> "C'est ravissant comme ça vous soûle
> D'aller ainsi dans ce cirque bête !
> Bien dans le ventre et mal dans la tête,
> Du mal en masse et du bien en foule.
>
> . . . .
>
> "Tournez, tournez ! le ciel en velours
> D'astres en or se vêt lentement.
> Voici partir l'amante et l'amant.
> Tournez au son joyeux des tambours."

The circus of merry-go-rounds was unfortunately *bête* for Verlaine, as it failed completely, and the worst result of the speculation was his wife's anger.   One of her admirers, spying the psychological moment, received the famous cut which was an outlet at once for the many bitternesses massed in the poet's heart and in the husband's.

The affair happened in Belgium.   It was, therefore, out of the depth of a Belgian cell that these admirable tears came to us : —

> "Il pleure dans mon cœur
> Comme il pleut sur la ville;
>
> .   .   .   .   .
>
> Il pleure sans raison
> Dans ce cœur qui s'écœure.
>
> .   .   .   .   .
>
> C'est bien la pire peine
> De ne savoir pourquoi,
> Sans amour et sans haine,
> Mon cœur a tant de peine."

From the same cell broke forth this beautiful cry : —

> " La tempête est venue.   Est-ce bien la tempête ?
> En tout cas, il y eut de la grêle et du feu,
> Et la misère, et comme un abandon de Dieu."

After this " abandon de Dieu " came the appeasement of " Sagesse."   He wrote for his wife, whom he so greatly loved, and loved to the end, " La Bonne Chanson."

> " Puisque l'aube grandit, puisque voici l'aurore,
> Puisque, après m'avoir fui longtemps, l'espoir veut bien
> Revoler devers moi qui l'appelle et l'implore,
> Puisque tout ce bonheur veut bien être le mien! "

And again for her " La Lune Blanche," and yet

again : "N'est-ce pas ? en dépit des sots et des mé-
chants." For her he sang of woods and flowers,
of the rapture of living, and then came the shadow
and afterwards the two years of "compulsory meditation," completed under the influence of the chap-
lain and the nuns who surrounded him during his
sojourn in the infirmary and in the prison.

Verlaine came out of this ordeal a new man.
The humble post of professor of English (a language he hardly knew) was offered him in the
Jura. Here he mused, he soared above himself,
he sought God ; and in finding Him, he also found
one of his own best veins. This strong spontaneous soul cried out his tender cry, his St. John's
cry : —

> "O mon Dieu, vous m'avez blessé d'amour ;
>
> . . . .
>
> O mon Dieu, j'ai connu que tout est vil ;
>
> . . . .
>
> Voici mon front qui n'a pu que rougir ;
>
> . . . .
>
> Voici mes pieds, frivoles voyageurs ;
>
> . . . .
>
> Vous, Dieu de paix, de joie et de bonheur,
> Toutes mes peurs, toutes mes ignorances,
> Vous, Dieu de paix, de joie et de bonheur,
>
> Vous connaissez tout cela, tout cela,
> Et que je suis plus pauvre que personne,
> Vous connaissez tout cela, tout cela.
>
> Mais ce que j'ai, mon Dieu, je vous le donne."

"Sagesse" overflows with this naïve, devout, and
tender sap: "Those who do not resemble this little
child will not enter the kingdom of my Father."

It was the supreme grace of Verlaine, in his generous repentance, as well as in his errors, to be
constantly the "little child" of the gospel. His
very *mea culpa* was devoid of that excess, the stamp
of vanity, which only too often tacks an ugly decoration to the apparent shame: his were the candid
weaknesses of Christ's disciples. He fell, and fell
again, because foresight and experience were things
that slipped by him, impotent to act upon his in-
fantine soul.

It was not that his impulses turned a deaf ear to
the counsels of experience, but rather that these
counsels were never in time to arrest impulse. A
friend with great difficulty managed to gather three
hundred francs to relieve Verlaine at a moment of
pressing distress. Verlaine took a cab, and hunted
up all his comrades to drive them round like a
wedding party. The procession stopped at each
wine-shop of the quarter, and it is easy to imagine
the condition of Verlaine by night-time! Still,
if in aid of a friend's need there was a call for
a "chanson" for the publisher Vanier, Verlaine
never hesitated, and the work (almost an effort
to him) once done was a proof that his heart strove
above the strange discrepancies here mentioned.

The childlike spontaneity of Verlaine's heart
constitutes the vitality of his poetry. It is a cry
of the soul from first to last. Herein, again, is
Verlaine revealed thoroughly French, for the exquisite chiseling of the form never for a moment
represses the intense sensibility at bottom. He is
never troubled by pride and its accompanying disguises. From this he was preserved by the flame

of naïve passion that he nourished. On the other hand, if this absence of pride is, in a measure, responsible for the *débraillé* of his life, he owed to it the flower of his talent, the suave grace of the verses of "Sagesse." The distinguishing note of Verlaine, and one which he alone among our poets possesses, is the loving faith of his religious poetry : —

"Mon Dieu m'a dit : Mon fils, il faut m'aimer ; "

and further down —

"Oserai-je adorer la trace de vos pas,
   Sur ces genoux saignants d'un rampement infâme ? "

and again —

"Il faut m'aimer ! Je suis l'universel Baiser."

I repeat that the disciple St. John and Francis of Assisi are spontaneously evoked in the mind of the reader by the tender effusions of this heart exclusively love's slave.

Lamartine, Hugo, Musset have had their hours for "singing" God ; but they sang rather than loved, adored rather than cherished. In Lamartine a pantheistic note is mingled with the song ; in Musset, despair and unrest. Verlaine is all engrossed in loving, and for this reason he introduces an infinitely more religious mood into his poetry than any of the others introduced into theirs.

The only comparison between Musset and Verlaine that forces itself into notice rests wholly on the use of absinthe, which will strike the reader as a sufficiently inadequate means of identification be-

tween two poets of violence and disorder. Neither
do the similarities of rhythm constitute similarities
of "essence." It is not in "Rolla" that we can
look for any suggestion of the Verlaine of the
"Fille." Still less does "L'Espoir en Dieu"
shadow forth the Verlaine of "La Vierge Marie."

Musset is the poet of a refined humanity, —
of a humanity in which innate brutalities have
yielded place to corruption; of a humanity in which
the traces of savage nature and the stallion nature have disappeared. Verlaine, perhaps, does
not see so far, but he sees as truly, as Musset. He
explains his own heart, and his heart is a very simple one, precisely because it is contradictory in its
enthusiasms, incoherent in its movements.

The souls that Musset paints are literary souls, —
souls that Musset met in gilded Bohemia and in
drawing-rooms. In his work, bright chandeliers
flash light on beautiful nude shoulders; and even
the pictures of nature that Musset paints are
always drawn from select centres. He does not
wander, like Verlaine's "Noctambule," in the
shadow of the morgue, in the dark twilight of
ignoble slums.

If a parallel were inevitable; if, in order to be
sure of the talent of a French poet of the day, it
were compulsory to compare him with a preceding
French poet, then our choice should fall on Marot;
not the Marot of the "Elégies," but here and
there, and by an occasional flash, the Marot of
the "Chansons:" —

> " Quel est cet homme bas de visage et
>   Bas de taille,

Qui T'ose ainsi saluer Seigneur ?
C'est un maraud."[1]

The delightful song of Louis XII.'s protégé, —

"Plaisir n'ay plus, mais vis en déconfort" —

evokes quite naturally Verlaine's

"Bon pauvre, ton vêtement est léger."

Nevertheless, taking a general view of both poets,
Verlaine as little resembles Marot as he does
Musset, or as Ronsard resembles La Fontaine.
They possess in common that "esprit naïf et
malin" which Sainte-Beuve holds to be the special gift of the French race, from Joinville to La
Fontaine; this gift creating between all these
writers more properly a similarity of atmosphere
than any real resemblance. Another likeness,
which is found not in their poetry, but in their
life, is that both Marot and Verlaine were sincere
in their devotional evolutions. Clément Marot.
turned Huguenot, endured exile and the greatest
poverty without flinching. Possibly, though, Verlaine might have shown greater delicacy of instinct
than Marot. He would not have allowed the poor
Duchess of Ferrara (Renée de France) to sell her
very garments to succor him. Marot and Verlaine, again, were admirable "goldsmiths;" not
triflers, like Jean Mechinot, Marot's contemporary, who "faisait des huitains bons à changer de
trente-huit manières," but finished jewelers, sub-
tile setters of gems. This was another point of
similarity between them.

Here, however, all comparison between the two

[1] The poet's play upon his own name.

poets ends. It is not by the old clothes for which
Madame de la Sablière substituted fine raiment,
nor by the unthinking negligence of their respective
lives, that we can match two natures so diverse as
Verlaine's and La Fontaine's. The constant care-
lessness in all the details of his existence was
revealed by La Fontaine in his most intimate
relations. The Fabulist had no deep feeling for
anybody. Verlaine, on the contrary, was a devoted son, an affectionate friend, throughout the
storms of his life. During the respite after one of
these tempests he sent for his mother. An old
farmer who had worked for Verlaine's father had
settled in Paris, where he kept a boarding-house.
Verlaine rented two rooms, and the "Little Saint,"
as the poet's mother was speedily called, set about
forming some sort of hearth for her son. The
homeless of the neighborhood received aid and
welcome from this little old lady, who, shriveled
by care, was rarely seen, except on her way to
church. This was a rural corner in the big city,
a corner of the Jura, a corner of simple beings
formed by this little group. But misfortune came
sooner than old age, and the little mother took to
her bed. The day God called her soul forth from
its prison her son was also ill, and unable to pray
beside her bed. He was compelled to let her cross
the threshold for the last time without accompanying her! Of the hurricanes and torments that
tore the poet the "petite dame sainte" suspected
nought. She was familiar rather with the son than
with the artist. Anxious for his beloved mother's
peace, he kept from her very nobly the Verlaine of

"La mort pour bercer les cœurs mal chanceux ; "

"Pauvres cœurs mal tombés trop bons et très fiers certes."

The despairing Verlaine, who was the poet, would
turn to her love after each fresh deception, but
tacitly and without confessions : —

"J'ai la fureur d'aimer. Mon cœur si faible est fou.
N'importe quand, n'importe quel et n'importe où,
Qu'un éclair de beauté, de vertu, de vaillance
Luise, il s'y précipite, il y vole, il s'y lance."

What unconfessed wounds a heart so capable of
loving must have hidden from this mother ! They
loved each other; this was the compensation of
enforced silences, in which the son's generosity
spared the mother's fragility : —

"O ces mains, ces mains vénérées,
Faites le geste qui pardonne ! "

verses of tender outpouring, in which, untrammeled, Verlaine's filial worship bursts and ex-
pands, and which are the sweetest cries of his
affectionate soul.

Once more, to love was the very essence of his
nature ; it was his grace and his attraction, — attraction which sprang from the feminine note of
his heart. Amongst his followers, amongst his
imitators, none have been able to imitate this
faculty. Neither Villiers de L'Isle-Adam nor any
of the others have filled their verses with this overflowing tenderness which distinguishes and endears
Verlaine to so many. He knew how to make those
who attached themselves to him anxious about his
fate. This is an exceptional devotion, which hardly
any but natures capable of valuing it can excite.

In Verlaine, ingratitude was not allied to dignity, as too often happens with brain-workers, whose pride leads them to regard kindness as a due foreseen and expected. Verlaine gave with a full heart to those around him, and the attentions with which the Count de Montesquiou surrounded the poet's last years were, indeed, the sanction of the feeling he inspired in Verlaine. Besides, — a detail which has not been sufficiently noted in the numerous inexactitudes written elsewhere, — before, long before, the alleviations of the last four or five years of his life, Verlaine's poor disciples had frequently defrayed their master's expenses. One of them, François Coppée's secretary, used to collect among twelve of them every month the two hundred and fifty francs, to which each one contributed twenty, and God only knows how difficult this louis often was to find for some of them, and how many comings and goings the poor secretary had to go through.

But delicate natures placed in a position to help, minds appreciative of the genius of Verlaine, and whom his poetry had attached, began to inquire into the services that might be attempted. The matter was not an easy one to manage. The poet's impressionable and impressionist nature rendered him refractory to all thought of foresight or order. The friends I refer to arranged his home, and brought comfort into it. "He died in a golden house," wrote Maurice Barrès. So it was, the last amusement of this big child having been to paint everything about him in liquid gold. It was not even an irony for him! His eyes dwelt on all this gold around his poverty with the pleasure of Flaubert describing the splendors of Salammbô! A child also by his candor; and one of the most touching proofs he gave only a few hours before breathing his last.

He was speaking of his wife, calling on her, invoking her. Suddenly he turned affectionately to one who, for the past two years, had watched over him: "It must hurt you to hear me ever thus calling out for her. . . . Pardon!"

A witness of this scene — one of those who formerly had undertaken the monthly collection — tells us that he was overcome with emotion by this double anxiety of Verlaine's heart at the very moment that his end was so near. The early tenderness endured throughout an existence whose weaknesses have been but too much dwelt upon; whilst on the other hand, the pain of distressing a poor human heart, whose devotion never once relaxed from the time of their association, left him no repose.

Love was the last movement of this heart, as love had been its first impulsion. This faculty of tenderness is felt through all his work; it imposed itself on Verlaine's friends, who in turn loved him as did Count Robert de Montesquiou. Some verses of the latter, published in the "Revue des Deux Mondes," reveal the note of a delicate singer, whom the vibrant nature—"woman" and "artist" — of Verlaine cannot but have fascinated.

What will be Verlaine's place in contemporary poetry? For Verlaine is no classic, still less a romantic. This is a secondary question, in truth,

which the future alone can settle. The centuries
have their mysteries. Ronsard and Marot were
only awakened out of their prolonged classic sleep
— prolonged since Corneille and Racine — by romanticism. Rousseau and Madame de Staël scattered over our national path pollen of the picturesque which brought to the French mind the
memory of Ronsard's "aubépines" and "rosées,"
and Villon's "clairs de lune." Taste turned to
evocation, and the sixteenth century reappeared.
With Verlaine the evolution has not stopped.

He touched the heart, and that is the road to
popularity. The pure formists address themselves
only to the lettered mind — to the special critic.
The true poet invites every one to respond to his
prayer; and the writer of "Ecoutez la chanson
bien douce," the writer of "J'ai revu l'enfant,"
the writer of "Chères mains," and of so many
other pieces, like Musset and like Lamartine, in
confiding to all the secret palpitations of his heart,
created an echo in the French soul.

To endure one must move. Feeling alone remains, and Verlaine, having found the key of the
French heart, has done more for his own immortality than in torturing formulas and a grimacing
play of rhyme, after the fashion of those who
borrow their fame from him without his sensitiveness.

Sentiment, however, is not the only note of his
own individuality left by him as an inheritance to
posterity; there is sensualism as well, a certain
violent outburst of the satyr, justifying the words,
"C'est une femme et un satyre." But what of

that? is it not a new proof of the perfect sincerity of the poet, and the thorough homogeneousness of the talent and the man? — strong instincts as well as beautiful delicacy of soul, and this last gift surviving through all to the end. There is more likeness in that association of the " Faun and the tenderness," there is more likeness in the alliance of these tendencies, between Verlaine and the English poet Greene than between even Verlaine and Marot. But, again, only an ephemeral likeness; *au fond* the soul of Verlaine is French.

He has sung for the French — love, joy, and despair; his manner in dealing with these is French. The justness of the poet's sensibility inclines to the nation he addresses; there is the basis of the durability of his work. Hence the fact that, save Shakespeare, who is human, and not English, — as Homer and Dante are human, and not Greek or Italian, — the English poets do not touch us, for tears and laughter are essentially national property. In a word, the sentimental humor of races is individual to each nation, and the indispensable condition for maintaining contact with the French soul is, first of all, to love and suffer as a true Frenchman.

I will end this sketch with some words of Zola touching this matter; they will more precisely fix the chances of immortality that Verlaine has because of this national turn of mind: —

"If poetry be but the natural outflow from a soul, if it be but music, a plaint and a smile, if it be the free fantasy of a poor being that suffers, that enjoys, that sins, that weeps and repents, Verlaine is then the most admirable poet of this latter half of the century."

Verlaine never labored either to experience quintessential sentiments or to paint them in a grimacing language; he was always Verlaine. Like Musset, "he drank from his own glass." He felt his own emotions, and recounted them to the public, without exaggeration, without effort or the use of tinsel; and thence the durable brightness that his poetic star will probably cast over France. During his lifetime, as it too often happens, his disciples rather dimmed him for the public gaze. Death is his resurrection; henceforth he stands upon his works. "Such poems," says Coppée, "are made to last. I assert that Paul Verlaine's work will last."

Yes, his work will live, despite some of his disciples, and solely because of the flame of what Verlaine had in his own soul, and of what he felt in his own heart. He loved through all; there is a spirit of life in that. He never drew himself to himself. He never retired from the touch of other human hearts. His palpitations in poetry never grew to be mere literary emotions. Though his outward life may have looked solitary, his soul never ceased to throb with other souls.

> " Mais, sans plus mourir dans son ennui,
> Il embarque aussitôt pour l'île des Chimères
> Et n'en apporte rien que des larmes amères
> Qu'il savoure, et d'affreux désespoirs d'un instant,
> Puis rembarque."

This last word is the moral epitome of Verlaine's heart, "puis rembarque." His sorrow for self always gave way to his living emotionalism — the tragic Golgotha of "all" appealed to him ever imperatively enough to drown "self"! That was the delicate treasure of his talent, — a gem hard enough to defy decay.